Data-Driven
School Improvement Series

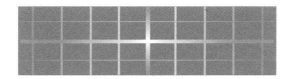

EXPLORING AND APPLYING CASE STUDIES

Peter J. Holly

ACKNOWLEDGMENTS

This workbook is dedicated to all those teachers and administrators in Iowa with whom I have worked to make school improvement a reality over the last ten years. In particular, I would mention the educational heroes of this book—Nancy Bradley, Vicki Sullivan, Chris McCarron, Lesley Stephens, Kristin Woodward, Susie Smith, Fay King, and the creative force in my life, Kay Forsythe—who, day in and day out, give of themselves unstintingly in support of the students and their learning.

Educational Testing Service
MS 18-D
Rosedale Road
Princeton, NJ 08541-0001
Web site: http://www.ets.org/pathwise

ISBN 0-88685-248-x

Printed in the United States of America

07 06 05 04 03 02   10 9 8 7 6 5 4 3 2 1

Table of Contents

GROUP PROCESS GUIDE

The PATHWISE: *Data-Driven School Improvement Series* is a set of tools designed to assist teams of teachers and administrators in the process of school improvement. Although an individual wishing to improve teaching and learning in a single classroom could undertake many of the activities, the activities are generally presented in the context of group work. The workbooks are sequential in moving through the school improvement process, and the activities are sequential within each workbook. Each activity is designed to build upon those that precede it and to add to the groundwork for those that follow. This **Group Process Guide** is provided to assist facilitators and team members in making the activities effective in achieving their intended purposes. In some instances the activities are intended to help teams identify areas for school improvement focus; other activities are meant to help the team members hone their skills in the group process.

The completion of activities by a school improvement team (referred to in this text as a Learning Team) should reflect the style and needs of that unique team. For a variety of reasons, different teams will move through the tasks with different time requirements and differing levels of commitment to the specific tasks. Some teams who use the materials may be coming together for the first time; others may be long existing and well functioning prior to using these materials as a guide in the school improvement process. It is important to allow your team to use the activities provided to assist your work, but allow your own style to influence how you accomplish each task.

Group Process Techniques

Ground Rules

Facilitators and team members can take advantage of a variety of group process techniques to assist them in moving through their development and thereby, ensure that they accomplish their intended purpose—to improve their schools. Most of these strategies and techniques are like the paddles of a war canoe and used only when appropriate and necessary. However, the foundation for all strategies, and therefore necessary at all times, are **GROUND RULES** (sometimes referred to as norms or group behavior expectations). Examples of ground rules are as follows:

- Seek opportunities to be involved.

- Praise others, no putdowns.

- Seek to understand, then to be understood (active listening).

- Include all members (a community feeling).

- Empathize—put yourself in another's place.

- Offer the right to pass.

- Ensure confidentiality—what is said in the group, stays in the group.

Groups should establish the ground rules that enable them to work together respectfully in all phases of development. It is the ground rules that assist a group in working through conflicts while maintaining the integrity of the group's work.

The Foundational Layer of Teamwork Skills

As stated above, group process strategies will be selected and implemented throughout this workbook depending on the activity to be accomplished. The following list of basic strategies, introduced in the first workbook, *Conceptualizing a New Path*, while an attempt to be comprehensive, is not exclusive. Facilitators and team members are encouraged to use other foundational strategies that they have found to be effective in the school improvement planning process. There are excellent resource materials available that provide further ideas (see, in particular, Johnson and Johnson, 2000, and Garmston and Wellman, 1999). The strategies included below, however, are the ones that will be referenced and utilized in the activities in this workbook.

Circle Configuration

The physical arrangement for the team when working should be as close to a circle as possible. Each member of the group should be able to easily hear all others when they speak. The facilitator should sit (not stand) in the circle. All members of the team have an equal voice and equal responsibility for the success of the team.

Groupings

In order to provide team members with the opportunity to reflect and clarify their own thinking as well as to understand that of the other team members, a variety of groupings within the team should be used during activities. At times, individuals should reflect on their own. Dyads (pairs) should be used to allow all members to share their ideas in the safety of a single partnership. Triads (groups of three) can be used for the same purpose. At times it is very effective to reflect alone, then share the reflections in a dyad or triad with that subgroup coming to consensus on their position. Then dyads can be combined into quads with further clarification and consensus on issues. Groups can continue to combine with other groups until one or two larger groups have been able to find their common ground...and thus the common ground for the team.

Facilitation Skills

It is critical that all team members have the opportunity to gain facilitation skills including reflective listening, clarifying, open questioning, summarizing, encouraging, and reporting. Many teams prefer to rotate the role of the facilitator among members; other teams agree on a single facilitator for a specific period of time. Other important team roles include chairperson, process observer, recorder/reporter, critical friend, engaged participant, and, when required, translator. Garmston (2002) emphasizes that having all participants understand and agree to meeting roles is one of his five standards for successful meetings; the other four, all relevant for this **Group Process Guide**, are as follows:

- Address only one topic at a time.

- Use only one process (strategy) at a time.

- Achieve interactive and balanced participation.

- Use cognitive conflict productively.

The above commentary is a summary of the basic skills of facilitation. Later in the **Group Process Guide**, there is a more comprehensive discussion about facilitation skills in the context of team meetings (see School Improvement Meetings).

 ## Go Round

Research has shown that those who speak aloud in the early part of any meeting are more likely to continue to speak and share throughout the meeting. The guidelines for a Go Round are that each person in the group responds to the prompt, in turn, without interruption or comment from the other members. Go Rounds are encouraged at the beginning of each session to bring all members into the group. Go Rounds can also be used at any time to get a sense of what each member of the group is thinking—or when one or two members tend to dominate the discussion, to ensure that *all* ideas have the opportunity to be shared. Go Rounds are an excellent strategy for mobilizing the interactive and balanced participation recommended by Garmston (2002).

 ## Team Listing

For some group activities, it is important to have one team member record each participant's ideas, suggestions, and/or opinions on poster-sized paper. This Team Listing can be posted on the wall for easy reference and revision as needed.

 ## Consensus Building

It is important to define consensus. Teams sometimes create problems (perhaps an intentional block to their success) by defining consensus as *everyone* in complete agreement on a course of action. While an admirable goal, this is rarely achieved. A more manageable definition of consensus is that of "sufficient consensus," defined as agreement among all members of the team that they will not sabotage the implementation of a course of action that is supported by the majority, even though there may be some skepticism regarding the likelihood of its success.

There are a variety of strategies that can be used to facilitate consensus and to determine if a majority opinion exists for a course of action. A Go Round with members stating their position on a scale of 1 (low support) to 10 (high support) can be very effective. Another technique is to have each member (on a count of three) give a signal, such as "thumbs up" for support; "thumb horizontal" for ambivalence; and "thumbs down" for non-support.

There are also many published strategies for creating a consensus opinion. These are available in many books on team building and group work. Examples include cooperative processing, nominal group technique, and brainstorming.

The Tambourine

This is an excellent group processing technique that can be used to enable a group of educators to meld their individual agendas and to find common ground. The technique is called the Tambourine because it resembles a tambourine when drawn on a large sheet of poster paper. The technique works as follows: the members of the group sit in a half circle around the sheet of paper—which can be pinned to a wall or affixed to a stand. It should look like the design below.

Then each individual, after careful consideration of the issues at hand, goes through his or her list of personal thoughts and ideas. The recorder/scribe writes these on the poster—within the small circle representing this particular member. This step is repeated for each individual until all the small circles are completed. Ten minutes are then devoted to silent scrutiny of what has been produced so far—with an eye to finding the "common ground" issues. Then, using a Go Round, members identify those items that are predominately in common and, if the majority of participants agree, the items are added to the inside of the larger circle—thus producing a shared agenda of common ground issues to which everyone has contributed.

Confronting Issues

Sometimes referred to as dealing with the "elephant in the living room," groups must be willing and able to identify those things that pose barriers to their effectiveness and to openly discuss the issues and seek mutually beneficial solutions. Confronting issues will often throw a team into chaos and can seem like a setback when a team has appeared to be functioning well. However, if the stages of group processing are thought of as a spiral, each time a group cycles through the phases they emerge at a higher level on the spiral than the last time around. Although difficult and challenging, it is the act of confronting barrier issues that increases the likelihood of long-term success of any team. The ground rules again become critical in helping the group discuss their problems and find solutions.

Celebrations and Closure

On an ongoing basis, groups should engage in celebrations of their accomplishments and as closure at the conclusion of their work. These celebrations should be as public as possible and should recognize the contributions of all team members. The nature of each celebration is determined by the culture of the group—from solemn, ceremonial celebrations to more party-like atmospheres.

The quality of shared decision making based on data is dependent on the quality of collaborative processes used. This **Group Process Guide** is intended to give teams the tools they need to develop quality group-work sessions. Teams are also encouraged to use other sources of group processing strategies and to avail themselves of learning/training opportunities for facilitation skills if available.

Techniques for Generating Ideas and Information Sharing

During the ongoing process of school improvement, there is a recurring need for team members to generate ideas and share information. Several techniques for generating ideas and information sharing are summarized below.

Brainstorming

According to *Pocket Tools for Education* (1996), brainstorming is the free, uninhibited generation of ideas, usually in a group setting, and is used to solicit ideas from the group members on a given topic. In terms of running a brainstorming session, it is important to follow these four steps: select a recorder and group facilitator, generate ideas, record the ideas, and organize the results.

The goals of brainstorming as described in the same publication are to

- generate a wide variety and extensive number of ideas

- ensure that everyone on the team becomes involved in the problem-solving process

- ensure that nothing is overlooked

- create an atmosphere of creativity and openness

In addition, the group facilitator should maintain the following rules:

- No criticism allowed.

- Equal opportunity to express ideas.

- Quantity over quality.

- Piggybacking or hitchhiking (adding to, elaborating or supporting someone else's idea) is encouraged.

Two variations on the brainstorming theme are described below.

Free-Wheel Brainstorm

Individuals are encouraged to spontaneously call out responses, remembering to abide by the following B.R.A.I.N. guidelines:

- Build on each other's ideas.

- Refrain from judgment.

- Aim for quantity.

- Imagine creatively and "out of the box."

- Note all suggestions.

Round-Robin Brainstorm

Each participant takes a turn in giving an idea or suggestion. An individual may "pass" at any time and may re-enter the process to give a response—again, at any time. Continue going from person to person in the group until everyone passes. Once again, the B.R.A.I.N. guidelines should be applied.

Round Robin

The round-robin approach can be used for purposes other than brainstorming and generating ideas (e.g., expressing personal opinions or sharing information). It is important to follow the agreed upon rules and, in so doing, protect each speaker and his/her contribution.

Directions for conducting a Round Robin: Designate a person to start (e.g., the person to the left of the facilitator or the person with a birthday nearest to the current date). Go around in a circle, giving each person a turn to share his/her opinions or information concerning the topic in question. There should be no response from anyone else, with the exception that the group member recording each contribution may ask questions for clarification.

The facilitator should model for all participants a non-judgmental attitude in listening. Attention should be focused on the speaker and what he/she has to say, with the facilitator remembering to avoid making negative or positive responses to the statements. The reason for this strict adherence to limited responses is that other participants might hear the response as limiting their contribution (thinking that what they've got to say will either be treated just as negatively or not viewed in such a positive light).

Round Table

The same procedure as for a Round Robin is followed with the exception that the opinions/ideas are first written on index cards or self-adhering notes and then shared.

Turn to Your Partner

Formulate: Think of your own answer individually.

Share: Share thoughts with one other person.

Listen: Listen carefully to another person's ideas/explanations.

Combine: Build on each other's thoughts and ideas.

Team Discussion

Talk it over; share your ideas. The important focus of the team discussion is that the team has a goal in mind; a specific outcome from the discussion such as, "What do we believe will be the best measure of success of our students' mastery of reading comprehension?"

Three-Step Interview

Group of 4–6 divided into pairs (dyads)

Interview: Set time limit per partner interview and round robin (usually 3–5 minutes per interview and 8–10 minutes for sharing).

Step One: Partner 1 interviews Partner 2
Partner 3 interviews Partner 4

Step Two: Reverse roles

Step Three: Each person shares the partner's response with the whole group (round robin) or with another dyad.

SCHOOL IMPROVEMENT MEETINGS

Structuring Learning Team Meetings

Before the meeting...

Adequate preparation before each team meeting by both the facilitator and team members will result in more productive team meetings. Based on the length of each team meeting, the facilitator must decide what material will be covered in the meeting and what material participants will need to cover on their own in preparation for the meeting. For example, in preparing for the first meeting, the facilitator might ask team members to read on their own, prior to meeting, the Introduction and the first section of Chapter One.

The facilitator must also decide which tasks/activities will be implemented in any given meeting. Each task in the workbook is organized as follows:

<u>Purpose:</u> (Why are we doing this task?)

<u>Grouping:</u> (How are we to work—on our own, in pairs or triads, or with the whole Learning Team?)

<u>Group process strategy:</u> (Which strategy will most effectively support us in accomplishing the work we are doing?)

<u>Directions:</u> (What are we doing?)

It is important for the facilitator to carefully study these four elements of a task prior to the meeting to ensure a smooth implementation of the task. Each group process strategy is explained in the **Group Process Guide**, which will serve as a handy reference throughout the use of the workbook. In addition, it is the facilitator's responsibility to ensure that any necessary materials, such as poster paper and markers, are ready for use.

During the meeting...

The group processing skills that have just been covered in the **Group Process Guide** are most frequently used in meetings. Indeed, it is in meetings that school improvement work is generally processed. For the benefit of all those concerned, such meetings need to be focused, purposeful, task-oriented, and productive. There is nothing that gives school improvement a bad name more than meetings that meander aimlessly into educators' personal time. Meetings—and the time used for meetings—are resources that we cannot afford to squander. At any school improvement meeting, therefore, the basic skills and techniques learned and applied in the first workbook, *Conceptualizing a New Path*, need to be practiced in combination to provide for structure, flow, and, above all, task completion. In each meeting, these simple procedural rules should be utilized:

- Assign team member roles.

- Review the ground rules.

- Conduct a focus activity or "ice-breaker."

- Review the goal(s) of the meeting and check for understanding.

- Select an appropriate process to match and accomplish the task.

- Record the conversation by displaying the key words and phrases used.

- Provide time to reflect at the end of the meeting.

Indeed, this checklist is a very handy tool for group facilitators to use when planning school improvement meetings. Moreover, during the reflection time at the end of the meeting, it may well be advisable to invite team members to evaluate the session using the kind of review sheet found on the next page.

Team Self-Review Sheet

For each of the following statements, circle the number which best indicates your view of how your group performed, using the continuum of "1" (Strongly Disagree) to "10" (Strongly Agree).

According to Garmston and Wellman, the facilitator's knowledge of "Self" includes a self-examination using such questions as

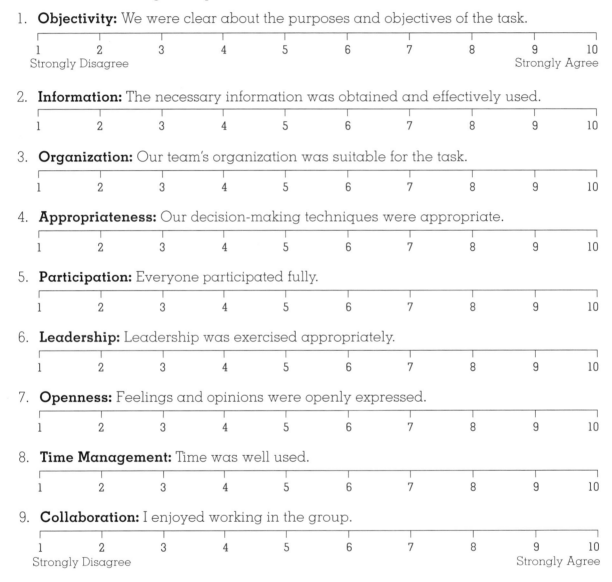

1. **Objectivity:** We were clear about the purposes and objectives of the task.

    1   2   3   4   5   6   7   8   9   10
    Strongly Disagree   Strongly Agree

2. **Information:** The necessary information was obtained and effectively used.

    1   2   3   4   5   6   7   8   9   10

3. **Organization:** Our team's organization was suitable for the task.

    1   2   3   4   5   6   7   8   9   10

4. **Appropriateness:** Our decision-making techniques were appropriate.

    1   2   3   4   5   6   7   8   9   10

5. **Participation:** Everyone participated fully.

    1   2   3   4   5   6   7   8   9   10

6. **Leadership:** Leadership was exercised appropriately.

    1   2   3   4   5   6   7   8   9   10

7. **Openness:** Feelings and opinions were openly expressed.

    1   2   3   4   5   6   7   8   9   10

8. **Time Management:** Time was well used.

    1   2   3   4   5   6   7   8   9   10

9. **Collaboration:** I enjoyed working in the group.

    1   2   3   4   5   6   7   8   9   10
    Strongly Disagree   Strongly Agree

10. What might the team do differently to improve the next meeting?

A Word About Teams

This workbook can be used on two levels: in off-site school improvement training sessions where the participants may or may not be from the same school or school district, or during on-site school improvement planning sessions where the teams will be the site-based teams. Whichever is the case, participants will get the most out of this workbook when they are members of a locally based team and are using the various tasks "for real" (i.e., they are using this workbook to actually do school improvement).

Participants—whether working directly in their schools or returning to their schools following the training sessions—may well want to work within the protection of the kind of Operational Agreement recommended in the first workbook in this series. An example is as follows:

This school encourages students, parents, staff, and community members to put forth a sincere effort to interact in the following ways:

- Have the best interests of our students as a central focus at all times.

- Be flexible and receptive to others' ideas through

  - active listening

  - honest and open exchange of ideas

  - sensitivity in the use of humor

  - acceptance of disagreements as a necessary part of the decision-making process

- Work toward inclusiveness by encouraging and welcoming the involvement of all.

- Respect the integrity of decisions made by other individuals and groups.

Establishing such a school-wide Operational Agreement is a high priority task for any teams embarking on the journey of school improvement.

INTRODUCTION

Exploring and Applying Case Studies is the sixth and last workbook in the PATHWISE® *Data-Driven School Improvement Series* on databased decision making in schools and school districts. Workbook Five: *Creating a Data-Driven System* begins by introducing a model for a data-using system at the local level and ends with a description of how this kind of model is used to support the learning of one particular student—Heather. This workbook reverses the process and, through the use of case study material, starts with several students and their recent learning histories and ends with a description of the support system for their learning at the classroom, school, district, and state levels. The students are Rebecca, Karl, Levi, and Virginia (these are not their real names but they are real students); the classroom is an integrated fifth grade class; the school is Bryant Elementary; the district is Dubuque Community School District (DCSD), and the state is Iowa.

Living and working in Iowa for over ten years, the author has had privileged access to each of these system levels and these case materials are a result of his participant observations, interviews, surveys, and reading of documentary evidence. In January, 2003, for instance, he was able to visit Bryant School and interview the principal, Lesley Stephens, the two data coaches for the school, Vicki Sullivan and Chris McCarron, and the two fifth grade teachers involved in the integrated classroom, while also observing the four particular students and the rest of their class in action in an integrated classroom setting.

Dubuque is situated on the eastern edge of Iowa. In many ways it is America's town lying squarely on America's river—the Mississippi. As one recent history of the town emphasizes, the majestic Mississippi River put Dubuque on the map, both literally and figuratively. Founded in 1788 by French Canadian fur trader, Julien Dubuque, who was attracted by its distribution potential, Dubuque has long benefited from its riverside location. Indeed, it is Dubuque's river location that has determined its cycles of affluence and relative economic hardship.

It was the river that brought large riverboats to its docks and determined that the city should become a hub of interstate shipping. It is also the river that, following a period of relative decline, is now bringing prosperity back to the region in the form of riverboat gaming and a brand new multi-million dollar entertainment complex—aptly named America's River—which is part history, part recreation, and part education. To understand Dubuque today is to know four things:

- ■ It has a traditional feel. Dubuque has been described as one of the most unusual cities of the American heartland in that, in the old part of town below the bluffs, neighborhoods look much as they did 50 years ago. With a rich variety of nineteenth century brick row houses, Victorian mansions, and a unique "roofscape" of steeples and towers, Dubuque has looked old enough to fill in for Boston as a movie location (*Field of Dreams*).

- After its early beginnings, Dubuque became an educational and religious center. Two Catholic colleges, Loras and Clarke, and the University of Dubuque, were founded by religious orders and still have a strong religious and educational influence on the city. This also led to the creation of a strong parochial school system.

- Following the economic decline of the late nineteenth and early twentieth centuries, the city is now enjoying a period of relative prosperity (it is the location for a large John Deere operation) and is beginning to feel the effects of an influx of new inhabitants, many of whom are coming from the Chicago area. An active Chamber of Commerce is determined to see this growth continue.

- The public school system is seen as a vital cog in these developments. Jane Petrek, former Superintendent, writing in the local publication called *Julien's Journal* (2000), has these words to say:

> We live in a unique and dedicated community of which Dubuque Community Schools are proud to be a vital part. Through endorsing, partnering, and nurturing relationships, we will continue to ensure that the community and our schools will grow and prosper. The most important resource our community has is its children, who grow and learn to become productive citizens. They will help attract new businesses and keep those already here going and growing.

Dubuque's students, then, are its future and, in all the schools across the city, students like Rebecca, Karl, Levi, and Virginia are being prepared in terms of their acquisition of knowledge, skills, and attitudes to be that future.

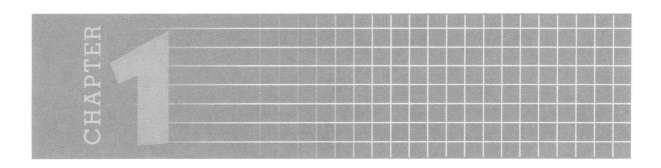

CHAPTER ONE: THE STUDENTS

Karl's Story

Karl is a fifth grader at Bryant School. He came to Bryant in the fourth grade, after a history of behavioral problems at another school. According to his records that came with him, Karl had many behavior problems, had a hard time focusing, was very disruptive in class, and his academic grades were below grade level. Behavior charts had been used to document behavior, help him stay on task, and behave appropriately. The charts, however, did not work and the negative behaviors had continued. In fact, Karl had been suspended from his previous school on two occasions.

When Karl arrived at Bryant, according to his class teacher, the same behaviors were evident, including inappropriate hall and recess behavior, like running down the hall and "sliding on his stomach like Superman." As a consequence, Karl was placed on Stage 3 of the district's problem-solving process (having been through Stages 1 and 2 at his previous school). The difference between Stage 3 and the previous stages is that, at this point, the parent(s) and consultants from the local Area Education Agency (AEA) have to be actively involved and the student is now on the formal route to special education identification, which can culminate in the student having an Individualized Education Plan (IEP). In the Dubuque Community School District (DCSD), it has to be said, the four-stage problem-solving process is used more to avoid special education placement than the alternative: the key to success is finding the right intervention for the right student, thus remedying the problem and moving on.

It is interesting to read the documentation that has accompanied (and recorded) Karl's travails. In grade three, for instance, Karl was placed on Stage 1 of the problem-solving process.

DCSD Problem Solving: Stage 1 (October)

Desired Behavior: Karl will exhibit self-control in the classroom, hallways, lunchroom, etc.

Plan of Action:

1. Contact Karl's mom with behavior concerns so she can follow up at home. Start a Parent Contact Log.

2. Later additions:

   3/12: Daily note on Karl's assignment calendar regarding behavior.

   3/26: Verbal reminder and 3 strikes plan. After 3 interruptions, Karl had to leave the room. He was responsible for missed work.

   4/17: Sent to office bench for inappropriate behavior choices.

Team conclusion after review of the data: How was the plan successful/not successful?

1. Not working well. Karl tries for a day and returns to former behavior choices.

2. 3/12: After several weeks, very little improvement.

3. 4/17: Little improvement.

Next step after interpretation of the data: move to Stage 2.

In grade four, therefore, Stage 2 of the DCSD problem-solving process was activated on Karl's behalf. In the meantime, Karl had transferred to Bryant School.

DCSD Problem Solving: Stage 2

Desired Behavior: Karl will exhibit appropriate behavior in the classroom, hallways, lunchroom and recess.

Plan of Action: October—January

1. Use behavior chart daily.

2. Provide reinforcement (recess) for appropriate behavior.

3. Provide consequence for inappropriate behaviors.

Team conclusion after review of the data:

1. Graph work demonstrates wild fluctuations.

2. Summary of information shared at parent meeting (as follows).

Meeting with Parents Regarding Karl

Date of Meeting: Thursday, January 31

Persons in attendance: Bryant's problem-solving strategist (Chris McCarron), Karl's classroom teacher, an AEA social worker, the school's guidance counselor, a special education teacher, and Karl's mother and stepfather.

Purpose of the Meeting: To review Stage 2 interventions and to plan for Stage 3.

Summary of the Meeting:

At the meeting, we reviewed the information that was collected from the file review. Karl's mother reported that the information was accurate. She agreed that all plans to address behaviors at this point have not been successful. We also examined the data that have been collected on the current Stage 2 plan. The behavior pattern is very inconsistent and no pattern can be noted. Karl also has such a broad repertoire of behaviors that the current plan did not address all the behaviors that Karl was exhibiting. Karl's mother shared that his behavior at home is as challenging as it is at school. She expressed concerns that because of his inappropriate behavior at school and at home, her interactions with Karl often have a negative focus. The entire team, including Karl's mother, agreed that there are not many positives in Karl's life right now.

We discussed Karl's inattentive, disruptive, and impulsive behaviors. It was agreed that most of these behaviors are attention-seeking behaviors, and that they are due to his lack of impulse control. We discussed the ADHD referral that was completed in second grade. The doctor who met with Karl diagnosed him with ADHD and medication was recommended. At that time this advice was not acted upon, as Karl's parents were opposed to medication. However, Karl's mother stated that since so many interventions have been tried and have met with such little success, she might reconsider a trial of medication. She also stated that Karl has asked if he could have medication to help him. Karl's mother added, however, that she thought Karl's father would be in opposition to a medication trial.

Some preliminary plans were made at this meeting. However, since Karl's father was not at the meeting, it was decided that we would meet again in a week and invite him to join us. As much as possible, it is important that all the significant adults in Karl's life are involved in the plans to meet Karl's needs. The next meeting is scheduled for 02/07.

Preliminary plans for Karl include:

- **Counseling.** Karl's mother is willing to seek counseling for Karl. There was discussion regarding the choice of doctors. After talking with one of these doctors, we will decide if Karl's counseling will be a combination of our school services and independent counseling or one or the other.

- **Increased Peer Interactions.** The school guidance counselor will facilitate meeting with a small group of fourth grade boys, on a weekly basis, that will include Karl. She will meet individually with Karl before each session to review group interaction skills with Karl to increase the likelihood of a positive group experience.

- **Opportunity for Positive Adult Interaction.** Karl will work with the custodian one day a week to complete a work job. Karl will be given recognition for his efforts and his service to the school.

- **Behavioral Support.** A behavior plan will be developed. The special needs teacher, the social worker, and the school's problem-solving strategist will all make observations of Karl in the classroom. They will try to select the most significant behaviors to address and will write a behavior plan. The special needs teacher will meet with Karl every morning to review the plan and to start his day off on a positive note. They will again meet at the end of the day to review progress. The behavior sheet will not be sent home daily. He will contact the parents if there is a severe behavior that warrants attention. Other inappropriate behavior will be dealt with at school.

- **Social/Emotional Assessment.** As part of the Stage 3 assessment plan, the social worker will meet with Karl to complete a variety of assessments. It is hoped that these assessments might assist us in programming for Karl.

It is at Stage 3 in the problem-solving process used in DCSD that the parents and AEA representatives have to be involved. It is interesting, therefore, to read the following AEA notes for Karl's plan:

Definition of desired behavior: Respect for adults and peers, which means that Karl will respect adults and peers both verbally and physically in all settings.

Interventions:

- Meetings with other students for social skills instruction

- Work with custodian, earning a certificate of service

- Counseling with a doctor, inside and outside of school

- Meetings with special education teacher (am) and reviews (pm)

- Behavior chart to monitor incidents of respect (positives and negatives)

- Weekly report to parents

- Special education teacher—verbal praise

- Major incidents—Karl to see special education teacher

Comments:

> During this intervention, Karl was also placed on medication for ADHD. There was an immediate, noticeable effect. His outrageous behavior (crawling around the room, lying on the overhead, etc.) decreased immediately. The chart also helped him to attend to his behaviors. Karl still has a tendency to blurt out answers and has some difficulties with his peers. It is recommended that he continue on a Stage 2 behavior plan to address these issues. Karl is no longer meeting with the special education teacher.

His new class teacher confirmed these observations:

> Once Karl was placed on medication for ADHD there was an immediate difference in behavior and on focusing issues. Now Karl is in the 5th grade at Bryant. He is having a successful year overall. Academics are at an average level, with some tutoring when needed. He had one of the leads in the 5th grade school play, which earned him respect from his peers. He has a very positive attitude and seems to like school a lot. We are now working on academic goals mainly because, due to his former hyperactivity and short attention span, he is having to catch up on a lot of skills.

Certainly the Karl that this author observed during his class visit was a model student. Sitting at the front of the class, he appeared interested, totally involved, attentive, and eager to answer the teacher's questions. He is also spunky enough to be the only student in the class to introduce himself to the visitor: "Hi," he said, "I'm Karl."

Karl's story is now taken up by his teacher's notes and records. One of these, for instance, was a copy of his fourth grade Iowa Test of Basic Skills (ITBS) results, which included these comments:

> Karl was given the Iowa Test of Basic Skills in October.... At the time of testing, he was in fourth grade at Bryant in Dubuque Community.

> Karl's composite score is the score that best describes his overall achievement on the tests. Karl earned a composite grade equivalent of 2.7 on the level 10 test. This means that his test performance was approximately the same as that made by a typical student in second grade at the end of the seventh month. Karl's Composite Iowa percentile rank of 11 means that he scored higher than 11 percent of fourth grade students in Iowa. His overall achievement appears to be well below average for fourth grade.

> A student's ability to read is related to success in many areas of schoolwork. Karl's Reading Comprehension score is somewhat below average when compared with other students in fourth grade in Iowa.

> A student's scores can be compared with each other to determine relative strengths and weaknesses. Vocabulary, Comprehension, Spelling, Punctuation, Usage and Expression, and Problem Solving and Data Interpretation seem to be areas of relative strength for Karl. Some of these strengths might be used to help to improve other areas. Compared to Karl's other test areas, Capitalization, Concepts and Estimation, Science, and Maps and Diagrams may need the most work, as can be seen in the following chart.

Tests	Scores		PERCENTILE RANK				
			Low				High
	IGE	IPR	1	25	50	75	99
Vocabulary	3.9	40					
Comprehension	3.2	25					
Reading Total	3.4	33					
Spelling	4.5	60					
Capitalization	1.3	4					
Punctuation	2.9	20					
Usage and Expression	4.0	44					
Language Total	3.1	23					
Concepts & Estimation	2.2	5					
Problem Solving/Data Interpretation	3.2	26					
Computation	2.5	7					
Mathematics Total	2.6	13					
CORE TOTAL	3.0	20					
Social Studies	2.7	14					
Science	2.1	6					
Maps and Diagrams	1.6	3					
Reference Materials	2.4	7					
Sources of Information	2.0	2					
COMPOSITE	2.7	11					

Legend: IGE = Iowa Grade Equivalent
IPR = Iowa Percentile Rank
Iowa Percentile Rank

At Bryant, all students identified as being below grade level (on ITBS and any other test results and assessments) are put into problem solving. When his behavioral issues were under control, therefore, his fifth grade teacher felt that the time was right to place Karl on Stage 1 of the problem-solving process in order to attend to the academic concerns. According to the teacher's documentation:

Problem Solving: Stage 1

Desired Behavior: Student will become more proficient in addition, subtraction, multiplication, and division facts.

Grade 5 (October 23): Plan of Action

1. Practice Monday (addition), Tuesday (subtraction), Thursday (multiplication), and Friday (division) with strategist for 5 minutes after review practice (approximately 10:40 am).

2. Time tests will be given every Wednesday to practice and monitor progress (graph results).

How was the plan successful?

	September	February
Multiplication	+21/60	+39/60
Division	+14/60	+26/60
Addition	+43/60	+54/60
Subtraction	+21/60	+43/60

Given the comparative success of this intervention, Karl's class teacher and the strategist agreed on further targeted efforts.

Problem Solving: Stage 1 (November 12)

Desired Behavior: Improve formation and connections of cursive letters.

Plan of Action:

1. Practice formation and connections of cursive letters every morning after Dimensions of Learning (DOL)[1] completion. [Practice] worksheets will be used. Initial instruction for the day will be done by the class teacher.

2. Practice worksheets will be corrected by the strategist.

How was the plan successful?

Karl is progressing well; however, he needs constant reminders to write in cursive, and not to print.

---

[1] Marzano, R. (1992). *Dimensions of Learning: A New Paradigm for Curriculum, Instruction, and Assessment.* Unpublished paper. Mid-continent Regional Educational Laboratory (McREL), Aurora, Colorado.

Problem Solving: Stage 1 (October 23)

Desired Behavior: Increase performance on [publisher's] fifth grade mathematics tests.

Plan of Action

1. Contact parents to describe mathematics performance concerns on grade-level assignments and tests (phone/letter).

2. Small-group instruction on specific skills, as needed, takes place in the regular mathematics class (re-teaching). The class teacher and the special education teacher are in a regular education, class team teaching situation.

3. After-school tutoring will take place as needed.

How was the plan successful?

1. Parents gave verbal/written support to address these skills.

2. After-school tutoring: Chapter 2 score: 53% (attended 3/3 tutoring sessions); re-take: 80%

3. Small-group work: Chapter 3 score: 55%; retake: 75%

4. Chapter 4 score: 70%

5. Chapter 5 score: 35% (attending five after-school tutoring sessions).

The Students
Task 1: Reflecting on Karl's Story

 Purpose: To discuss Karl's story and compare it with those of students who are well known by the participants.

Grouping: Work individually and then meet with your Learning Team.

Group process strategy: Use the Go Round technique (refer to the **Group Process Guide**).

<u>Directions:</u> On your own, respond to the following questions, using the space provided below to record your responses. Then meet with your group to share your responses.

- Can the prescribed interventions for Karl be currently considered a success? Explain why or why not.

- As a student, how does he compare with boys and girls that you have taught in your classes?

- What do you consider to be his long-term prospects for each of the following areas?

  Academic:

  Social:

  Emotional:

  Vocational:

Rebecca's Story

Rebecca is in the same fifth grade class as Karl. In many ways she is an exemplary student. She is well behaved, respectful, hard working, enthusiastic, and helpful at all times, but she has a learning problem. Indeed, if it were not for Bryant's comprehensive early warning system, she could have easily slipped through the net. While other more demanding students garner more than their share of attention, Rebecca is the kind of student who could easily meld into the background. According to her class teacher: "Rebecca is a very average student who is very quiet and respectful in the classroom."

As an observer in the classroom, this author can certainly attest to this statement. Sitting toward the front of the class, Rebecca certainly has a pleasant disposition, is attentive and polite, and remains on task at all times. She is interested, involved, and always ready to learn. Yet, says her teacher:

> [She is average when it comes to ITBS, although] she is on the ball with math; [she is also] somewhat anxious—she's the twin of a high achieving talented and gifted student....We wouldn't have caught her if it hadn't been for the listening test. There are lots of overwhelming problems in the fifth grade and it would have been easy for her to hide in the pack. She's a model student; never says 'boo.' Although she's of average ability, she's quiet—we wouldn't have known her problem. The red flag was the listening test, which she flopped. She didn't know how to focus; it's her listening ability—she is not an auditory learner. Our task was to equip her to be successful long term.

As her teacher continues:

> There was no evidence of a problem until she took the first unit test in reading (10/22). She received +0/6 on a listening comprehension test. Rebecca re-took the test just to see if it was a bad day or she wasn't feeling well. On the second try she received +1/6. This was a concern and her name was brought up at a problem-solving meeting. The school strategist had an intervention to try with Rebecca, which helped her focus on specific items to listen for.

Problem Solving: Stage 1 (December 3)

Those present: Rebecca's class teacher, the strategist, and her parents.

Desired Behavior: Increase listening ability to improve scores on [publisher's] listening sections of tests and to improve attending skills throughout the day. Improve Rebecca's self-perception.

Plan of Action:

1. An IRI (Individualized Reading Inventory) listening test was given to Rebecca by the school's problem-solving strategist. On this IRI, Rebecca's independent listening level was found to be between the second and third grades. She was able to retell at the second grade level, but as the text became longer and more difficult, she only remembered the information provided at the outset of the story.

2. Her parents are considering an ADD packet and will contact the school if they choose to pursue it.

3. Her parents were given the option of having Rebecca see the school guidance counselor. They will notify the school if they want the counselor to meet with Rebecca.

4. Discussed the possibility of having Rebecca tutor a younger student. Her parents will discuss this with Rebecca.

5. Rebecca will be taught specific skills to give a retelling.

6. The classroom teacher will meet with Rebecca three days a week for six weeks.

7. Rebecca will be provided with a visual prompt to assist her (see below).

Story Retelling

Tell WHO or WHAT the story is about.
Tell the TIME or PLACE of the story.
Tell the IMPORTANT PARTS of the story:
    Beginning
    Middle
    End

Retellings

1. WHO/WHAT
2. TIME/PLACE
3. IMPORTANT PARTS
4. DETAILS

How was the plan successful?

January—Using the listening tool was very successful.

Mid-year test: Listening Comprehension= +10/10 = 100%

We will continue to monitor progress not using the tool, but with a few reminders about WHAT to listen for.

According to the teacher's documentation of the intervention results:

Rebecca undertook 13 story retellings between 12/06 and 1/27. Out of a total of 8 points (2 points each for 4 criteria), she scored a '6' five times, a '7' four times, and an '8' four times. In the [publisher's] Level 11, Unit 2 Test (given 12/19), she scored +4/6 for the listening section and in the mid-year assessment (given 1/27) +10/10.

Rebecca's teacher concludes:

After the intervention was given for six weeks, Rebecca showed considerable improvement in the area of listening comprehension. She scored +10/10 on her mid-term reading listening comprehension test.

There are two significant aspects to this story.

First, there is its simplicity. According to her class teacher, "Rebecca just had to be taught how to listen. Sometimes kids need it laid out for them."

While there are different kinds of skill deficits, many respond to the simplest of treatments. What is often required is a simple structure to follow, some scaffolding for learning.

Second, in many cases the interventions do not have to be highly sophisticated or complicated. In this specific situation, the problem-solving strategist designed Rebecca's intervention virtually on the spot. Because it worked so successfully with Rebecca, however, the tool has since been used with other students with similar problems.

While Rebecca may never be as high an achiever as her sibling, her listening block (which impeded her learning and clearly affected her confidence and self-image) has been removed and she can continue with her learning. While her difficulties with auditory processing may never disappear, she now has a way of dealing with her deficit so her learning process is not impaired. It will be interesting to see how this release acts exponentially over time to activate and motivate her learning.

Levi's Story

Levi is in the same fifth grade class as Karl and Rebecca. He is a different kind of learner again. He is what could be called a "slow processor"; learning doesn't come easily to him. While he is not identified as a special education student, he does need a great deal of ongoing support. He is in Year 3 of Problem Solving. Many interventions have been tried, yet he continues to struggle. According to the school's problem-solving strategist, he is one of those students who may need multiple problem-solving interventions over multiple years. Concerning the current situation, according to his class teacher:

> Levi is in the medium to low average math class in 5th grade. We became concerned about Levi when he started scoring low on chapter math tests. He went on a Stage 1 in Problem Solving, which involved small group re-teaching interventions and tutoring after school. We also noticed that Levi has a hard time focusing for a long period of time. He is now being observed and tested for ADHD. The interventions seem to be working, but they need to be repeated for each chapter. We are still trying to help Levi in this area.

The impression is that Levi will continue to struggle and need ongoing support for his learning.

Problem Solving: Stage 1 (October 23)

Desired Behavior: Increase performance on [publisher's] fifth grade mathematics tests.

Plan of Action:

1. Contact parents to describe mathematics performance concerns regarding grade-level assignments and tests (phone/letter).

2. Small-group instruction on specific skills, as needed, takes place in the regular mathematics class. The class teacher and the special education teacher facilitate this type of instruction by team teaching in the regular education classroom.

3. After-school tutoring will take place as needed.

How was the plan successful?

- Parents gave verbal/written support to address these concerns.

- After-school tutoring:

    - Chapter 2 score: 56%;

    - Attended 3/3 tutoring sessions; retake: 60%

- Small-group work:

    - Chapter 3 score: 65%; retake: 80%

- Chapter 4 score: 100%

- Chapter 5 score: 45% (Levi is attending five after-school sessions with the special education teacher)

During the observed lesson time in the integrated classroom, the class teacher spent some time kneeling by Levi giving him "positive strokes" (her words) and coaxing him through his mathematics assignment. According to his teacher, his home situation is not helping matters. She explains: "They need to get straightened at home. With enabling families like Levi's, we're the bad guys. There is total lack of respect; he treats his parents badly even in front of teachers. In terms of his behavior, there are lots of issues."

Virginia's Story

Virginia is in the same integrated classroom as the other students. She is an "entitled" special education student and has an IEP. According to her teacher's notes:

> Virginia is identified for special education services in the area of math skills. She was in a small transition group working in the general education curriculum taught by the special education teacher in the special education setting. This year she is in the general education curriculum taught in a team teaching setting in the general education classroom. This continues the transition plan for Virginia so that she may gain the skills and confidence to work independently in the grade level classroom without special education services. When Virginia feels rushed or pressured or unable to grasp a concept immediately, she has the tendency to shut down and start missing homework assignments. She has had fewer emotional shutdowns this year, but indicated in the IEP conference that she was still often feeling insecure. It is hoped by the end of the year in this transition program that Virginia will realize her potential and maintain an emotional balance for independence without special education services. To push her too fast will only make her too frustrated.

Reportedly, Virginia has an interest in horses and, according to all those concerned, does seem more confident and appears to feel good about herself this year. Her teacher reports that she is a good helper and worker. Virginia's mother would like to see her be able to achieve well in mathematics, complete assignments on time, and have confidence in her ability to do grade level work before she leaves sixth grade. In fact, Virginia and her mother would like to see her exited from special education services before she attends junior high school and want her education to go beyond high school. In terms of her current functioning, according to the latest report on her progress:

> Virginia has taken four chapter math tests in the general education math curriculum. She has achieved the following scores: 80%, 73%, 75%, and 94%. On weekly grade-level math probes, Virginia has achieved a score of 79 correct digits, which puts her above the 75th percentile for 5th grade norms. On 2-minute timed tests of basic facts, Virginia scored 32/60 division; 34/60 multiplication; 38/60 subtraction; 42/60 addition facts. In 4th grade on ITBS, Virginia had national grade levels of 3.3 in concepts, 3.2 problem solving, 3.2 total and 3.8 computation. In 5th grade on ITBS, she has levels of 5.2 concepts, 6.0 problem solving, 5.5 total and 3.9 computation. Although Virginia's skills have greatly improved, she has a tendency to shut down when she does not feel confident.
>
> Goal: By December, Virginia will average at least 70% accuracy on all 6th grade general education curriculum math tests.
>
> Evaluation Procedures: Chapter tests from general education mathematics curriculum.
>
> District standard and benchmark related to this goal: Number Operations and Relationships—Students will use numbers effectively for counting, estimating, and problem solving; demonstrate accurate computational skills (including addition, subtraction, multiplication and division); and explain their thinking to another

person. Perform and explain operations on whole numbers, including: addition and subtraction (four digit), multiplication (two digit times three digit) and division (two digit divisor).

Short term objective: By May [of this school year], Virginia will average at least 70% accuracy on 5th grade general education math chapter tests.

It would seem that Virginia is well on the way to achieving her and her mother's wishes for her development in mathematics and ensuing exit from special education services.

While Karl, Rebecca, Levi, and Virginia are four fifth graders in the same integrated class, they are *not* part of a homogeneous group.

- For a variety of reasons they have all experienced impaired growth in their learning.

- This impaired growth is either short-term or long-term.

- They receive in-class and out-of-class support. In the integrated classroom setting, however, the latter is now used infrequently; in fact, in-class "pull-asides" are much more frequently used than out-of-class "pull-outs."

- They have all been identified as being "below grade level" and placed in problem solving for either reading or mathematics—or both.

- In terms of their ITBS results, they are all in the "marginal" group, i.e., those students scoring below the 40th percentile cut score, and therefore, in Iowa, they are among those students not deemed proficient. In fact, all four students are in the group often referred to colloquially as the "bubble kids" and, given the demands of the federal *No Child Left Behind (NCLB)* legislation, this is a group likely to receive a great deal of attention. Put candidly, these are the students whose scores, if increased, could dramatically improve a school's (and, therefore, district's) "proficiency" numbers. What is impressive, however, about the approach (problem solving) used in Bryant School is that it was in place long before *NCLB* came along.

- The four students, however, are not in this marginal group for the same reasons. The staff at Bryant have undertaken an intense study of all the students achieving immediately below the 40th percentile cut score and have found that some are vastly underachieving, some are overachieving, some are at the limits of their capability, some (given their learning histories) are developing, and some are deteriorating. It is a fluid situation, which underlines the importance of individual attention and the provision of in-class, flexible, needs-based groupings.

- They are all responding to the learning support provided, but at different rates.

- Although involved in the problem-solving process, only one of the four students has been identified as being eligible for special education services.

- All four students have responded to the targeted, personalized interventions that are very much part of the Bryant support system and are certainly characteristic of the particular fifth grade classroom in which they find themselves.

- They are four of many students at Bryant who are receiving support for their learning. One student being helped in similar ways to Karl, Rebecca, Levi, and Virginia is the son of one of Bryant's teachers and a transfer from the parochial school system. When her husband, impressed by the time and attention and the level of support being given to their son, commented on this fact, he was told by his wife, "But we do this for all the students....That's what we do at Bryant."

The Students
Task 2: Levels of School Support

<u>Purpose:</u> To compare the level of support offered to Bryant's students with that provided in the participants' schools.

<u>Grouping:</u> Work with your Learning Team, first meeting in pairs or triads, and then meeting as a whole group to share responses.

<u>Directions:</u> As a group, respond to these two central questions:

- Is the level of support given to students at Bryant matched by what is done in your own educational setting? Give specific examples to support your response.

- The vehicle for this support at Bryant is problem solving. What are the equivalents in your own setting and how successful are they?

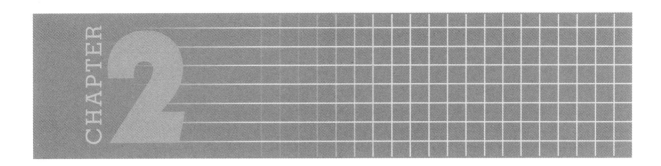

CHAPTER TWO: THE CLASSROOM

Walking into this upstairs, fifth grade, integrated classroom is no different than walking into thousands of classrooms across the country. It is large to be sure. It is neatly arranged and the walls are covered with visual aids. A clue that this classroom may be different is the layout of the room—some desks are arranged toward the front of the room (for whole-class instruction), some are arranged to one side, and there is a large table surrounded by chairs toward the back of the room for small-group instruction. The focus here is always on meeting the needs of individual students.

There is a plaque above the door. It is a framed picture and newspaper article about the retirement of one of Bryant's most respected teachers. She retired a year ago, still volunteers at the school (she helped with the recent fifth grade play). A year before she retired, during an in-service session on writing, she turned to all her colleagues and exclaimed, "If I knew there was a better way to help these kids, I wouldn't be able to sleep at night until we'd done something about it."

This attitude has certainly rubbed off on the rest of the faculty. Indeed (and this is so typical of Bryant School), how the classrooms look is not the real issue; what is crucial is teacher attitude. The classroom teacher of Karl, Rebecca, Levi, and Virginia applies several crucial understandings:

- She is dealing with individual students with widely differing needs—and these needs are permutations of social, emotional, behavioral, and academic factors.

- These students have to be grown one-by-one. It is a case of nurturing them, but it is nurturance toward high expectations.

- As a colleague of this teacher explained, it is also a case of dealing with one problem at a time—over time—in what she calls a layering approach. You deal with one problem, take stock, and then deal with the next one. This process, however, has to be ongoing and, therefore, lasts much longer than one school year. As a consequence, the teachers have to communicate well across the grade levels, have to be aware of student histories and what has been done for them previously, what is being done for them now, and what will need to be done for them in the future. What this means in practice is the students are "owned" by several teachers. As an interesting aside, a paraprofessional asked recently whether it was still *not* okay to talk about kids in the lounge. The answer she received says so much about Bryant School. "There are two kinds of conversation," she was told, "collective problem solving for a child or everybody complaining about a child. Let's keep it to the first."

■ The key to this approach is diagnostic teaching, which involves teaching explicitly to the students' specific needs. It is a never-ending cycle of teaching, diagnosis, and re-teaching, followed by more diagnosis. It is a matter of establishing kid-by-kid intensive support for learning. As one colleague remarked, "It's pretty simple really; you find out what they don't know or can't do and teach it to them."

■ Low achieving students (those designated "below grade level" or below the 40th percentile in ITBS) are seen as low achieving for a variety of reasons, all of which may need to be treated in different ways. There is no "one-size-fits-all" approach that works for these students.

■ Given the responsibility of meeting widely differing needs, this classroom teacher understands that she cannot go it alone. She has established a team-teaching arrangement with her special education colleague, and they both receive constant support from the school's problem-solving strategist.

The Classroom Teacher

It is this classroom teacher's second year at Bryant. After teaching out west for ten years, and at another school in Dubuque for three years, she had the opportunity to join the Bryant faculty. As she recalls, "People said to me, 'Why would you want to go to Bryant? Their expectations are so high.' But I knew what I was getting myself into....I'm a hard-working person and I'm willing to learn."

With her present fifth grade class, she team-teaches mathematics with a special education teacher. In fact, they co-teach. On the day of my visit, the special education teacher was the lead teacher for mathematics while the classroom teacher toured the room, helping individual students stay on task, and monitoring their individual progress. Formerly, the five special education students in the class were pulled out for mathematics. Now they are back in general education—in the team-teaching situation—and receive in-class support. According to the special education teacher, when she is the lead teacher for mathematics, she can cover the necessary content but use the kind of language that is accessible to the special education students. According to the classroom teacher:

> We team-teach math every day; we flip-flop the chapters....We often switch roles—as lead teacher and support. I was nervous to begin with, but we soon became comfortable with each other. Now we're learning from each other; we even talk to each other about the work in front of the kids, like: 'How can we do this?' We've developed an interactive, problem-solving style. We also have paraprofessional support; she works with those students who didn't get it yesterday, supported by Chris McCarron [the problem-solving interventionist].

In her interview, the special education teacher also confessed to early nervousness, but emphasized that the system is working so well that she wouldn't go back. She feels that the special education students are making the same kind of academic gains, but in an integrated setting with all the personal, social, and emotional gains that that brings. In her interview with the author, she made the following points:

■ The math class is a real example of inclusion at work.

■ We have to produce and use our own materials as we consider the [publisher's] materials too abstract and verbal.

■ The class has to be very organized in terms of the pacing of the work and the clarity of the tasks and assignments given. "It all has to be very concrete," she explains.

■ The five special education students in the class are passing all the tests. In fact, they are outperforming some of the general education students.

■ The special education students feel good about themselves.

■ Co-teaching, she admits, "...brought me out; I'm more creative now."

■ The downside is that we always need more planning time.

There are several factors at work in their classroom that make it a special place for learning.

■ The "layering" approach to helping the students develop need-by-need is clearly at work. According to another colleague at this school:

> One layer gets dealt with; then the next grade deals with the next layer until you get to the center of the student. We don't stop until the kid's needs have been completely met and we've totally figured out how to help each kid.

■ A major feature of this classroom, and of Bryant School in general, is the understanding that approaches normally associated with special education can be used most effectively with the general education population. Problem solving and progress monitoring are two such approaches. In a speech to the Bryant staff, this author (2000) described Bryant as the Problem Solving School.

■ Given the influence of special education, it is the custom at Bryant to continually take stock, know specifically what was learned and what was not learned—and by which students—and to adjust instruction accordingly on a day-to-day basis. Sometimes known as "precision teaching," this is a very specific, step-by-step, skill-by-skill approach to student learning.

- Arising from the influence of special education and progress monitoring and further stimulated by the district's Data Coach Training sessions, databased decision making is embedded at Bryant at the classroom level. Clearly, Karl, Rebecca, Levi, and Virginia have all benefited from this approach and their fifth grade classroom is no exception. Needs-based data-driven instruction (diagnostic teaching) is the norm at Bryant, partly due to the unavailing efforts of the first two data coaches to be trained, Chris McCarron and Vicki Sullivan, a sixth grade teacher. As all her colleagues attest, Vicki has done the most with data, but she is always willing to help other teachers with their data needs. Indeed, it is interesting to note Vicki's comments about her first impressions of Bryant School:

> **I came here seven years ago after spending thirteen years in the Catholic system in Dubuque. It was like coming home. I'd formerly lived in the area and I'd been wanting to move on. I was thirsting for the professional development opportunities offered here, the focus on kids, and the intellectual stimulation. I knew that the perception out there was that Bryant is all business, hard-nosed, and has lots of difficult families. And that's exactly why I wanted to come here!**

More recently, Vicki has devoted her energies to developing an electronic student database, which is fast becoming the main data support for instructional decision making and continuous improvement at the classroom level.

- Given the influence of special education, differentiated instruction is the norm at Bryant. A variety of interventions and strategies are used, including in-class and out-of-class flexible, needs-based grouping. Curriculum and instructional modifications and accommodations are the norm. Two particular features of the classroom are relevant here:

  - As mentioned previously, data are used constantly to make classroom decisions regarding individual and group needs. This ongoing process is an invitation to the educators involved to "assess to learn" (Stiggins, 2002). They learn about the students' learning needs (so they can intervene effectively to enhance the learning process) and, in so doing, learn about their own instructional needs.

  - What is also noteworthy is that they keep it simple. A specific need is met with a specific strategy, which is more often than not homegrown. The staff at Bryant (ably supported by the problem-solving strategist, Chris McCarron) does not fall into the trap of thinking that all interventions and strategies have to be highly sophisticated. As special education teachers have learned, the right strategy for the right situation is what counts, however small scale it may be. Chris McCarron's strategizing for Rebecca (as described earlier) is a good example of this fact. "Whatever works" is the motto.

As Peter Block (2001 and 2003) has reminded us, we often know more than we realize (in terms of what to do in such situations), yet we are often led to believe that the answers lie outside us and have to be discovered and imported and at a price, both financially and psychologically. Not so, says Block; many of the strategic answers that we need are already within us. They worked before and they will work again (or they will work in an amended form); they are part of a professional toolbox.

■ The selection of strategies (in terms of both what to choose and the pool of ideas available) is also enhanced because of the team settings in which Bryant teachers find themselves. There is the team-teaching/co-teaching team, described earlier in this chapter, of a classroom teacher and a special education teacher. They are supported by Chris, interventionist, and they are part of the fifth grade, grade-level team. These two teachers have also been added to the team that goes to data coach training and are also supported by the work of the original two data coaches, Chris (again) and Vicki. And they can count on the general support of other colleagues at Bryant. The teaming arrangements seem easy and natural, but, according to Vicki, a lot of hard work has gone into their creation. She explains, "When we started we had to be structured, prescriptive, and formalized. Then it became what's expected and now it just happens."

In other words, they didn't just fall into these arrangements; they had to work on them.

Reading a recent article by Dorothy Kerzner Lipsky entitled "The Coexistence of High Standards and Inclusion" (*The School Administrator*, March 2003), this author realized that what he witnessed in Bryant School is exactly what Lipsky is talking about. What is being offered at Bryant is an inclusive education in an inclusive school. According to Lipsky (2003):

> A whole-school approach requires all staff in the school to share responsibility for meeting the needs of both general and special education students. To meet the requirements of individual education plans, school districts can use several models or variations of teacher collaboration and school staffing. **As general education teachers gain familiarity with a wider range of adaptations and supports for all students and special education teachers learn new content-area skills, approaches to inclusive education shift to meet the realities of individual needs.**

This is exactly what is occurring in Bryant. Teachers are learning how to use special education approaches to help all the students in their classes, and the special education teacher is getting to use the content necessary for success at the specific grade level with her special education students as part of the class at large. Again, as though she were talking about Bryant, Lipsky (2003) continues:

> Teachers in inclusive schools report collaboration is a powerful means of personal and professional development. The benefits of collaboration for teachers include reducing the isolation of being a solo practitioner; sharing the responsibility for the teaching of a diverse group of students; learning new skills and approaches; reflecting upon practice with non-supervisory colleagues; and adding enjoyment to teaching.

Lipsky goes on to discuss the various kinds of collaborative arrangements that can be made. The most common models of inclusion, she says, are the following:

- Co-teaching (full-time or part-time) that places a special education teacher and a general education teacher in the same classroom, jointly sharing responsibility for the entire class.

- Indirect support from a special education teacher providing consultative guidance, including the development and adaptation of materials and alternative instructional strategies.

- The team model in which a special education teacher is included in a team of teachers serving a cohort of students.

- The staff as a group takes on responsibility for all students, teaching in a variety of configurations, from lecturing to a large group to tutoring individuals or small groups of students.

At Bryant, some teachers are using an amalgam of these approaches, including co-teaching, indirect support from Chris McCarron, and the use of the grade-level team as another form of support and collaboration. While this particular model is not being generally applied throughout the school, other variations are certainly appearing and Chris's expertise is available to all staff members.

Lipsky (2003) concludes by providing a description of the kind of classroom generated by the kind of collaborative arrangements described above.

> The traditional practice of an individual teacher in a classroom shifts to colleagues working together to address the needs of all students in inclusive classrooms. Teachers share their

knowledge, step out of their old roles, learn from fellow professionals, and become interdependent.

The inclusive classroom is differentiated. The needs, intelligences, and learning styles of students differ; curricular materials, instructional strategies, and assessment must vary as well.

This description is uncannily similar to what is happening in Bryant on a daily basis.

In an insert to Lipsky's article, she summarizes the "Traits of Inclusive Schools."

- School administrators assume responsibility for the planning, implementation, and outcomes of the education for all their students.

- Programs and procedures are planned to meet the needs of all students, not a one-size-fits-all approach.

- Classrooms are differentiated and use a wide range of curricular materials and instructional strategies.

- Peer learning and cross-age tutoring support classroom learning.

- Instructional technology is infused into the curriculum.

- Collaboration between and among school personnel brings greater expertise to instruction and allows for professional development.

- Accommodations and modifications in testing are used to measure what students know and can do.

- Such an inclusive school provides a unified educational system, including a range of services, not a place or a program to which special education students are sent.

While Bryant is moving toward being an inclusive school (in terms of Lipsky's definition), it will be important to retain some flexibility in its approaches. For example, in the same edition of *The School Administrator*, Thomas Hehir (2003) counsels against the use of a "one-size-fits-all model of full inclusion" that may not be appropriate for some students. Pullout services, he says, may well be required for students who need intensive help in reading. There should be a shift to inclusionary education that recognizes the full range of needs of the disability population: put simply, the students and their needs should come first. While integration in regular classes with appropriate accommodations and support should be the norm, Hehir (2003) concludes, certain disability-related skills might need attention outside the regular classroom.

In other articles in the same edition of *The School Administrator* (March 2003), Judy Elliott wonders whether the imminent reauthorization of the *Individuals with Disabilities Education Act* will mesh with the demands of the *No Child Left Behind* legislation, thus providing an opportunity to bridge the divide that exists between special and general education (something which is clearly already happening at the school level); Jim Surber describes "Flexible Service Delivery" in Iowa's neighboring state, Illinois. According to Surber, the innovative service delivery model known as the Flexible Service Delivery System (or "Flex"), initiated in the 1997–1998 school year, is enabling increasing numbers of students with academic and behavioral challenges to succeed at school. The goal of Flex is to shift the focus from categorizing and labeling children with disabilities to a system that provides necessary modifications and adaptations to make more children successful in a general education setting. The approach is very similar to what is occurring at Bryant:

■ Flex focuses on the functional assessment of student needs, in part by providing more useful information to classroom teachers and through the development of classroom-based interventions.

■ Collaborative problem-solving teams (which include parents, teachers, related services personnel and an administrator) are responsible for identifying the needs of diverse learners.

■ As one principal remarks in Surber's article: "Flex is not necessarily an easier way of providing services to our at-risk students, but it clearly is a better way."

■ Everyone is responsible for the education of all the children and most of the referred students receive curricular modifications without being placed in special education programs.

Again, similar to the work at Bryant, central to the Flex model is a problem-solving process. As Surber emphasizes:

> The problem-solving component is an interactive and ongoing process whereby the team works together to meet the needs of our diverse learners. Typically, grade-level teams schedule time on a weekly basis to meet, solve problems, develop interventions, and collect data that allow them to evaluate the success of the interventions and make future decisions about the needs of the student. The problem-solving meetings cannot be viewed as an end or a one-time event but rather as an ongoing process.

As in the Flex approach in Illinois, problem solving goes to the heart of what Bryant is about. Three related characteristics make up the Bryant model:

■ The problem-solving model itself, which was first designed as a state-wide initiative in the early 1990s, was divested through the auspices of the special education divisions of the Area Education Agencies (AEAs), and, thereafter, implemented at district, school, and classroom levels. This is a noteworthy example of a statewide initiative that has taken root at the local level.

■ As part of problem solving, the use of the "ICEL" (Instruction, Curriculum, Environment, and Learner) diagnostic frame is to specifically identify—on a child-by-child basis—the nature of the learning problem.

■ There is deployment of a problem-solving strategist to assist staff members in diagnosing learning problems, designing appropriate interventions, and modifying instruction accordingly.

The Classroom
Task 1: The Influence of Special Education

Purpose: To reflect on the influence of special education at Bryant School.

Grouping: Work with your Learning Team. Select a recorder.

Group process strategy: Select a brainstorming technique (see the **Group Process Guide**) and create a team list.

Directions: As a team, brainstorm and compose a list of the benefits that accrue through the application of special education approaches in general education settings at Bryant School. Have your recorder create a team list on poster-size paper.

Chris McCarron, the problem-solving strategist at Bryant, has had a major role to play in its journey toward being an inclusive school. As a former paraprofessional, general education teacher, teacher of students with severe and profound disabilities, and talented and gifted (TAG) coordinator, she has a wealth of experience to call upon. She joined the Bryant staff as a kindergarten teacher, then became the TAG coordinator and one of Bryant's first data coaches, and is now a part-time strategist at Bryant while establishing similar approaches in other schools across the district. It is fascinating to read her reflections concerning her educational travels:

The journey of becoming one of Dubuque Community School District's first data coaches has been an interesting professional growth process for me. The staff development provided by Peter Holly and Mary Daily Lange served as a conduit for me to reflect upon my current practices as an individual teacher, a member of Bryant School's staff, and as one link of the greater Dubuque CSD personnel. The reflective process along with the assimilation of new knowledge has left me feeling confirmed in many situations, redefining and clarifying my action in other areas, and challenging my own thinking and practices in still other areas.

When reflecting upon my role as an individual teacher, I think I have always used data as one of the main driving forces in decision-making. Perhaps my passion for data grew from starting my teaching career as a teacher for students with severe and profound disabilities. To most of the world, the students who I taught were 'unteachable.' Many individuals thought that providing services to these students was a sheer waste of time. I think that my first attempts of data collection were to 'prove' to the world, and perhaps even myself, that indeed, I was making an impact on the students I taught. I sought to prove that learning was occurring. I dissected the data, finding even the slightest trends that I could use to document improvement. Through the dissection of the data, I found that I could even predict success or failure based on days of the week, medication changes, seizure activity, and visits home. I discovered through the data analysis what were optimal teaching times, and then found myself not only individualizing student goals, but also designing my teaching differently for specific students. Data collection and analysis changed from being the 'proof' of my success, to my 'plan' for success.

Later, as my students and I moved into more inclusive settings, my data collection continued to serve as a planning agent for my teaching. However, as I pored over the student achievement data, I felt that it didn't really capture all of the growth that I was observing in my students and the general education students with whom I was now interacting on a regular basis. I was not capturing the affective growth—the changes in perceptions and the increases in interactions between the two diverse populations. As I started to share with others what I considered the 'real successes' of inclusion, I realized I had not captured all of that growth in my student achievement data. It was then that I started to understand the importance of using what the data coach trainers refer to as perception data. Including this type of data collection in relationship to my students helped me to have a more accurate, complete picture. It was confirming to hear Peter and Mary discuss the need for a variety of types of data. I know that if we do not collect a variety of data, we limit the picture it can paint for us. Using one kind of data is like trying to capture the sunset in a painting with only the color yellow. Yes, it can give us the essence of the picture, but it is only when we add the oranges and the purples that we truly see the significance of the event. Student achievement data alone does not create a whole picture.

As her teaching assignment changed, however, her need for data was to take an unexpected twist.

My transition to the world of general education initially changed the way I viewed data collection. I naively thought that now the scrutiny of my students' success would be decreased. I would no longer need to prove anything to the world. I started to use data much more internally. I used it to help me drive my instruction, but felt that the audience for my data had narrowed. Well, that was until I awoke one morning to the headline in the *Telegraph Herald* that read, 'Fulton Fourth Grade—Lowest Scores in the District.' (At the time, I was one of the four fourth grade teachers at Fulton). That headline and onslaught of editorials that followed all targeted the lack of academic growth, not for some hypothetical 'at-risk' students, but for MY students. One editorial even suggested that the teachers at Bryant and Fulton should trade places to give students at Fulton the opportunity to have 'good instruction.'

In the days that followed that infamous headline, I found myself confronted with students who were convinced that they could not achieve. They held up that headline as the data that confirmed what many of them felt about themselves. They were convinced that they now had evidence to prove that their efforts at trying to achieve more were useless. I found myself needing to use the data that I had collected in my classroom for different purposes than I had ever intended. Perhaps for the very first time, I started to use student achievement data to shape student perceptions about themselves. I started meeting with students, and also parents, showing them the data. I showed the students where they had started the year and the progress they had indeed made. We compared data on classroom performance with ITBS data and determined if they told the same story. If the two types of data were different, we brainstormed why that might be. I helped students to write individual goals and helped them to document their progress (now I know that to be progress monitoring). Kids started to see their own achievements. Success started to breed success. My students started to make growth that even I wasn't sure was possible. I found that I, the one who had been so appalled by the headline, had also subconsciously been guilty of looking at their 'at-risk' profiles and limiting them just as so many others had done. I don't know if my students would have faired any better in the rankings that year if they had had the chance to retake the ITBS in May, but I do know, and more importantly, my students began to know, that they were capable of growth and of meeting their goals.

Ironically, Chris's next port-of-call in her voyage of discovery around Dubuque Schools, was to be Bryant School. As she explains:

Not because the newspaper mandated, but as part of my journey for new challenges, I left Fulton to join Bryant School staff as a kindergarten teacher. I remember my first conferences as a kindergarten teacher. I can't forget the blank stares I encountered as I pored over the 'data' that I had compiled on each student with his/her parents and enthusiastically explained the six-page report card that I had created to use as document of student progress. I explained each child's individual progress in each minute area; I compared their child's performance with the performance of his/her classmates; I shared my goals for their child and my plan to get there. I expected the parents to be thrilled, and to be as awed by the data as I was. I was not prepared for their stares and confusion. They were only interested in knowing if I 'liked' their child and if he/she was 'happy.' That day taught me much about evaluating the audience for data. What I needed to know as a teacher was not the same as what those parents needed to know. And, even if they did want to know it, I needed to put the data into a format that was much easier for them to understand. With that in mind, as schools continue to work with the student profiles that are being created as a result of our data coach training, I think that we need to be sure we know the intended audience. Our profiles then need to be created in a way to best share the information that the designated audiences need and want. Perhaps, in the end, we will even need a variety of profiles for different audiences.

Dealing with questions and scrutiny from the parents of my kindergarten students was nothing compared to the interrogation I received from some of my parents when I became the TAG facilitator at Bryant. I was placed in the TAG position at the time the district was creating a new model for serving talented and gifted students. The district was just beginning to require that a personal education plan (PEP) be written for all students who were identified as 'talented and gifted.' I soon learned that data collection now had a very different meaning for me. Student scores now were the gatekeepers to services. A certain score came attached with the label of TAG, or if the score was not high enough, the lack of the label. A number started to be more important than everything we knew about a child. Even though we had a balance of data available to us, we were being asked to limit the evaluation of the data. Fortunately, Lesley Stephens [Bryant's principal], and a group of parents and teachers helped me to rewrite Bryant's service delivery model for TAG programming. We used a more balanced approach to our data evaluation that included perception data, classroom performance data, and parent, teacher, and student nominations. Again this experience supports the need for our schools to push ourselves to be not only broad in the data we collect, but also to be thorough in analyzing the data. As a district, I know that there is some data that we spend a good deal of time collecting, but we seldom analyze the results....As we continue with the staff development of our data coaches, I think that it would be beneficial to include a review of the data that is available to our schools and the ways that it can be helpful in learning about and planning for our students.

Finally, in her new role as problem-solving strategist at Bryant, Chris is helping other colleagues collect and use data for classroom-based, data-driven decision making as she explains below:

In all of my teaching roles that I have reflected on, the data that I interacted with was data I owned. It was data about my students, reflected my teaching, and became the driving force in my decisions as a teacher. Now, in my role as problem-solving strategist at Bryant school, I am charged with a very different role. The role that I have served in as problem-solving strategist has been that of a 'data coach,' even before it became the official title. Using data for yourself and helping others to use data are two very different tasks. Becoming an effective data coach is a process, one that has many subtleties that I am still discovering. Understanding what data tell us and how data might be used are strengths that I brought to the position from my variety of previous experiences. What I have needed to learn and continue to need to improve upon are my skills to help others to move through stages of learning to understand and use data. I need to nurture them through the process, just as I learned through the process of change over time.

The Classroom
Task 2: The Role of the Problem-Solving Strategist

Purpose: To reflect on the work experiences of Chris McCarron and their effect on the way she performs her professional role today.

Grouping: Work on your own and then meet with your Learning Team to share your reflections.

Directions: On your own, make a list of the key experiences in Chris McCarron's teaching career and explain how each of them may have influenced how she now performs her strategist role at Bryant.

Key Experiences   Resulting Influences

The Problem-Solving Classroom

The chief responsibility of the problem-solving strategist at Bryant is to actively support the problem-solving process in classrooms across the school. The problem-solving process is Dubuque's version of the Iowa Department of Education/AEA initiative referred to previously in this chapter.

According to an introductory booklet on Individual Student Problem Solving put together by Chris McCarron and Donna Shaw (representing the LEA) and Tina Brestrup, Ruth Neagle and Carolyn Oppedahl (representing the AEA), the process is grounded in seven Belief Statements and consists of four stages (see below). If these stages are completed, placement in special education may well be the result. This eventuality, however, is neither inevitable nor, in many cases, desirable. Indeed, the problem-solving process often serves to remedy a situation prior to special education placement even becoming an option. The process neither prevents those students who are deserving of special education placement from receiving this level of attention nor precludes those students with specific academic and/or behavioral needs from receiving appropriate attention outside of special education programming.

Belief Statements

- All students are **entitled** to the best education possible in the most appropriate, least restrictive setting.

- The **best education** may occur in general education, special education, or a combination of both.

- Students should be **supported** according to their needs.

- Services **follow the student**, not the teacher, not the school, not the program, and not the curriculum.

- **Student need** determines the length of time that services follow the student. As the need changes, so does the service.

- The Problem Solving Team/IEP Team decides when to begin and end services.

- **Teachers** (general education as well as special education) working with the student, along with the rest of the Problem-Solving Team (**including parents**), are to be involved in problem-solving **decisions**. (According to Iowa law, all entitlement decisions must meet criteria outlined by the AEA.)

2001–2002

Consultation Between Teachers and Parents
Stage 1

■ Concern about a student is expressed

■ Communication with parent through notes, phone calls, conferencing

■ Intervention is designed, carried out, and documented

2001–2002

Consultation with Other Resources
Stage 2

■ Stage 1 intervention was not effective

■ Teacher requests assistance from team

■ Communication and parent involvement

■ Intervention is designed, carried out, and documented

2001–2002

Extended Problem-Solving Team
Stage 3

■ Stage 2 intervention was not effective and/or additional resources are needed for intervention success

■ AEA Support Staff involvement

■ Formal problem-solving approach is utilized

2001–2002

> ## Due Process IEP Consideration
> ## Stage 4
>
> ▪ Insufficient improvement with interventions and/or maintaining intervention success requires resources of special education
>
> ▪ Assessment to determine need and eligibility
>
> 2001–2002

The Problem-Solving Classroom

How to establish classrooms that cater to the needs of diverse learners:

- Special Education/General Education blending

- Problem Solving/Child Find/planned interventions

- The equivalent of IEPs for all students

- Individual student goal-setting through self- and teacher assessment

- Differentiated instruction

- Accommodations and modifications

- Continuous progress model

- Choices/options in terms of learning opportunities—catering to different learning styles and multiple intelligences

- Flexible, needs-based grouping

- Learning in a real-life context

- Teacher as leader/facilitator; student as worker

(The above list is an extract from a speech given by Peter Holly in 1998 to an audience of special education teachers and administrators.)

Problem solving is a cyclical process. At each of the four stages, a three-part cycle is utilized, similar to that recommended by Deojay and Pennington (2000). These authors describe a three-step framework in which those involved 1) specify the current level of student performance; 2) create an action plan; and 3) evaluate and communicate progress. As can be seen from Appendix A, each stage of the cyclical model used in

Dubuque has three similar components: a problem statement/the desired behavior; the plan of action; and the team conclusion after the review of data and various forms and documentation that have been designed to expedite the process.

In a recent presentation to another school's staff, Chris McCarron (2003) reminded them of the following:

- Problem solving (in Dubuque Schools) has become a general education, not special education, initiative, and it is the responsibility of general education teachers to initiate, guide, and sustain the problem-solving process.

- Problem solving is not just for students we expect to qualify for special education; many never reach "entitlement."

- Problem solving is an approach that should be utilized to address *all students* who are not meeting grade-level expectations.

- Teachers must be vigilant in monitoring student progress. Done well, problem solving is simply good diagnostic teaching.

- When a student's achievement is not meeting grade-level expectations, it is the responsibility of the general education teacher to begin the problem-solving process.

- Problem-solving interventions begin with interventions that occur within the general education classroom, using general education materials.

- Many problem-solving efforts will enable children to be successful within the general education classroom.

- Problem solving is a very real attempt to "leave no child behind." In saying that, while the focus is often on the individual student, groups of children can receive the same intervention if it fits the identified (collective) need.

- Above all, problem solving should not be viewed as an add-on: it is a way of doing business.

- As such, there is an ongoing need to document our problem-solving efforts, to record those interventions that work and those that don't, thus leaving a blueprint for future educators.

- The essence of problem solving is that the teacher identifies a concern, selects interventions to address the concern, implements the interventions, and collects data to determine the effectiveness of the interventions. It is this final step that constitutes "progress monitoring": the frequent and repeated analysis of student performance data for the purpose of evaluating the effectiveness of an intervention.

■ The ongoing application of problem solving leads to the creation of classrooms characterized by differentiated instruction. According to Carol Ann Tomlinson (1998 and 1999), differentiation involves personalized instruction: the creation of different roads to the same learning destination, while striving to maximize the capacity of each learner. It involves modifications for struggling and advanced learners, taking into account their interests and their learning profiles. It is crucial, she says, to develop and deliver curriculum and instruction that are responsive to individual learning needs, i.e., diagnostic teaching.

In the same presentation, Chris McCarron (2003) also reminded her audience of the important role that the ICEL frame for problem analysis can play in the problem-solving process. ICEL is an important tool that can be used to examine probable explanations for the discrepancy between what an individual student is expected to accomplish and what he or she is actually accomplishing. ICEL stands for Instruction, Curriculum, Environment, and Learner and is used purposefully in this order to analyze where the problem lies. As a consequence, those educators doing the analysis do not start and end with an examination of the individual learner when the instructional strategies and approaches being used, the curriculum content being covered, and the learning environment (both at home and at school) may well be contributory factors.

Possible Issues in Each Domain

Instruction	Curriculum
Materials	Content
Pace	Expected outcomes
Clear instructions	Intent of curriculum
Teacher delivery	Format
Amount of practice	Difficulty
Curriculum placement	

Environment	Learner
Room arrangement	Motivation
Furniture/equipment	Academic skill levels
Rules	Social skills
Management	Cultural concerns
Routines	Vision
Expectations	Hearing
Task pressure	Ability

2001–2002

The widespread use of the problem-solving process has contributed to the growth of two major characteristics that are the essence of Bryant classrooms: teaming and data-driven improvement.

Teaming

At Bryant School, **different kinds of teams** are used as **professional learning communities** to bridge the gap between **school improvement policy** and **classroom practice**.

Every year the **whole staff**, working as a collective team, studies current and trend-line data and identifies school-wide goals. Each of these goals then becomes the focus of an **action team**, the members of which study both external data (where we should be and what we should be using in this goal area) and internal data (where we actually are currently). The ideas generated by the action team are then translated into classroom practice by individual teachers (possibly working within **team teaching** arrangements and definitely supported by the problem-solving strategist), while working within the context of a **collaborative grade-level team**.

The practice of teaming that has been established at Bryant—particularly the grade-level arrangements—is very similar to the latest theory on what it takes to establish professional learning communities. Indeed, it can be said with some authority that this is an area where the latest research is converging with the best of school and classroom practice.

As Keiffer-Barone and Ware (2002) have summarized:

- Traditional forms of staff development have little impact on school culture and/or student achievement.

- What appears to improve teaching and learning is restructuring schools to create professional development that is ongoing and built into the day-to-day work of teaching (NPEAT, 2000).

- Organizing schools in collegial teaching teams is one way to improve instruction and student achievement through collaborative problem solving (Johnson and Johnson, 1999).

- Such teams become adult learning communities that focus on continuous improvement, a key to effective staff development (NSDC, 2001).

- Decision making about instruction can be effectively decentralized to teacher teams, working to the district's academic and behavioral standards.

- Collaborative teamwork in Cincinnati schools has led to the development of strategies for making improvements in targeted areas based on student data, e.g., the analysis of student test results (Keiffer-Barone and Ware, 2002).

According to Richard DuFour (2003), school-based teams are increasingly operating as professional learning communities. In a learning community, he says, participants

- have a clear sense of the mission to be accomplished and a shared vision of the conditions that they must create to achieve their mission.

- work together in collaborative teams that engage in collective inquiry into both best practices for accomplishing their goals and the current reality of the conditions in their organization. Any discrepancy between best practice and the reality of their school spurs them to take action to reduce the discrepancy.

- work together in a cycle of continuous improvement involving the gathering of data, the identification of areas of need, and the development of strategies to address these concerns, and support each other as they implement these strategies, gather new data, and assess the impact of the strategies.

- engage in an ongoing process that drives the daily work of people throughout the organization and includes the evaluation of the results of their efforts.

Both DuFour (2003) and Becky Burnette (2002) have presented case studies of schools that are operating as learning communities in ways similar to Bryant. In DuFour's case (the study of a suburban school district), the following actions were undertaken:

In establishing a focus on learning, three essential questions were posed:

- What is it we want all students to learn?

- How will we know when they have learned it?

- How will we respond when a student is not learning?

It was the responsibility of each school to monitor the learning of each student on a timely basis, develop systematic procedures to give additional time and support— during the school day—to any student experiencing difficulty, and create a system of needs-based interventions.

While the format was left to each school's discretion, collaborative teams (whether course specific, grade level, interdisciplinary, vertical, or departmental) were formed and given the same charge: to focus on a specific, measurable student-learning goal.

Using a four-step process, as follows, these teacher teams were encouraged to focus on results.

Four Steps Toward Team Engagement

1. Clarify the essential outcomes that each student is expected to achieve as a result of completing a course, a grade level, or a program.

2. Develop common assessments to be given to all students on at least four occasions during the year.

3. Define what it will take for the students to be deemed proficient in terms of the assessments.

4. Analyze the results and develop improvement strategies. Each team is required to review student performance on the common assessments, to identify the strengths and weaknesses of all the students tested, and to develop relevant implementation strategies. Each member of the team would be called upon to assess the performance of his or her students in comparison to the group, to seek help from teammates in areas of concern, and to offer teammates suggestions and help in those areas where his/her students have excelled.

In an article entitled "How We Formed Our Community," Burnette (2002) describes her own school's story in terms of a seven-step process:

1. In small-group discussions about the school, team members responded to these trigger questions:

    ■ What makes this a good school?

    ■ What can we do to make it an even better school?

    ■ As your new principal, what do I need to know and understand about this school?

2. A schedule was built that contained common planning time. Grade-level teaching teams in grades one through four now had a guaranteed one-hour collaborative planning session each week. In addition, multi-grade team meetings were held on a monthly basis, as were faculty meetings to share what the teams were doing.

3. The members of each team were encouraged to determine how to spend their planning time (by defining their purpose and direction) and to develop protocols and norms to apply to their group process. The kind of agreements established were as follows:

    ■ We will be on time and prepared with all necessary materials.

    ■ Everyone is expected to participate by sharing ideas and concerns.

    ■ We will discuss school issues in school only, maintaining confidentiality at all times.

- We will reach decisions by consensus after all opinions have been heard.

- We will maintain an atmosphere of mutual respect.

4. Critical questions were established for focusing the team efforts.

   - Are we clear on what students are to learn and the evidence they must show that they have learned it?

   - Based on our analysis of student achievement data, what are the strengths and weaknesses of our students' performance?

   - How will we judge the quality of student work?

   - How does our curriculum align with state standards and state tests?

The teams were also given suggestions concerning the "products" on which they should work: common assessments; reports on student achievement and the specific strategies to be used to improve the results; rubrics to guide student assessment; and new curriculum units aligned with state standards.

5. The next move was to create a feedback system. Each team was asked to complete a weekly report containing the issues being considered, identifying problems being faced, and suggesting resources that could help them in their work. The principal promised to respond to their reports, thus ensuring ongoing, two-way communication.

6. Team leaders were asked to represent their colleagues on the School Improvement Committee. As Burnette (2002) comments:

> Teachers often see improvement initiatives as additional burdens, placed on them when they are already straining to meet the demands of their position. We attempted to diffuse that reaction by presenting the professional learning community initiative within the context of the existing school improvement framework. [Moreover] we linked our professional learning community initiative to existing school, district, and state programs, requirements, and expectations. By integrating our work within the context of existing structures, we avoided creating extra work. We worked smarter, not harder.

7. In terms of a focus on results, each team was asked to commit to a specific, measurable student achievement goal, to identify the action steps teachers would take to achieve the goal, to outline the evidence they would monitor to assess their progress, and to be ready to share and celebrate when positive results emerged from their work.

In schools like Bryant and those described by DuFour and Burnette, learning communities (mainly, but not exclusively, in the form of grade-level teams) are the way to do business. Moreover, in Cincinnati, where teaming has changed the way teachers and students learn, according to Keiffer-Barone and Ware, 2002, "The real learning for teams comes in their daily practice and team problem solving."

Problem-solving teams are the crux of the matter. In most cases, "problem-solving teams" is the generic title given to teams that are undertaking such activities as action research and continuous improvement; in Bryant school, however, they are this and more—the more being the specific approach referred to in Dubuque Schools as "problem-solving" for individual students. Such teams link policy and practice, school improvement, and classroom improvement. By keeping their work as close as possible to what teachers have to do on a day-to-day basis, problem-solving teams are not seen as yet another thing to have to do—to add to plates that are already overflowing. They are seen as part of the solution, and not as a contributing factor, to overload. Part of the secret of success is to keep the work focused on student learning. According to Anne Lewis (1998), therefore, there is wisdom in using student work as the basis for collaborative discussions about teaching and learning. Lewis explains:

> If you go into any group of teachers and ask, 'Could you be doing your job better?' you will lose most of them immediately. But if you ask them to look at student work and talk about how it could be better, then teachers become really student focused.... Teachers have always examined student work, of course. But they've almost always done it alone, for the purpose of grading an individual's work. The practice of teachers sharing and discussing student work with fellow teachers, however, has become more common with the growing use of portfolios as an alternative or supplemental assessment tool.

The collaborative screening of student work can be used, she says, to gauge whether content standards are being met, to learn more about the students and their needs, to craft useful feedback for students, and to help teachers think about their teaching. Lewis's argument is that teachers are more inclined to look at their own contribution to the learning process by looking first at what the students are doing. Catherine Lewis (2002), in agreeing with her namesake, cites the Japanese lesson study approach as a similar vehicle for unlocking how students learn and, therefore, how teachers should instruct. Francis Duffy (2003) maintains that the essential ingredient in this process is what he calls **situated learning** (i.e., learning in an everyday context) within a "community of practice." A community of practice (see Lave and Wenger, 1991) is a small group of practitioners who share a common practice or have a common learning interest. Such teams, says Duffy, are a powerful tool for supporting and bridging personal and organizational learning and development.

DuFour (2002) agrees. He emphasizes that working in teams is more likely to provide the participants with the feelings of self-efficacy necessary for responsibility. He says: "School improvement may begin when a principal accepts responsibility for student learning, but it is only when the entire staff embraces that responsibility that sustained school improvement takes place."

In a series of challenging articles, Schmoker (2002, 2003, and 2003b) has taken these arguments one major step further. In arguing that lengthy, complicated school improvement plans have failed to produce school improvement (Schmoker, 2003b), he claims that the work of school improvement that really impacts student achievement—the hard work of improving instruction—gets done in small teams. Such school improvement plans, he says, supplant what does improve instruction and raise levels of achievement—a team of teachers meeting regularly, and continuously, to design, test, and adjust their lessons and strategies in the light of their results. Such teams, he continues, need to become the essence of what schools are about. Talking about the school improvement plans that he's seen, he declares that schools need to "make these simple collaborative structures the soul of their improvement planning; most don't include them at all." Echoing Peter Block (2001), Schmoker (2003b) argues:

> It is time to close the gap between what we know and what we do to promote learning. It is still the rare school that recognizes that teachers, working together, have the capacity—right now—to improve instruction. We need to give them this opportunity. We need to ditch much of what we now do, in exchange for regular times, at least monthly, for teachers to design, refine, and assess their instructional strategies. And then, just as regularly, we need to honor and celebrate each team's success as its members develop and share better lessons and strategies with their colleagues. It is no overstatement to say that in most schools, such practices would yield immense, often immediate benefits.

In his most recent article, "First Things First: Demystifying Data Analysis," Schmoker (2003) poses the question: "What do small teacher teams do to be productive?" He provides several responses. Such teams, he says

- use data to focus on a few simple, specific goals. The effective use of data, he says, depends on simplicity and economy.

■ use data to put first things first—the improvement of teaching and learning.

■ use data to give their members the answers to two important questions:

   ▪ How many students are succeeding in the subject/class I teach?

   ▪ Within those subjects/classes, what are the areas of strength and weakness?

The answers to these two questions, he says, set the stage for targeted, collaborative efforts that can pay immediate dividends in achievement gains. Almost as an aside, Schmoker (2003) makes a crucial observation, as follows:

> Why don't most schools provide teachers with data reports that address these two central questions? Perhaps the straightforward improvement scheme described here seems too simple to us, addicted as we are to elaborate, complex programs and plans.

Being able to receive ready answers to the questions would enable a grade-level or subject-area team of practitioners to establish high-leverage goals; for example, moving the percentage of students passing a mathematics or writing assessment from a baseline of 67% in 2003 to 72% in 2004. Setting such goals may be the most significant act in the entire school improvement process, he argues, greatly increasing the odds of success. Keeping the goals simple focuses the attention and energies of all those involved and frames their next decision—what to work on and where to direct the team's collective attention and expertise. It is at this stage that the participants need to remember what they found in their data. Where do the greatest numbers of students struggle or fail? Where are the gaps in student achievement? As Schmoker (2003) reminds us:

> Every state or standardized assessment provides data on areas of strength or weakness, at least in certain core subjects. Data from district or school assessments, even grade books, can meaningfully supplement the large-scale assessments. After team members identify strengths and weaknesses, they can begin the real work of instructional improvement: the collaborative effort to share, produce, test, and refine lessons and strategies targeted to areas of low performance, where more effective instruction can make the greatest difference for students.... [Thereafter] Using the goals that they have established, teachers can meet regularly to improve their lessons and assess their progress using another important source: formative assessment data. Gathered every few weeks or at each grading period, formative data enable the team to gauge levels of success and to adjust their instructional efforts accordingly.

As Schmoker (2003) concludes, such a simple approach to school improvement goes a long way to solving the overload problem and puts the focus where it needs to be—on real students with real learning needs. It was interesting to observe, therefore, when the Bryant team read through several articles on data-based decision making during a recent data coach training session, it was the Schmoker (2003) article that they considered to be the closest description to, and a vindication of, their own approach. They warmed to his preferred version of school improvement that is stripped down, team-based, data-driven and focused on improving instruction in order to enhance student achievement.

Data-Driven Decision Making at the Classroom Level

A second major characteristic that sets Bryant classrooms apart from many classrooms in other schools is the thorough and extensive use of data to guide decision making. Over the last three years, Bryant School (along with two other sites in Dubuque) has participated in a pilot project that has focused on the use of classroom action research as the vehicle for improving teaching and learning. An important offshoot of this work has been the development of a Student Profile—a database that contains all the relevant information concerning the students in each class. It is interesting, therefore, to read Chris McCarron's description of how the faculty has grown into using these databases for instructional decision making.

> I am very fortunate to work with a highly dedicated and talented group of teachers at Bryant. They want to do what is right for students and are willing to invest the effort to do that. Therefore, one might think that this journey to data-driven instruction would have been an easy one for the staff. It has not. Rather, it has been a real growing experience over the past three years that has dramatically altered the way we 'do business' at Bryant School. Even at that, we are just toddlers on this course of development.
>
> Bryant staff began our infant stages of using our data to prove what we already knew. For example, if we thought a child was having difficulty with reading, we collected all kinds of data that showed the child was having difficulty. Our data seldom held surprises for us. This use of data was an easy one for us. The Bryant staff likes predictability. The staff was also fairly comfortable at looking at student achievement data. I think that this was also generally a predictable source of success. We have a long history of high student achievement. Looking at this data was again a safe venture.
>
> At the end of last year, I believe that we have finally moved to 'unsafe' data territory. When we decided to suspend the plan and look at what the data was telling us about our school, it was a

real turning point for us. The meeting where all staff (teachers, secretaries, and paraprofessionals), PTA, and site council joined together in one room for a discussion about our school data was a historical moment in our school. I don't think any outsider could really understand the importance of that shift. There was no way to plan the outcome, no way to protect ourselves from scrutiny. Some people may think that fear of scrutiny is because Bryant staff thinks or feels they are above scrutiny. When in fact, this group of people believes that if there are some unanswered questions or an area where there needs more attention, it is because they have not worked hard enough at it. Work harder and faster could be the Bryant motto. And when they are exhausted and can't dream of working harder or faster, they close up. They look to the predictable. They want confirmation that their hard work is paying off. Being as vulnerable as they were at that meeting was a great risk, but the risk paid off. The success of the common dialogue started us on a new journey.

The journey continued with our student profiles. We have used the profiles this year to tell us the story of our students, the whole story. We haven't just selected the data that told us the story we wanted to hear. We are asking ourselves more questions, starting to look at some of our subgroups, disaggregating our data. We are allowing ourselves to say that we don't know the answer, even if only in a whispering voice. I am seeing people give themselves permission, not to work harder, but to work differently.

This change was really evident in the individual efforts at action research. Many individuals have ventured into new strategies, and teaching interventions that are outside of their predictable past. I can't tell you how many times I have reassured various staff members during the past months that it is okay to try something that may or may not meet with success. Helping them to understand that we can learn a great deal about a child from an intervention that is not successful has been a challenging task. People have been so very apprehensive that they are doing it right, that my job as support person has been to encourage them to rejoice and take pride in the fact that they are simply doing it! That is why it was so important that they take this first sharing of their action research to a small, safe audience. Each individual needs to see, hear, and know all of their hard-working, dedicated peers experienced the same vulnerability and that they are stronger for having done so. I appreciate that we were given this first opportunity to share alone. The questions that we will be using for our sharing get at the heart of not only action research, but at the process of using action research as a tool to stretch our own thinking.

Vicki Sullivan, a sixth grade teacher, along with Chris McCarron, one of the original data coaches, has done the most to champion the development and use of an electronic database (Student Profile) at Bryant. As part of her commitment to action research, Vicki worked on the database in order to be able to engage in data-driven decision making at both classroom and school levels. She was the first Bryant educator to see the potential of data aggregation and disaggregation—and the power of technological applications to aid these processes. In her own classroom, Vicki set out to be able to monitor the following:

- individual student progress, including specific learning needs and the implications for the problem-solving process

- group needs, i.e., those students with the same learning needs and deficits

- correlations across fields—for example, the possible link between low reading performance and being at-risk

- the progress of students in various subpopulations (including gender, socioeconomic status, students with IEPs, ethnicity, mobility, and so on) in the context of *No Child Left Behind*

- the performance of her class on a national standardized test (ITBS), including the grade equivalencies of her sixth grade students and an item analysis in terms of her students' performance on various items over several years—thus providing specific trend-line data on her students' achievement levels, their strengths and weaknesses over time, and, therefore, her level of success as their classroom teacher

What is impressive about Vicki Sullivan's approach is the amount of pertinent documentation (records and other paperwork) that she generates. This documentation includes: letters to parents; mathematics and reading "pretesters" for potential TAG students; line and bar graphs to plot student progress during problem-solving interventions; conferencing sheets used with the students; and a massive amount of recorded classroom assessment data that is used formatively to guide instruction.

The Classroom
Task 3: Data Collection at the Classroom Level

Purpose: To provide evidence of similar data collection and monitoring approaches being used in classrooms in the participants' schools and school districts.

Grouping: Work on your own and then meet with your Learning Team.

Directions: Working individually, list the classroom activities/approaches in your own school(s) and/or school district that are designed to collect student data and monitor student learning. Use the space provided to record your list. Then, in your team, share your individual lists and identify those activities/approaches that occur most frequently across the classrooms in your small-group sample. Compare your list with the types of approaches/activities being used at Bryant.

Should some of your listed activities/approaches be removed? Identify which ones and explain why. Are there any activities/approaches that you want to add to your list? What are they and why should they be included?

Classroom Data Collection and Monitoring Activities/Approaches

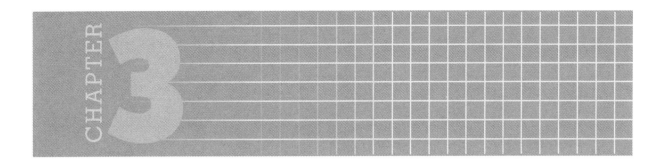

CHAPTER THREE: THE SCHOOL

You don't have to be in Bryant for very long before someone will make reference to the school's culture. According to Kent Peterson (2002), a school culture is the set of norms, core values and beliefs, rituals and ceremonies, symbols, and stories that make up the persona of a school. Every school has a culture, Peterson confirms, which includes those unwritten expectations that are built over time, maintained by those involved, and shape everything about the school for good and bad. By influencing the ways people think, feel, and act, a school's culture can be a positive or negative force. Roland Barth (2002) points out that a school's culture acts for or against improvement and reform and, as the title of Peterson's article suggests, "Culture: Underlying Attitudes Can Stop or Start Progress."

> When a school has a positive, professional culture, one finds meaningful staff development, successful curricular reform, and the effective use of student performance data. In these cultures, staff and student learning thrive. In contrast, a school with a negative or toxic culture that does not value professional learning, resists change, or devalues staff development hinders success. School culture will have either a positive or a detrimental impact on the quality and success of staff development (Peterson, 2002).

In their definitive article entitled "Good Seeds Grow in Strong Cultures," Saphier and King (1985) identify twelve norms, which collectively form a "strong school culture [that] provides a foundation that supports significant and continuing improvements in instruction." These norms include the following:

- collegiality

- experimentation

- high expectations

- trust and confidence

- tangible support

- reaching out to the knowledge base

- appreciation and recognition

- caring, celebration, and humor

- involvement in decision making

- protection of what is important

- traditions

- honest, open communication

Moreover, Richard Elmore (2000) draws our attention to the research conducted by Susan Rosenholtz (1986). She discovered two distinctively different school cultures:

- The first type of school culture is characterized by norms of autonomy, with ambiguous goals and no attempt to develop a shared teaching technology. There is no agreement among teachers and principals about the outcomes they seek and the means for reaching them. In such a setting, therefore, definitions of teaching success and the manner in which it is attained are highly individualized and the epitome of "loose-coupling."

- The second type of school culture is characterized by an emphasis on collaboration and continuous improvement. A kind of normative climate develops in such schools where teacher effort, through a variety of principal actions, is focused on skill acquisition to achieve specific goals. In these schools, experimentation and occasional failure are expected and acceptable in the process of teacher learning. Further, seeking or giving advice is not a gauge of relative competence, but rather a professional action viewed as desirable, necessary, and legitimate in the acquisition of new skills.

According to Elmore (2000), Rosenholtz concludes that collegial support and professional development are unlikely to have any effect on the improvement of practice and performance unless they are connected to a coherent set of goals that give direction and meaning to learning and collegiality. Effective schools, she argues, have tighter congruence between values, norms, and behaviors of principals and teachers, and the activities that occur at the management level are aligned closely with, and facilitative of, the activities that occur at the technical level. Significantly, her findings show that a principal's level of collegiality with teachers affects school performance only when it is connected to activities that focus the school's purposes and that translate those purposes into tangible activities related to teaching. The principal and teachers need to explicitly create a normative environment around a specific approach to instruction, while underlining a view of teaching as a body of skill and knowledge that can be learned and developed over time (as opposed to an idiosyncratic and mysterious process that varies with each teacher).

As DuFour (2003) has recently underscored, it is often a matter of embracing forces that are seemingly opposites: accountability and autonomy, tightness and looseness.

> I am convinced that the parameters—the focused purpose and big
> ideas—that should drive school districts today are found in the
> concept of the professional learning community....The strategy
> proven most effective is one that is loose and tight, a strategy that
> establishes a clear priority and discernible parameters and then
> provides each school and department with autonomy to chart its
> own course for achieving the objectives.

Teamwork—the lodestone of professional learning communities—is the bridge between
what DuFour (2003) calls big ideas/purpose and innovative autonomy. Teams also form a
crucial bridge between

- the school as an organization and individual teachers

- planning and implementation

- policymaking and policy enactment

- overall strategy and day-to-day tactics

- the school and the classroom

- administrative leadership and leadership in the classroom

DuFour (2003) also argues that teamwork provides the platform for creating shared
knowledge by bridging the understanding of what works now and what could work in
the future. Team members, he says, can read research articles and books, attend
conferences and workshops, and surf the Internet, and, by sharing this information, build
shared knowledge and a common vocabulary. Shared knowledge, he says, is the
prerequisite for an effective decision-making process.

In agreeing about the cultural significance of professional learning communities,
Peterson (2002) underlines that their participants value learning, work to enhance
curriculum and instruction, and focus on students. According to Peterson, such a culture
possesses

- a widely shared sense of purpose and values

- norms of continuous learning and improvement

- commitment to and a sense of responsibility for the learning of all students

- collaborative, collegial relationships

- opportunities for staff reflection, collective inquiry, and sharing personal practice

- a common professional language and extensive opportunities for quality
  professional development

In making many of the same points, Keiffer-Barone and Ware (2002) refer to the characteristics of highly effective teams identified by Supovitz and Watson, 2000:

- There is no substitute for a good leader.

- The purpose of effective team meetings is continuously improving instruction.

- Effective teams identify resources they need to provide quality instruction and to find ways to obtain these resources.

- Effective teams find "extra hands" to help them meet their students' needs.

- Collaboration is essential.

- Just as they expect their students to learn, effective team teachers keep learning.

At Bryant, while knowing that their school culture is essentially a positive force for change, staff members also question whether there are some aspects of their culture that they have to "unlearn" (see Duffy, 2003) and which may be holding them back. Chris McCarron, as quoted earlier, alludes to their liking for predictability, although, as she herself admits, this propensity is counterbalanced by their deep desire to do "right things for kids."

As the author (1991 and 2003) has argued, this combination of "conservative radicalism" may be a more improvement-oriented stance than that of so-called "change omnivores" who chase every change that comes along. There is one aspect of a change culture, however, that no one finds easy: the task of confronting colleagues that are not pulling their weight. As Fullan (2001) has pointed out, collaborative cultures are required unless the collaboration is used to mask and protect ineffective practice. As he says:

> Strong teacher communities can be effective or not depending on whether the teachers collaborate to make breakthroughs in learning or whether they reinforce methods that, as it turns out, do not achieve results. In other words...strong communities can make matters worse if, in their collaboration, teachers (however unwittingly) reinforce each other's bad or ineffective practice. This is why close relationships are not ends in themselves. Collaborative cultures, which by definition have close relationships, are indeed powerful, but unless they are focusing on the right things they may end up being powerfully wrong.

All the commentators mentioned above, whether explicitly or implicitly, cite the role of leadership in creating a change culture. Fullan has explored this key role in *Leading in a Culture of Change* (2001). Bryant, it has to be said, is blessed with fine leadership at every level of the organization. Bryant's principal, Lesley Stephens, is very experienced and has exactly the right background to lead a school of diversity. During her working life, she has worked with Native Americans, and she has been a factory worker, a civil rights activist, a parochial school teacher, a reading clinician, a special education teacher, and a teacher in several schools in Dubuque. She has been an administrator for thirty years, thirteen of them at Bryant. Teaching students is what she calls her "ministry"; she has a deep, personal commitment to her "kiddos" (a word she uses frequently). When kids are treated badly, she says, "...it hurts me deeply." This commitment is her mission, her focus, which she admits is very strong, as she explains: "You have to keep your eye on the kids." When asked about her leadership style, she says it is about modeling, about "living and showing." According to Stephens, it is about

- asking a lot of questions

- being directive when the occasion demands

- setting high expectations

- setting parameters and giving people the empowerment and the authority to get to the expectations ("You don't have to task analyze for them," she says.)

- trying hard to find strengths in everyone and "then taking them to the edge"

- asking for change in small incremental steps ("People are all at different places," she observes.)

- giving suggestions concerning the next steps

- being "political" when necessary (While she doesn't feel comfortable at such times, she knows the importance of support and help from the outside. She admits, "You can't cut cords—you need resources; you can't totally isolate yourself [especially when it comes to finding resources for the students and their learning]....While I have high expectations," she says, "I'm not doing things for accolades for myself. It's not about me. I try not to emote, but I do feel very deeply.")

Interestingly, according to her colleague, Vicki Sullivan, setting the expectations started with her interview. Says Sullivan:

> We talked about the culture. There was a lot more of her talking to me rather than me talking to her. She wanted me to know what I was letting myself in for. It was a case of me having raw potential and her willing to provide professional development. She described my 6th grade colleague and said she was looking for a fit—in terms of my personal style.

This is a wonderful example of what Saphier and King (1985) meant when they said that "leaders with culture-building on their minds bring an ever-present awareness of these cultural norms to their daily interactions, decisions, and plans, thus shaping the way events take place." Stephens displays an intuitive awareness of what it takes to lead in a culture of change. In Fullan's terms (2001), she knows—and demonstrates—the importance of moral purpose, understanding change, relationship building, knowledge creation and sharing, and coherence making and, in so doing, displays the attributes of energy, enthusiasm, and hope.

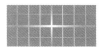

The School
Task 1: Builders of Change Cultures

<u>Purpose:</u> To reflect on the ways that principals can be builders of change cultures.

<u>Grouping:</u> Work on your own and then meet with your Learning Team. Select a recorder.

<u>Group process strategy:</u> Use a brainstorming strategy (see the **Group Process Guide**). Create a team list.

<u>Directions:</u> On your own, reflect upon and list the ways in which principals can establish cultures that are conducive to change in schools like Bryant. Use the following space to record your thoughts. Then meet with your team to share your reflections. Have your team recorder create a team list.

The Culture of Bryant School

The fact that Lesley Stephens talked about the school's culture with Vicki Sullivan during her interview clearly had a lasting impression. Several years on, during a recent site-based in-service session, Vicki Sullivan celebrated the "hallmarks of Bryant's culture" for and with colleagues. In terms of "who we are and what we say and do," she lists eight characteristics:

- love of life-long learning

- high achievement/quality work

- student centered

- continuous improvement

- tenacity

- collegiality

- willingness to grow and change

- gratitude

As a consequence, during his time in the school interviewing colleagues and observing Bryant at work, the author looked for evidence of each characteristic—none of which was hard to find.

Love of Life-Long Learning

When asked about this ingredient of Bryant's culture, colleagues readily provided examples:

- Staff members are on action teams and, as such, are

  - researching best practices;

  - attending classes;

  - working on advanced degrees;

  - showing a willingness to attend relevant workshops, conferences, and so forth;

  - willing to tell the students what they like to do; and

  - modeling learning.

■ The school's long-term engagement with Expeditionary Learning (EL) is another example of ongoing learning. Bryant was one of the original pilot sites for EL in Dubuque and everything done in the school has been influenced by the ten "Design Principles" of Expeditionary Learning Outward Bound: The Primacy of Self-Discovery; The Having of Wonderful Ideas; The Responsibility for Learning; Empathy and Caring; Success and Failure; Collaboration and Competition; Diversity and Inclusion; The Natural World; Solitude and Reflection; and Service and Compassion.

■ There is a reverence for learning. "People here," the author was told, "are anxious to learn; they're well-read—they read journals. We share after every workshop. We don't like dullness—we like bright people, and common information helps the conversation."

■ New teachers are encouraged to become involved in professional development activities. According to the teacher who described herself as the "newest kid on the block":

> This school is a perfect fit for me—it's progressive, state-of-the-art, with dedicated teachers everywhere. Teachers are willing to embrace new researched ideas and take them by the horns.... I've definitely found my niche! Even 'seasoned' newcomers like me take part in mentoring [according to the district's policy]. I joined the Writing action team; it's been a wonderful growing experience for me. I've been to conferences in Chicago and Madison—there was a freeze in my former district! The principal definitely sets the culture—it all starts with her. She's very encouraging and dedicated to the kids.

The same teacher also produced a list of the professional growth opportunities that she has been able to attend in the six months she has been at Bryant. The list included classroom observations; Classroom and Behavioral Management Level II training; the DCSD Professional Mentoring Program (several sessions); an introduction to action research at Loras College; training sessions for new Title I teachers; district training sessions on center management and phonemic awareness; and in-service sessions on an assortment of topics including problem solving, individual student progress reports, PWIM training, mandatory reporting of child and dependent adult abuse training, reading fluency, handwriting without tears, Iowa Teaching Standards, and ETS PATHWISE: A Framework for Teaching (based on Danielson's book, *Enhancing Professional Practice: A Framework for Teaching*).

■ More experienced colleagues are constantly challenged to breathe new life into their teaching and their careers. As one teacher announced in her interview: "I was a first grade teacher for twenty years. Then I decided to go for Reading Recovery training with the AEA and now I'm responsible for eight Title I kids—first graders. It was an interesting, bold decision—a great leap. What's more, teachers don't retire here—they just volunteer!"

■ The staff members are committed to passing on their love of learning to the students and their parents through the use of Student Portfolios. It is fascinating, therefore, to read the following conclusions of the Bryant Portfolio Task Force when its members reported back to colleagues.

Bryant's Portfolio School Plan

Our philosophy is to improve ongoing assessment. Bryant students will develop a portfolio, which will be a purposeful collection of authentic work, systematically organized as a vehicle for engaging students in the process of self-evaluation and goal setting, which shows growth over time.

As of May 2002, Bryant's Portfolio Task Force reviewed the established school plan and made the following recommendations for Fall 2003 implementation.

■ There will be a working portfolio that will be housed in the classroom in two covered bins. Portfolios should include a sampling of a wide variety of work in all curriculum areas. Both students and teachers may choose selections. All work must be dated. It will be left up to individual teachers as to how they want to organize the student portfolios.

■ Non-classroom teachers who have as their responsibility a student's math, reading, or writing program are responsible for producing evidence of progress for the portfolio regularly. Said teachers are responsible for maintaining the portfolio in their teaching areas and preparing the portfolio to be sent home (three times yearly) in collaboration with the timeline established by the student's homeroom teacher.

■ A minimum of three times a year, students in grades 2 through 6 will write an organized self-reflection on a collection of their work. This will be kept in the classroom in the student's portfolio. (Samples to help organize the reflections are in your portfolio packet.)

■ The classroom teacher is encouraged to conference with each student periodically throughout the year. A sample to help you organize your conferences is in your packet.

---

continued

- Portfolios must go home a minimum of three times per year. Suggested times are: before or after parent-teacher conferences, end of an expedition, at a brown bag lunch, or at the request of the parent. Portfolios will be transported in an envelope provided by the school. Filling out order forms for the following year is each classroom teacher's responsibility. Order forms are included in the packet.

- At the conclusion of the school year, all student work will be sent home in their envelopes. The empty bins and colored inserts will remain in the classroom. The empty hanging files with students' names will be sent on to the next grade.

- This portfolio plan will be shared with parents at the pre-entry conferences in August. Parents will also be given guidelines on critiquing their child's portfolio. This is included in the portfolio packet.

High Achievement/Quality Work

According to various staff members interviewed:

> Our business is student learning and we go about it in a very businesslike manner. We have high expectations.

> We pride ourselves in continuing to climb the ladder (of achievement), despite changes in our population. We're looking at things differently; letting go of some things.

> EL (Expeditionary Learning) is about doing quality work. When we entered EL, that was a whole-group decision. We created it on the ground floor and it's played a big part in a lot of the changes here. Now it's embedded and probably invisible to an outsider; it's just part of the way we do business here. The staff does their take on it—that's healthy.

> We have a nice balance of process/product, including depth of content and high standards. We ask the students: 'Is that your best work?' and we're smiling and challenging them at the same time. We're working together (with the students) toward 'quality' which is both our common goal and yet objective—outside us. High quality of work is what we're all after.

> As a colleague said recently: 'Nothing gets swept under the rug at Bryant'; every kid is swept up and dealt with.

There is high quality of instruction at Bryant. It's very structured (it's what the kids need). After the 'pre-test' we talk about how many missed a particular item.

In the sixth grade we have four groups for language arts and, with special education staff involved, that allows us to do some specialized programming and needs-based grouping, including Seminar (TAG).

Student Centered

Comments received during interviews include the following:

- According to the same new teacher, teachers are so high energy for their students. As she reflected in the interview:

  Problem solving (I'd never experienced that before) is the key: every child is given the help wherever—and whenever—it is needed. Follow through is also provided, so their [the teachers'] dedication goes somewhere. The amount of time spent by teachers on *every* child (not just the most needy) is most impressive. The needs of a lot of kids get met—elsewhere they might have fallen through the cracks.

- Kids come first at Bryant. As the principal, Lesley Stephens, points out:

  We don't give up on any kids; giving up on kids is not an option. On a kid-by-kid basis we ask the same question: 'Is their annual growth sufficient?'

- According to other colleagues:

  The problem-solving model/process has been turned into a problem-solving system at Bryant. We were a pilot school originally. Now teaching—testing—re-teaching—tutoring—retesting is a way of life here. Three-quarters of the kindergarten class are currently in problem solving; we're trying to get to their issues early. There are no 'normal'/average kids anymore; they all have issues—they're all fascinating. The student population has changed so much—many have 'issues' in their lives. Although we're still a neighborhood school with some 'downtown' kids (we've also got some autistic kids on the spectrum), the percentage of kids receiving free and reduced lunches has risen from 1% to 30%. Although the perception out there is that we're a 'cream puff' school, that's certainly not the case.

We've adapted problem solving—it was a special education initiative originally—and are now using it for general education as well. We've got a knack for using special education approaches in general education classrooms. Now problem solving is celebrated, reinforced, and grown/nurtured over time, because we know it meets kids' needs and it allows us open, sharing time. Now tools are getting reused and making interventions has become part of our normal way of life. As part of problem solving, we use various assessments: CBMs (Curriculum-Based Measurements) and probes, DIBELs (Dynamic Indicators of Basic Early Literacy Skills), and progress monitoring.

■ According to the principal, Lesley Stephens:

The kids' needs can't be met if the teachers' needs can't be met; they have to feel supported. In order to reach the kids, you have to want to come to work. You have to feel affirmed and be ready to talk candidly about the students' strengths and weaknesses. It's about sweeping up kids, not sweeping their issues under the carpet. You have to feel able to take risks, innovate. There's a guilt level involved; in some places, kids can sit forever—that's not the case here. No child falls through the cracks; no child gets left behind. It's like you can't help scratching the itch—you can't let it be if the kids need help.

During an early morning problem-solving case conference involving the principal, strategist, three teachers, and two AEA consultants, after much useful discussion, the principal interjected and said: "What's the data showing? Let's look at work samples. What's the child actually learning?"

Continuous Improvement

Continuous improvement at Bryant is without question needs-based data-driven. The work of the trained data coaches is foundational. In fact, Bryant's four data coaches have done more than most with the training that they've received over the last three years.

■ They have pulled together all the data—collecting it, analyzing it, sharing it, and organizing staff discussions on the strength of it.

- They return from the training sessions, report on what was covered and use the same exercises (distributed in the training) with their colleagues. As Vicki Sullivan points out:

  > They [the teachers] don't have to wonder what we do when we go to the training sessions—we're not big keepers of something. Everything we've learned, we've integrated. We've used all the ideas in an abbreviated form—so they are doable. We've translated them for staff, made connections for them. It's a big maze to get through.

- Now that there are four data coaches, they feel more inclusive, more knowledgeable, and more linked to the action teams. They feel they are in "collaborative leadership" roles when dealing with the action teams and their members.

- They built the **intensity matrix**, Guidelines for Bryant School's Action Team Work (see Appendix B), of which they are justly proud. This is the "grand strategy" for school improvement over several years—the means by which the overall focus for school improvement at Bryant is being transferred from problem solving to the new, major data-driven school goal—writing.

- They have worked painstakingly on the Student Profile—now referred to as the electronic student database—which is now being used during parent conferences, another source of pride and satisfaction.

- The data coaches also designed the "plan of attack" in 2003 to take the analysis of ITBS results to colleagues, including the awkward fact that there is under-performance at one grade level compared with the other grades. They also led what could not have been an easy session.

In acknowledging that continuous improvement at Bryant is data-driven, it is important to note that assessment data are used in two ways: to make decisions on an everyday basis and, when collected together and recorded, to make medium-term decisions about what to do over the next few months. Classroom assessments include BRIs (Basic Reading Inventories), CBMs/probes, DIBELS, plus the Student Profile/electronic student database (which was used during parent conferences before the start of the school year) and student portfolios (the product of a former action team/task force) which go home prior to conferences and contain writing samples, an interest inventory and—at the end of the year—a letter to the student's new teacher.

Bryant is also a pilot site for the district's new Individual Progress Report that is aligned with standards and benchmarks and with the district's grade-level expectations. As one teacher remarked: "We use the data in order to look at both what we've accomplished and what we need to accomplish. It's important for progress monitoring; it provides verification for your gut feelings."

For continuous improvement to be data-driven at various organizational levels, three factors are at work at Bryant.

1. The same data is used to inform different kinds of decision making.

   Take, for instance, Bryant's ITBS results. Part of the art of the scientific use of data at Bryant is to go two ways with it. This approach was recently endorsed in the National Staff Development Council's (NSDC) *Results* publication. In an article entitled "The Secrets of 'Can-Do' Schools," seven traits of high-poverty, high-performing schools in Louisiana are presented (Richardson, 2003). One of the traits is described as follows:

   > Analyzing student data was the first step and the driving force in the professional learning process. **The schools analyzed data, especially looking at test results, to identify areas of broad, common needs and each student's specific strengths and weaknesses.**

   In Bryant's case, the same data (ITBS results) are used to inform whole-staff decision making and the creation of whole-school goals (A) and the identification of individual learning goals for each student by each classroom teacher (B). As a consequence, another dimension is generated. Classroom goals (C) are the confluence of the teacher's responsibilities relative to implementing the whole-school goals in his or her classroom and the identification of multiple individual goals, i.e., group needs, for the students in the class. At this third dimension, the goal, for example, may be writing, but it is geared to the actual writing deficiencies of the students in the class. These three dimensions can be referred to as

   - the **standardized** use of data (A), which, in terms of ITBS, involves the identification of major, school-wide content deficits and, therefore, school improvement goals.

   - the **personalized** use of data (B), which leads to the pinpointing of specific deficiencies of individual students.

   - the **customized** use of data (C), which establishes—through item analysis—group needs in the classroom. Group needs can also be interpreted two ways: they can be the same need shared by a group of students and they can be the needs of a particular subpopulation of the students, e.g., at-risk students.

2. Bryant staff members, led by the data coaches, are taking the initiative to make technology work for them when it comes to data use.

   The Student Profiles (since renamed the electronic student database) are being used in aggregate and disaggregated forms to create the three levels of data use. As Denis Doyle (2002 and 2003) has pointed out, while schools are awash in data, the data are often not used in any effective way. What is needed, he says, is purposeful organization and, for this to occur, technology is required.

   > **Few schools have the information technology infrastructure, including hardware, software, and trained personnel, to take advantage of the power inherent in school data (Doyle, 2002).**

   Bryant, according to Doyle's remarks, is in a minority of schools that do have the technology and the training to use it. Even then, says Doyle,

   > **Technology is easy, culture is hard....Because data have been used historically to point the finger of blame, it is difficult to convince educators that the next round of data collection will be used as a resource, as an opportunity to trumpet successes and seize opportunities.**

   Again, the Bryant experience would belie these comments. Attitudes to the use of data have clearly changed at Bryant and the availability of technology has helped in this process. The Bryant experience would suggest, therefore, that while culture change is hard, technology makes it easier.

3. Moreover, Bryant educators have created a culture of data use.

   It is striking, therefore, to see the similarity between what has been done at Bryant to create this culture and the list of characteristics of school systems that use data well provided by the Education Commission of the States in a research report published in 2001.

What Effective Data Users Have In Common

- Strong leadership committed to using data for decision making

- Supportive school and district culture for using data for continuous improvement

- Strong service orientation toward principals and teachers—provides specialist knowledge and supports to use in data analysis

- Partnerships with universities, businesses, and nonprofit organizations

- Mechanisms for supporting and training personnel to use data

- Close accounting of every student's performance on academic standards

- Focused flexibility on how time is used

- Well-defined, data-driven school improvement process

Tenacity

Tenacity is another attribute of the Bryant School culture. Indeed, said, one participant, the work ethic at Bryant is not for the faint of heart. There is a hunger, a thirst, said another, to improve what we do in the interests of kids. There were many other similar comments made:

> There's always some way to do things better.
>
> It's sheer will on the part of my teaching partner; she's relentless in pursuit of her goals.
>
> This is a staff with resiliency—when they're knocked down, they spring back up.
>
> Sometimes there's friction over people doing the same tasks. We have to learn that we can't go through the door at the same time!
>
> When I was told at my interview that people work hard here and was given a synopsis of the culture, I thought: "This must be a big deal."
>
> People are willing to put themselves on the line. Our core values are honesty and perseverance.
>
> We don't do anything in half-measures—that wouldn't be Bryant.
>
> I made a student confront a bad test result with his parents. It's all part of him taking responsibility for his learning.

While being selective and not climbing on board every bandwagon that comes along, the Bryant staff, once they have settled on what to change, stick tenaciously to their changes over time. When asked: "So what are the major changes that you're investing in right now?" the answer, predictably enough, was problem solving, writing, and data coaching. Another staff member commented: "The Progress Report Card is not a huge shift for us and Character Education is out there but is not a great driving force."

Problem-solving activities are a constant reminder of the staff's tenacity to help the students, particularly those academically at-risk students in the 13th to 25th percentile range from whom entitlement has been withdrawn.

Collegiality

According to one staff member: "We work together as though we are subject to an unwritten agreement or covenant that 'it's for the children'." "It's a form of peer pressure," said the same person. There is a surprising amount of collegiality, said another: "We're an independent bunch of strong people with lots of leaders. We respect each other and there are no put-downs. Our opinions differ but we discuss things openly and reach some kind of consensus."

So how are decisions made at Bryant? Well, replied one of the teachers: "In roughly four steps: we gather information, mull over it (we think about it and reflect on the possible consequences of particular actions), discuss our differences, and then **sufficient agreement** emerges.

How do new people get on board? "By osmosis," was the response. "It's a case of figuring it out. You watch your grade-level partner teacher, you talk to your mentor, you observe other colleagues—it's a bit like the Stepford wives!"

Collegiality is also structured into the daily life of the school in three ways:

1. Action teams explore the research and share best practice.

2. Grade-level partners and team-teaching pairs work in support of each other.

3. Problem-solving teams have changed the way they do business at Bryant. One teacher explains:

> The very existence of the teams signals that you don't have to be alone with all this. Other people care and there are answers out there. Needs are recognized that weren't recognized before. Chris is the catalyst; she'll say, 'Have you noticed this?' Then we brainstorm interventions—ideas, tools, strategies are available. When we had a conversation about BRIs, there was an expectation that we were going to do something about it—but together. Being on a problem-solving team has added a whole new dimension to instruction.

As another colleague confirmed:

> Whatever's needed for the kids—we talk about it as grade-level teams. During planning time every other week (when the 'specials' have our kids), the grade-level team and Chris become a collective problem-solving body and we spend 45 minutes going through the kids and asking questions such as: 'What does the data say?' 'What shall we do next?' 'Who's going to do it?'

According to Forsythe and Holly (forthcoming), student resiliency is more likely to be fostered by resilient teachers working in resilient schools. And teacher resiliency is fostered, they argue, by working in the kind of small teams described above. Such teams, they say, have definite advantages. They are

- small enough to be intimate and supportive

- natural enough to be part of everyday relationships

- close enough to be part of the ongoing daily action in classrooms

- frequent enough to create a strong sense of attachment

- real and relevant enough because the partnering teachers are faced with the same grade level expectations and can share the same students with all their attendant problems

Willingness to Grow and Change

According to Vicki Sullivan, their approach at Bryant is summed up in the song by Billy Joel titled "An Innocent Man." As the words to the song say:

> *Some people stay far away from the door*
> *If there's a chance of it opening up*
> *They hear a voice in the hall outside*
> *And hope that it just passes by*

As Vicki comments:

> Those wonderful words [from Billy Joel] sum up this place. There's a readiness to stand in the door—to face the risks and opportunities—knowing there are safer places to stand. Take Chris McCarron's unerring focus on kids—her course is true. And she continues to work with more rooms, gathering more work, more learning, and more collaboration.

Both Vicki and Chris are currently taking further degrees. "I always wanted to do it," says Vicki. "My family support group said, 'Just do it!' It was really tough though when my son turned to me one evening and, without a hint of sarcasm in his voice, said, 'Thanks for dropping by'."

Even veteran teachers at Bryant are willing to put themselves on the line for their students. Said one teacher:

> They're open to new ideas and interested in things that work with kids.

A colleague agreed:

> Yes, it's for the kids; I need to feel like I'm helping them—you get the feedback from the parents later. Once a particular learning disability is dealt with, many of the kids move on and prosper—that's what it's all about. You feel more professional in this kind of situation. It's not as scary to say I made a mistake.

As the Billy Joel song ends:

> *Some people hope for a miracle cure*
> *Some people just accept the world as it is*
> *But I'm not willing to lay down and die*
> *Because I am an innocent man*

Reprinted by permission of Billy Joel.

Gratitude

This letter from a parent to the fifth grade teachers is indicative of the depth of parent gratitude.

> Dear [Fifth Grade Teachers],
>
> This was Expeditionary Learning at its finest! Our Bryant fifth grade children looked to be playing as they learned immense life skills in the production of *Bones*. As a parent helper, I was in awe of what I observed: no snapping at each other's missteps. No complaints of it being no fun, no one telling someone else that their work was not valued.

Some precise children measured skeletal bones to create a model for the x-ray screen. Others painted cardboard sheets to create a lab set. Some students huddled at a corner desk writing a distinct, succinct description of the play as an introduction for the program brochure. Makeup was tested and application techniques were revised three flights up, while yet another group practiced lines with the ever nimble light crew adjusting the field to best spotlight the current star performer. A special talent sung the woeful lament of a broken bone, too tired to go on, as another sang of the importance of just keeping in step. And indeed, each and every child did just that.

In the end, as students danced to the...choreographed finale, each and every participant strutted their stuff. And that "stuff" was great!

Thank you. Thank you. Thank you, for teaching our children.

The School
Task 2: Elements of School Culture

<u>Purpose:</u> To compare the elements of Bryant's school culture with those of other schools.

<u>Grouping:</u> Work with your Learning Team or other school-based small group. Select a team recorder to develop a team list.

<u>Directions:</u> Working in small teams (hopefully as colleagues from the same schools), list the elements of the culture of your school—as Vicki did for Bryant—and note whether each of these elements works for or against school improvement. Give a short rationale. Use the space provided below for notes.

<u>Elements of Your School Culture</u>   <u>Impact on School Improvement</u>

Establishing a Culture of School Improvement

It is fascinating to read Lesley Stephens' Executive Summary that introduces Bryant School's 2002-2003 Comprehensive School Improvement Plan.

Reflections on Comprehensive School Improvement

William A. Foster once remarked, 'Quality is never an accident, it is always the result of high intention, sincere effort, intelligent direction, and skillful execution; it represents the wise choice of many alternatives.'

As I think back over the last ten years (our first School Improvement Plan was that long ago) and this year most especially, I believe it is now accurate for me to say, 'I think we finally get it and have it together.' Why, I question, has it taken so long? Only to someone involved, can the answer be obvious. School Improvement is the most challenging, most difficult, most affirming, rewarding, professional challenge of one's career.

At this point in time, our school comes to the common ground of uniting our vision with our practice and in so doing has created a learning culture within our school that embodies what current research is telling us. In the business world, culture stands out as a strong predictor of financial result. So true for education. Numerous studies have identified the organizational culture as critical to the successful improvement of teaching and learning. Visionary institutions are places where cultural values infuse all aspects of everyday practice.

The Progress Review on our School Improvement Plan cannot occur without emphasizing the value and the role 'culture' plays at this school. Culture is for us 'the way we do things around here.'

The Foster quote is most appropriate. Bryant's high quality work is the result of vision and high purpose, sincere effort, intelligent leadership, and skillful execution—all of which are applied to the school improvement process. And the school improvement planning process at Bryant is the vehicle for enacting the vision in practice, extending the school's learning culture, and impacting teaching and learning so that, as Lesley Stephens explains, the culture of the school (which she has done so much to create) infuses all aspects of everyday practice. This, of course, is the ideal: when the school's vision is enacted on a daily basis in real teaching and learning situations. School improvement planning at Bryant, it can be said, is not only part of the culture but is also the vehicle for cultural transmission and enactment.

As Lesley Stephens admits, however, this hasn't always been the case. Producing impactful school improvement plans has been a lengthy learning process in itself. Several years ago School Improvement Plans in Dubuque schools suffered from many of the defects recently listed by Schmoker (2003). The plans were often the lengthy products of what was largely a paper exercise. Staff ownership was minimal, the plans were interest-based as opposed to data-based, and, without any clear focus, the plans lacked the ability to impact at the level of practice. Ten years on, much has changed. By now the plans, Bryant's included, are:

- "phat" (important), not fat (They have been "skinnied up," to use Nancy Bradley's apt description.)

- thoroughly grounded in data (baseline, up-close, and trend-line)

- the platform for far more staff involvement and engagement

- highly focused on teaching and learning

- geared to provide for accountability at the school level in terms of the measure of impact on student achievement

- inclusive of support mechanisms—including targeted professional development activities—to enable all those involved to be skilled enough to be successful (Building staff capacity to be successful is a crucial ingredient of these new-style plans.)

- achieving optimal capacity—high focus, high use of data, high engagement, high skill development, and high impact on student achievement—and, therefore, high accountability (The school improvement plans in Dubuque schools, as elsewhere in Iowa, are the vehicle for embracing high levels of both local autonomy and accountability—a combination which is probably unprecedented across the nation.)

Far from distracting from, or even supplanting, the real work of school improvement (as Schmoker claims), these plans are well capable of galvanizing real school improvement, i.e., teachers working together to improve their instruction in order to improve student learning (process) and student achievement (product).

April 17, 2001, was a real watershed in the history of Bryant School's school improvement efforts. Vicki Sullivan and Chris McCarron, working with their principal, Lesley Stephens, at a data coach training session, had decided that their school improvement plan wasn't good enough (too unfocused, too interest-based, too lacking in impact). They decided, therefore, to take a timeout—to go slower to go faster—and to re-energize their efforts by creating a comprehensive collection of data from which they would select their new focus areas. April 17, 2001, was the date chosen to bring everyone together (teachers, support staff, and site council members) to decide the future direction of Bryant School. Prior to the event, all participants received the following communication.

Preparing for Our Meeting

On Tuesday, April 17th you have an opportunity to be part of shaping the future of Bryant School. On this date, teachers, support staff, and site council members will join together to determine goals for our school plan. The goals that we select will be the primary focus of our collective efforts for approximately the next five years.

To aid us in coming to a consensus on goals for our school, we have collected a variety of information relating to Bryant School. There are two distinctly different types of data to examine. First, we have perception data, the summary of the surveys which were completed this year by Bryant staff, parents, and students. This data allows us to compare and contrast how these three stakeholder groups view Bryant School. Secondly, we have hard data, the collection of testing results and other concrete data from a variety of sources. Both sources of data provide us vital feedback regarding Bryant School.

While knowing the information provided in each source is crucial in our decision making, we are also aware that examining and discussing every piece of data as a group would be an impossible task. Therefore, to aid in the process, we have taken the data available to us and have summarized the results of the data. In doing so we have invested every effort to summarize the results rather than to interpret the results.

Interpreting the results is the responsibility of every teacher, member of the support staff, and site council member who will be a part of creating the next Bryant School Plan. Included in this packet of information are the survey summary results for each of the three groups (staff, students, and parents), a matrix which highlights the summary results for the surveys, and a summary of the hard data resources. We would encourage each person to read the information in the packet and to ask him/herself what this information reveals about our school.

At the meeting, people will be asked to point out what information indicates the strengths of Bryant School. We will also ask what information points to needs or areas of improvement. Once our strengths and needs are listed, the group will be asked to come to a consensus on a broad goal for each of the three district categories: high student achievement, citizenship and character development, and communication and collaboration. After the broad goals are selected, it will be the responsibility of each action team to determine the more specific plan for addressing the goal.

This is an exciting adventure for Bryant School. Each person has the opportunity to [contribute] his/her voice to the plan for Bryant. No voice is more or less important than another's voice. It will be through the sharing of our individual, various perspectives that we will arrive at the collective action that will shape Bryant's future.

continued

Should you have questions regarding the data, please feel free to contact Chris or Vicki.

Agenda

Opening

Review of Agenda

Determine Strengths

Determine Areas of Concern, Interesting Information, and Challenges

Determine What the Implications of the Data are for Bryant School

Come to Consensus on Three Goals:

     High Student Achievement

     Citizenship and Character Development

     Communication and Collaboration

Closing

The session certainly met the organizers' expectations. Strengths and challenges were identified (see below) and three broad goal areas were selected (see the following page).

DATA RESULTS	
Strengths	**Challenges, Areas of Concern, Interesting Facts**
■ Know expectations	■ Parents lack of knowledge regarding IEP/PEP
■ Parents support students	■ How I compare with others
■ Teachers care about kids	■ Difference between the learning of boys/girls
■ Technology—parents/students	■ Spelling on ITBS
■ IEP—very pleased	■ 81% did not pass the writing assessment
■ Scores maintaining	■ Talk with me (student) frequently about progress
■ Reading	■ Relationships
■ Strengths in curricular area entering Junior High	■ Feedback/assignments
■ High expectations	■ Staff and students understand expectations, but not communicated to parents
■ Goals aligned	■ Technology—staff
■ Teachers hard on selves	■ PEP parents
■ Teaching children to be life-long learners	■ Parent/teacher perception of curricular areas
	■ Concerns about class size
	■ Math
	■ Teachers hard on selves
	■ Language
	■ Social Studies—staff
	■ Science—staff
	■ Problem solving focus

BRYANT SCHOOL LONG RANGE IMPROVEMENT GOALS

1. Improve Student Achievement PK–12

   Brainstorming

   ■ Writing

   ■ Math—math computation

   ■ Science

   ■ Social Studies (intermediate v. primary)

   ■ Spelling

   Comments

   Science and social studies may be addressed under problem solving.

Goal: WRITING

2. Nurture and support a positive learning environment based on mutual respect, active citizenship, and demonstration of good character.

   Brainstorming

   ■ Make every child feel included

   ■ Steps to Success program

   ■ Expeditionary Learning

   Comments

   Inclusion and gender may be addressed in Steps to Success

Goal: STEPS TO SUCCESS

3. Strengthen communication and collaboration within the school system and with families and the community to support student learning.

   Brainstorming

   ■ Problem solving as a way of doing business

   ■ Portfolios

   Comments

   Bring kids on board as active participants. Technology issues may be addressed as part of problem solving.

Goal: PROBLEM SOLVING

In order to build on this success, however, three further moves were made.

1. Staff members were asked to volunteer to join one of the three goal-based action teams (not volunteering was not an option) and charged with the responsibility of specifying their short-term goals and success indicators.

2. The data coaches produced what they refer to as the "Intensity Matrix" (see Appendix B) that incorporates the life cycle of a school improvement initiative

(study and planning, further planning, and early implementation, full implementation, further implementation and modification, and maintenance) and ensures that each of the goals—in any one year—would not be demanding the same level of attention as the others.

3. As part of Bryant's involvement in an action research pilot project (starting in the fall of 2001), real efforts were made to bolster the school improvement efforts at the classroom level. The author introduced the new work by emphasizing that the project aimed to

    ▓ build on previous work in three pilot schools

    ▓ continue school improvement efforts that are needs-based data-driven, but this time underneath the School Improvement Plan

    ▓ use action research as the process vehicle

Put simply, he explained, action research helps educators become more effective in the identified areas of need of their instructional practice (see Workbook Three: *Engaging in Action Research*).

All participants in the three action research pilot sites—the Bryant School staff included—attended an introductory session in August 2001 and received the following handout.

Dubuque CSD: Classroom Action Research

Introduction: Classroom Action Research and School Improvement

■ It is often the case that school improvement efforts do not have an impact at the classroom level.

■ Even when goals are commonly agreed upon at the school level, they are implemented differentially and inconsistently at the classroom level.

■ What is required are bridges that link "policy and plans" and "practice."

■ One such bridge is **action research**, especially if it is conducted on a school-wide basis, while, at the same time, garnering individual commitment.

■ The whole staff can then share the same goal and commit to collaborative implementation. The action research allows for supportive reflection-in-action and reporting on progress.

■ It also links the staff to the world of new ideas outside the school.

---

continued

Classroom Action Research Project in Dubuque CSD

Given the points raised above, the purposes of this initiative are as follows:

- As a natural progression from the school improvement/data coach training, take data based continuous improvement to the classroom level.

- Help teachers improve what they do in order to help students improve their learning.

- Provide the vehicle for collaborative, "change-as-you-go" implementation.

- Carefully match internally identified needs (the "problems") with externally generated, research-based strategies and interventions (the "solutions").

- Increase the depth of personal ownership, commitment, reflection-in-action and, therefore, the likelihood of successful implementation.

- Enhance teacher effectiveness, thereby linking with professional growth plans and Track 2 of the Dubuque teacher evaluation system.

Action Team Responsibilities

- Collate internal data concerning current information regarding both student learning results and instructional practices. (Where we are now.)

- Collate external data (research-based strategies/best practice information) for both student learning and instructional practices. (Where we could/should be.)

- Complete Emily Calhoun's SAR (School-wide Action Research) Matrix as a summary document, including success criteria for both student performance and the learning and instructional environment. This should include a clear definition of the "model"/strategies to be implemented.

- Transfer ownership and resources to those responsible for everyday implementation—the classroom teachers.

Individual Teacher/Small Team Responsibilities

- Commit to undertaking mini-classroom action research projects.

- Select strategies to implement and methods of tracking the implementation.

- Frequently/regularly collect up-close data and the subsequent determination of midstream changes.

- Make connections with professional growth plans/peer coaching opportunities/teacher evaluation procedures.

Following the launch of this project, the discussion guide reproduced below was constructed to enable Bryant staff members to reflect on their progress with action research projects.

Action Research Discussion Guide

Reflection on student performance:

- What does the data that you are collecting suggest about the effects of the interventions?

- How did the student(s) respond to the interventions?

- What would be the next step in your interventions?

Reflection on your personal growth:

- What were the greatest challenges in your project?

- What were the greatest rewards?

- How did you stretch yourself?

- Did you use any external resources to help you in determining your interventions? If so, what, and were they useful? If not, what might have been a good source for your project?

- If you were going to have the same group of students next year, what might you select for an action research project to begin the year?

Reflection on the Bryant School community:

- Were the students and parents included in your planning, discussion, and review of your project? If so, how? If not, could they have been?

- What benefits does action research hold for Bryant School?

It soon became apparent, however, that the Bryant leadership team wanted to adjust the action research project to fit with its chosen direction. The team made three valid points:

1. The action teams that had been set up to pursue the three school goals could certainly apply the advice concerning the responsibilities of action teams in going forward. Indeed, it is interesting to note that the Writing Action Team has since done exactly that during its study/planning phase.

2. The problem-solving process being applied so extensively in classrooms across the school was seen as exactly the same process as action research but directed more specifically at students and their learning needs, with concomitant implications for the adjustment of instructional practices.

3. The work on Student (Classroom) Profiles—the electronic student database—which was also being initiated, could act as the catalyst for instructional decision making at the classroom level. Consequently, an in-service session (see the plan below) was organized for October 24, 2001, to involve staff in planning how to take the next steps.

Agenda for Early Release
October 24, 2001

Setting the stage. "Talking turkey." (10 minutes)

Discussion of why we collect data. (5 minutes)
Share that we have data at the district, school, classroom, and individual levels. Bottom line—data should be used to increase student achievement. Ways that data is useful. Past/present/future.

Group activity: What data can we use? Where is the data located? (20 minutes)
We will divide the staff into two groups. Grade levels will split and special education and other support staff will split between the two groups. Chris and Vicki will each facilitate one group. The group will brainstorm the data that they use to make decisions and then determine where that data is located. They will be completing the following chart that will be drawn on chart paper.

	What data can we use?	Where is the data located?
Data that tells of past performance:		
Data that tells of present performance:		
Data that can predict future performance:		

Using data to drive instruction through classroom profiles—a grade-level example. (20 minutes)
Vicki will share how sixth grade determined what data was important to them when making their instructional decisions. She will share how the data was collected and how they used the data in their decision making. She will share how the classroom profile looks and how it can be sorted by special fields.

Grade-level teams determine what data is important for their classroom profiles.
(35 minutes)
Vicki will give the directions for the activity of grade levels determining the data sources that they will use for their classroom profiles. Give assignments of support staff to the grade level.

Where do we go from here? (10 minutes)
Share how the action research and action teams come together. Distribute handout. Share that we will work together as a staff on the profiles during a staff meeting on November 21st. Their profiles will be entered into the computer and the sorts will be made for them.

The staff at Bryant continues to ratchet up its school improvement efforts. Indeed, during two sessions in February and April, 2003, with the demands of the *No Child Left Behind* legislation very much in mind, faculty members analyzed their Iowa Test of Basic Skills (ITBS) in some depth—in order to "go both ways" and inform goal setting at both the whole school and classroom levels. In the first session (02/26/03), several background papers were used. The session ended with faculty members filling in the *Analyzing and Reporting Our Data—Response Sheet* included below.

Analyzing and Reporting Our Data
Response Sheet

Name: _____   Data analyzed by: _____

Data collection period: _____   Date of analysis: _____

1. What do you notice when you look at these data? What can you say about student or staff performance based on these results?

2. What additional questions do these data generate?

3. What do these data indicate students need to work on? Based on these data, what can we infer teachers need to work on?

4. What do the results and their implications mean for our school?

During the second session (04/09/03), the fruits of the previous session were presented to colleagues plus other pertinent observations. This session proved to be another watershed in the history of Bryant's school improvement efforts. It was the session in which a particular lower-performing classroom was exposed for all to see. This is a turning point in the growth of any organization—when the "collective" identifies and begins to deal with individual deficiency. It is a sensitive, highly risky juncture from which most schools shy away. But it is only by grasping such opportunities, however difficult and embarrassing they prove for all involved, that growth can occur. This is accountability at work in its most foundational form.

Reflecting Upon Bryant's School Improvement Efforts

The continuing school improvement efforts at Bryant have four clear strengths:

- The somewhat unique, homegrown approach of "going both ways at once."

- The enthusiasm, leadership, and organizational skills provided by the data coaches.

- The readiness to accept the ongoing advice and feedback from an external critical friend.

- The fact that school improvement really is "how we do business around here."

Going Both Ways With School Improvement

A hallmark of Bryant's school improvement efforts is the way that data are used to "go both ways": to inform decision making at the whole-school and classroom levels. This enables the staff to be working simultaneously on two kinds of goals: whole-school goals (e.g., writing across the school/curriculum) and personal/instructional goals. ITBS data, for instance, is used to identify whole-school goals (and then to track their progress over time) and to generate instructional targets at the classroom level. The writing goal is an excellent example of a whole-school initiative.

- Writing was a need recognized by all staff during the pathfinding data "summit" in April 2001.

- Concerning the ongoing work on the writing goal, the 2001-2002 school year was a study year.

- As part of the study process and the exploration of external data, the writing action team involved staff members in looking at various whole-school approaches to writing. The Northwest Regional Educational Laboratory's Six Traits approach and the Iowa Writing Project were both examined. Neither met with unanimous support. As one member of the staff said during the interview, the Bryant approach is to look at various approaches, select the best parts of each, and customize them for use at Bryant.

- Staff also looked at the district curriculum's process for writing, an in-service was organized on the subject of holistic scoring, and rubrics have been created for the holistic scoring of both writing content and mechanics. The writing mechanics rubric is presented below.

■ Such rubrics are now being used to score the written work of each and every student. Baseline data are being collected and group and individual needs identified. In the meantime, problem-solving interventions are being readied to support the work on writing. At this stage, therefore, by working both ways, school improvement efforts at Bryant come together at the classroom level.

BRYANT WRITING MECHANICS RUBRIC						
Number of Sentences	**1**	**2**	**3**	**4**	**5**	**Total**
Capitalization						
Usage						
Punctuation						
Spelling						
Subtotal						

Description of Categories

Capitalization:

1. The first word of a sentence (*The boys are tall.*)

2. Proper names (*Jonathon Doe, Dubuque, etc.*)

3. The word "I" (*Linda and I are working on the project.*)

4. The first word in a quote (*Jack said, "The crowd is being difficult!"*)

5. Titles

Usage:

1. The sentence should be written as we speak (using correct grammar). (*He goed. = 0; He goes to the store every day. = 1*)

2. The meaning of the sentence is clear.

3. The sentence is a complete thought.

continued

Punctuation:

Ending marks

- Period (.)

- Question mark (?)

- Exclamation mark (!)

Within the sentence

- Quotation marks (" ")

- Commas in a series (paper, pencils, pens, and erasers)

- Commas in dates (Today is August 6, 2001.)

- Commas between city and state

- Commas within compound sentences

- Commas following introductory words

- Commas used with appositives

- Periods after abbreviations

- Apostrophes to show possession

- Apostrophes in contractions

Spelling:

Correct spelling is used for each word in the written product.

The Leadership Provided by Data Coaches

Everyone agrees that without the unstinting efforts of the data coaches (formerly two, now four), school improvement at Bryant would be nowhere near as advanced as it is today. While constantly putting themselves on the line, they have earned the trust and respect of their colleagues. They constitute a superb example of what Richard Elmore (2000) calls "distributed leadership" in that they exercise their leadership and organizational skills within the body of the staff. They are "of" the staff and work for the staff in a coordinating capacity. Their hard work, commitment, and dedicated service to their colleagues are demonstrated on a daily basis.

No wonder, then, that one of the original data coaches has been drafted into the Central Office to perform a similar role for other schools across the district and the other is already being considered as a strong future candidate for a school principalship. And now two new recruits are being encouraged to follow in the footsteps of their pathfinding colleagues. A crucial understanding on the part of the data coaches is the need to always keep their colleagues informed. Communication, they know, is a key activity.

The Guidance of an External Critical Friend

The author has served in the role of critical friend for the Bryant staff for almost ten years. Besides being the lead trainer for the off-site data coach and action research sessions, he visits Bryant at least three times a year to endorse its work and provide pointers for improvement. Another of his roles is to provide feedback on its School Improvement Plan. The most recent feedback report is reproduced below.

Dubuque CSD
2002-2003 CSIP Review

School: Bryant

<u>Strengths</u>

- Excellent Executive Summary—very informative and reflective.

- The summary of what the school database evidences (e.g., excellent attendance, strong parent participation, etc.) is most useful.

- The mixed economy approach to writing (taking the best from various approaches) is to be applauded, especially the incorporation of researched best practices (the work of the action team?).

- Outstanding Progress Review sheets and very comprehensive School Profile data.

- The sequenced, intensive focus on problem solving, writing, and citizenship is to be applauded (as symbolized by the excellent Guidelines for Action Team Work—incorporating SEIM).

- The two-level approach—the work on problem solving and the use of an electronic student database—puts Bryant in the vanguard of those schools trying to individualize student learning plus the fact that school-wide baseline data for writing is guiding whole school efforts.

- The intensity of focus in the plan is its greatest strength.

---

continued

Challenges

■ Keeping it all going in the face of the School Board's strategic plan and *No Child Left Behind.*

■ Continuing application of the SEIM design (mathematics?).

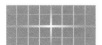 **The School**
Task 3: Strengthening School Improvement Efforts

Purpose: To use the story of Bryant's school improvement efforts to identify what activities are currently happening under the name of school improvement in the participants' schools and school districts.

Grouping: Work in small groups with your Learning Team or other building or district-based team. Select a recorder.

Directions: In small building-or district-based teams, use the details of Bryant's school improvement efforts over time to list what could be done to strengthen the school improvement efforts in your school or school district. How or why would these activities be effective? Have your team recorder record your list on poster-size paper

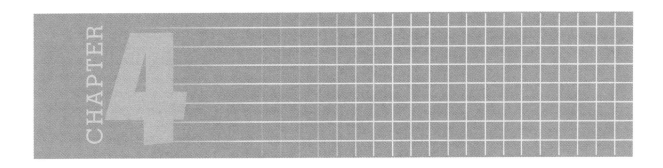

CHAPTER FOUR: THE DISTRICT

School Improvement—A Three-Stage Journey

Bryant School's journey with school improvement is one subset of a larger journey—that of Dubuque Community School District (DCSD). What has emerged from the author's research on the history of school improvement efforts in Iowa is that over the last fifteen to twenty years—in Dubuque and elsewhere in Iowa—it has often taken the form of a three-stage journey. All three stages are different versions of localism or, in Iowa, what is called "local control," i.e., control of education by the local community and locally generated school improvement efforts.

The first stage (Autonomy 1: the central control stage) was followed by a burst of school-based autonomy (Autonomy 2). In turn, a third stage (Autonomy Plus) developed that was not only a combination of some of the features of the first two stages, but also has some new characteristics of its own. It is this third, more systemic stage in which the full potential of locally generated school improvement is exhibited. These developmental stages are epitomized by what has occurred in Dubuque—as elsewhere in Iowa—over the last fifteen or so years.

Stage One: Central Control

The first stage was characterized by hierarchical, authoritarian relationships and conformity to centralized commands at the local level. In another river town similar to Dubuque this stage was characterized as follows:

During the late 1980s the district, according to one participant, was in a very centralized, top-down mode of operation. The superintendent was seen as a strong, directive, and authoritarian administrator who "got the job done and accomplished many things." Some of the achievements for which he was recognized were the implementation of both an instructional and a curriculum model, the closure of a school that had a declining student population, and the raising of teacher salaries. Along with the successes of this take-charge leader came the requirement that all employees had to conform to district (i.e., Central Office) decisions and directives. For example, all decisions regarding textbook adoptions were uniformly imposed throughout the district, and the budgeting process was firmly in the hands of those in the Central Office. This was the stage, then, when the school district was directed by a paternalistic, centralist regime at the local level. All changes were imposed and centrally controlled. Local [mandating] might sound like a contradiction in terms but, given the decentralized nature of education in Iowa, it was the dominant—and dominating—style of local leadership.

While more changes of superintendents were involved in Dubuque (a pattern that interestingly hasn't changed), the characteristic leadership style was the same.

Stage Two: School-Based Control

In the early 1990s, however, the second stage was initiated in Dubuque with several moves being made in the direction of site-based decision making and building-based management.

1. Each school was encouraged to set up a Site Council, and Jim Mitchell was drafted to train school teams in how to make the Site Council process as effective as possible. His advice during the training sessions included the following points:

    ■ Keep the work of the Site Council focused on student achievement.

    ■ Ensure that all constituencies (teachers, support staff, administrators, parents, students, business partners/community members) are represented and have an equal voice on the Site Council.

    ■ Encourage each member to represent and communicate with his or her constituency.

    ■ Make certain that staff and parents are made fully aware of the identified work of the Site Council.

    ■ Encourage Site Councils to keep looking for ways to improve.

    ■ Emphasize that the main work of the Site Council is to develop, implement, and support the School Improvement Plan, by

        ■ gathering input for the development of the School Improvement Plan;

        ■ reviewing and examining school data;

        ■ writing the School Improvement Plan (or designating a group to write it based on the Site Council's established priorities);

        ■ creating Action Teams to accomplish the goals of the School Improvement Plan;

        ■ determining that the Action Teams know their responsibilities, one of which is to report progress to the Site Council. In turn, the Site Council provides the Action Teams with support, encouragement, and feedback on the action plans.

    ■ Charge Action Teams with the responsibility of accomplishing the school's goals as identified in the School Improvement Plan.

■ Encourage each school to create a database of information about the school and its students to guide in setting future direction and to measure progress toward goals.

■ Emphasize the importance of having four participant roles on the Site Council: facilitator, chairperson (often the principal), recorder, and process evaluator (the "keeper" of the operational norms).

In addition, Jim Mitchell nicely summarized the steps that Site Councils should take to get started on all this work.

■ Select membership that represents constituencies.

■ Assign roles.

■ Develop operational norms.

■ Define and communicate essential work.

■ Develop the School Improvement Plan.

■ Support and coordinate the work of Action Teams.

■ Receive data collection and analysis from Action Teams.

It is worth noting that, ten years on, schools in Dubuque have hardly wavered from this original advice. Site Councils are being run in ways that are very similar to Mitchell's guidance materials.

2. Contemporaneously with the training given by Jim Mitchell, consultant Pat Dolan was advising the district to set up an "anchor document" (see Dolan, 1994) that involved the three "anchors" (Central Office, School Board, and the local Teachers' Association) in signing off on a document that declared their intention to collaboratively pursue site-based decision making and individual school improvement. This "Memorandum of Understanding" (which was originally dated 2/22/94 and was slightly revised in 2000) declared:

The Dubuque Community School District and the Dubuque Education Association (DEA) agree to continue the process of decision making that deliberately places considerable authority and responsibility for education and related decisions within the school itself or within the educational delivery unit. They will jointly continue to explore changes in structures and procedures that will facilitate the goals of

■ providing better educational services through collaboration;

■ placing the decision making closer to the teaching and learning;

---

continued

■ creating an environment that can listen better and respond more quickly to the needs of parents and students;

■ improving the work environment of administrators and teachers, which is ultimately the learning environment for children.

The parties also believe that in the process of this continued collaboration around the implementation of School-Based Shared Decision Making (SBSDM), there will be a growing sense of openness of communication, growing trust, and ultimately a developing ability to problem solve for the improvement of quality education in the Dubuque Community School District.

We are not trying to dismantle a good system, but working with a good system, deliberately continuing a process that will collaboratively help us learn how to better deliver quality education in a responsive way. We believe that those involved are the best designers, and that we will all learn from their successes and their mistakes.

The memorandum also covered the establishment of a district level Oversite Committee and similarly structured councils at each site, thus drawing the Site Councils within the working of the agreement. School Councils, it was agreed, would be composed in such a way "that all groups are represented in a ratio sufficient to guarantee authentic participation." Moreover,

...the size of the school, the size and complexity of its instructional staff, and the school's organizational structure will all influence the council composition.

The teachers and the principal will establish a fair system for selecting representatives who will, in turn, be responsible for regular communications with the broader constituencies. It is important that teacher membership includes active association representation and that parent membership is available to all parents regardless of affiliations with the local parent organization. In general, the school council is to make certain that more quality decisions are made, as appropriate, at the school level and that the process provides for decisions to be made close to where the students are educated, through the participation of those most directly concerned with students and within the context of district, state, and federal parameters.

3. From the mid-1990s onwards, teams from every school in Dubuque attended school improvement workshops led by consultants (the author included) from the

New Iowa Schools Development Corporation (NISDC), a nonprofit organization set up at the state level to assist schools and school districts in their school improvement efforts. The expectation was that the members of each building team would receive the training and apply the lessons learned by returning to their schools and involving their colleagues in creating a School Improvement Plan using a common format (the CREATE model introduced in Workbook Two: *Creating a Process*).

This training, according to Nancy Bradley, took up where Jim Mitchell's training left off. Building teams now had the tools to go back and commit to inclusive planning activities at the school level. It is interesting, therefore, to read the reflective comments of some of the original workshop participants. As one middle school teacher remarked:

> The shared vision concept is a relatively new idea for the Dubuque Community School District, much less for the individual school. Before, decisions were made from the top down with little involvement or input from school staff. It had been this way for years. Visions were something that nobody really had much time for—educational fads seemed very much in vogue and certainly were not long lasting. Nuts and bolts issues were topics of most discussion, not where the school as a whole was headed but more like, 'How will we get through this school year—never mind the next five.' We realize there have been some longer range plans out there in the past, but they always appeared to be nebulous and really didn't involve staff as such.

Another participant commented along similar lines:

> The school improvement planning that took place over the school year was, in itself, a new concept for me. I must be honest and say that, at first, I had little knowledge about what school improvement meant or was. I came from another state where teachers had little to say about school improvement. Things that happened at schools were decided from a higher source. There was little ownership of an overall school vision.

Both of these participants were reacting to the workshops as a result of their previous (Stage One) experiences when the top-down approach to decision making—even at the local level—meant that there was little staff involvement, little knowledge of school improvement, little sense of a shared vision, and still less sense of ownership. This new training, however, along with the work of Dolan and Mitchell, obviously contributed to the creation of the second stage of development (Stage Two) where the locus of power shifted in the direction of more building-based autonomy.

The emphasis during the NISDC workshops was on the generation of the school improvement **process** at the individual building level with different buildings reacting relatively **autonomously** by learning from their unique data and developing in different ways. "Process" and "autonomy" are the central concepts at this stage. While the district did demand a measure of process accountability (each school had to have a Site Council and produce a School Improvement Plan), there was little emphasis, at this juncture, on results in terms of student achievement.

Not that gains had not occurred. More inclusive involvement in the school improvement process was an early benefit and one much appreciated by many of the participants. As one enthusiast observed:

> No longer does our Site Council sit in isolation....This has been a pivotal year for our council in that we have veered from the self-contained to the 'staff, faculty, students, community' contained. It has become more structured as we try to stick to our agenda, put our priorities in order, and deal with the vision aspect of our school's mission statement—not the daily issues of our school day. As the Site Council evolves into an all-school vision, it will include everyone, whether on the actual council or involved in the various teams in order to further the reason we are in existence—to help our students learn with dignity, responsibility, and diligence....For the first time the staff is really empowered and has ownership. Because of our NISDC training, we have felt empowered to include all staff through our endeavors, thereby having 'site' educated individuals ready to step into the council when our terms expire. Eventually, the whole school will know how to embrace the new 'site-visionary' concept.

An elementary teacher echoed many of these sentiments:

> This has been a tremendous year for my own personal growth. I believe that being a part of the Site Council and a part of the training will stay with me for life. I have a new found appreciation for what a Site Council does and how important the job is. I also have a new found appreciation and respect for school principals and administrators....This planning is a very serious and deliberate process that can be completed easily. Site planning that is done effectively should impact our school and children for life.

Moreover, the fact that the training sessions empowered the participants to enter new territory of needs-based, data-driven, school-based improvement efforts proved a heady experience for many of the participants. The training engendered a real sense of release and a renewed sense of purpose. According to an elementary representative:

> In my twenty years in education many initiatives have come and most have remained with more piled on top of those previously introduced. The site-based decision-making model advocated by the NISDC consultants, Peter Holly and Stan Burke, shows us how to take what we are doing, throw out the chaff, and keep what is needed for institutional excellence. The major focus I internalized was the **need for data to drive all decisions**. So many times an idea became the model of the day simply because someone had read an article about a successful school which found new ways to impart knowledge to its clients. The thought that all achievement for students comes from an organized plan conceived with forethought and data was not exactly new, but this workshop brought such common sense attitudes forward in my thinking. I especially was pleased to note that data should be obtained from many sources, not just a parent survey or ITBS tests. As an Expeditionary School, we must obtain data on the efficacy of our E.L. stance. We discussed this along with all modes of data collection and found that we do have much of this data in hand. Now to centralize this data into a usable form to help us write future plans....The trainers gave the participants permission to find the things which are important to the particular setting and to seek excellence in that setting. Demographically different sites are now able to find what fits their needs and to write a plan, which assures them of a focused path to success. Also apparent was the need to continue these plans over a reasonable length of time so that in their maturity the ideas can become practice and be internalized.

The same participant talked about the need to make all stakeholders feel ownership of the plan so that they too will invest in it and want to "monitor its path, either consciously or unconsciously." In other words, the more it is "our" plan, the more we want to know if it is working and being successful. This was a most welcome departure: the growing understanding that data can be used not only to identify needs and, therefore, goals, but also to monitor and evaluate whether those goals are being and—more down the line—have been achieved. Along the same lines another school participant realized that the data being collected by her and her colleagues could be used for reporting progress to outside agencies such as the State Department of Education. She explained:

Through this process we have devised a school profile form that we will begin using next school year. The school profile will also help me in my current job. As the at-risk strategist for the school, I use much of the information for reports to the state. These reports are data-driven and we have included the following: enrollment; socioeconomic groups; student attendance, and tardiness; class size; student referrals; students in special programs; test data; reading proficiency levels; numbers of computers; members of staff, etcetera.

This growing readiness to use data to report on the progress being made by an individual school occurred during the second stage of development; it also acted as a precursor of the third stage. The growing use of data was to lead to the growing appreciation of the need for more accountability including more comparability across schools and school districts. And for comparability to occur, schools and school districts need to be judged in the light of the same quality criteria.

The District
Task 1: School Improvement—1985 to 1995

<u>Purpose:</u> To compare school improvement events in Dubuque with those in the participants' own school districts.

<u>Grouping:</u> Meet with your Learning Team.

<u>Directions:</u> In small discussion groups, compare what happened in Dubuque in the first two stages of school improvement with what was occurring in your own school district(s) circa 1985–1995.

Growing Dissatisfaction with Stage Two

While the power of school-based autonomy was still widely acknowledged, its limitations were also becoming clearer. When there is high autonomy and low accountability (the central characteristic of the second stage of development), there is great potential for variability of performance and inconsistency of effort across sites. Excellence in one site can be easily matched by mediocrity in a neighboring site. As Elmore (2000) has contended, this "loose-coupling" was the bane of education as it masked such differential levels of achievement. What was now required, it was acknowledged, was "Autonomy Plus" (less autonomy plus more accountability).

For instance, one Dubuque school—Irving Elementary—had used its newfound freedom to become a high performance school, eventually being recognized as a National Blue Ribbon School of Excellence. The Irving team was in the first group of schools to receive the NISDC school improvement training, and it took five years of very hard work to attain such a high standard of achievement. Talking about their school improvement efforts, when asked what made the difference for them, staff members mentioned:

- They committed to school improvement as "a very serious and deliberate process that cannot be completed easily...it all takes time with all the attendant student problems to deal with."

- They continued to be data-based in order to identify internal needs and select focused goals on which to work.

- They were "research-based" because they sought research-based strategies to use in meeting the identified needs.

- They were energized by the commitment that comes with involving people both inside the school and in the local school community.

- A Site Council with a clearly defined role orchestrated their school improvement efforts.

Ironically, however, the more successful that schools like Irving became, the more obvious it was that other schools were not showing the same level of initiative. Sites like Irving were over-performing schools in under-performing school systems. Put another way, if the true potential of such individual sites was being realized, the potential of the system around them was being underutilized. While some "parts" were thriving, the "whole" was not. And the trick is to achieve both at the same time so they are in some kind of synchronicity. What can be concluded, therefore, is that the very success of the second stage of development leads to the understanding that the balance between system and subsystem at the local level is out of kilter and needs to be redressed. This understanding is evidenced by the following participant's observations.

> As students are to take responsibility for their own learning goals and visions, so, too, do schools need to do the same. This is where the school improvement plan comes in. It no longer gives staff tunnel vision but opens the horizon to tailor-made goals and expectations for each school while still able to remain within the larger general goals the district has set for the Dubuque Community School District and its students.

What this participant is referring to is the "nestedness" that can occur between building and district goals. By working independently, those in the schools and, indeed, those in the Central Office, came to see the need for more interdependence. If *dependence* is the hallmark of Stage One, and *independence* is the central characteristic of Stage Two, as Covey (1989) has pointed out, then *interdependence* epitomizes Stage Three.

Stage Three: An Integrated School System

Two sets of observations by Central Office administrators, both made in 2000, would suggest that at this point the third stage of development was well under way. In a speech at the April 2000 NISDC Showcase (in which teams of teachers and administrators from around Iowa described their school improvement efforts), Nancy Bradley, the local torchbearer for school improvement in Dubuque, pointed out: "We're still evolving; we're not perfect and we're continuing to tweak the system, but we are proud of our process and our efforts over time." In her speech, she listed six reasons why everything was coming together as follows:

1. The common format for school improvement planning (involving goal setting and the establishment of supporting activities, timelines, success criteria, and staff development arrangements) had been in place long enough, in almost the same form, for it to be institutionalized. "It's our road map," she said. "It's like an IEP for a school."

2. We're ready, she admitted, to work with data now. "We were given the message before, but now we're more ready to hear it and act on it." Those involved, she said, are more inclined to ask the basic question, "What data can we pull together to learn more about ourselves?"

3. Using the recent state legislation (known as House File #2272 or just "2272") as the impetus, Comprehensive School Improvement in Dubuque now involved the dovetailing of district and school improvement plans. For the first time a District Improvement Plan had been put together, which would be supported by the building-level plans or "contributions." Taken together, she said, the two parts formed the Dubuque System Plan. The new District Plan mirrored the school format, modeled what items to include (and how to include them), focused on five district goals to which the schools had to respond, and laid out everything to be attempted across the district in the foreseeable future ("No surprises!" had been the request from the building principals).

4. Two new district-level committees were overseeing all these activities. The so-called "Chapter 12 Team" contained district and school representatives (one of whom was Bryant's principal, Lesley Stephens) and was charged with coordinating the local response to the changes in Chapter 12 of the state's educational laws—especially the mandates concerning district improvement planning, annual reporting to the state and the local community, and increased

accountability. A District Advisory Council, containing parent, community, and business representatives, was also set up to provide guidance on improvement matters.

5. For the first time, during site-based consultation sessions, all eighteen schools in Dubuque had received individualized feedback on their school improvement plans. These sessions took the form of mini-workshops on how to work with data and how to select appropriate success criteria. As a consequence, according to Nancy Bradley, "The schools are much better prepared to go forward."

6. With the ongoing use of data to inform decision making and the commitment to being systemically aligned, it was now possible for all those in the district to be more finely tuned in their attention to the specifics of student learning and student achievement. Consequently, she said, it was much more likely that different instructional strategies and interventions could be selected and deployed to meet specific learning needs and therefore create high achievement for all students.

Four months later, Superintendent Jane Petrek wrote an article for *Julien's Journal* (published in the September 2000 edition) under the new logo of "Dubuque Community Schools: Learning—Leading—Living." In this article Petrek observed:

> As we look forward, I can't help looking back, reflecting on the past school year. Improvement in our world is continuous. There is wisdom in maintaining successes, modifying programs and practices to better fit the organizational philosophy, and leaving behind those things that may have overpromised and underdelivered. I call it 'refinement of practice' which is simply aligning everything we do with our mission and beliefs.
>
> The mission of the Dubuque Community School District, I believe, is straightforward and succinct:
>
> *To educate students, in collaboration with the family and the community, to achieve success in a challenging program.*

The language of improvement has changed in interesting ways: alignment with mission and beliefs is now the key concept. While the site-based initiative has been retained (Stage Two), the power of the district as an entity has returned (Stage One), but this time as an integrated system operating within system-wide expectations (Stage Three), not as a bureaucratic hierarchy.

Petrek continues by emphasizing that the system beliefs (see the following) are also clearly defined and form the basis of the district's mission statement.

District Beliefs

The Dubuque Community School District believes that all children can succeed when provided a learning environment:

- Which emphasizes respect for individual rights and responsibilities, instills a desire for life-long learning, and develops involved citizens for today's changing world.

- In which all children are challenged to perform to the best of their ability and receive instruction in core knowledge and basic skills and have the opportunity to learn the critical thinking and problem-solving strategies essential for living in a global society.

- Which promotes mutually respectful relationships and values individuality and diversity.

- Which includes an active, meaningful, integrated and rigorous instructional program and scientifically-valid, research-based curriculum with interventions based upon assessment results.

- In which children are taught by talented and well-educated staff members committed to continuous improvement who have access to the resources necessary to deliver high quality programs.

- Which is safe and supportive and promotes excellence and equity.

- Which recognizes the critical role of parents and teachers as role models and promotes collaboration and partnership among students, staff, parents, and community members.

According to Petrek's extended commentary there are three areas that represent major shifts and improvements during the 1999-2000 school year: new state legislation; instructional program development; and leadership change, including organization restructuring.

New Legislation

Petrek summarizes the new state legislation as follows:

> New state legislation, referred to as 'Chapter 12,' challenged all districts in Iowa to review their standards, assessments, accountability, parental and community involvement, and integration of state and federal programs. This legislation supports high student achievement and goals determined by the

local districts. Dubuque Community School District's School Improvement Advisory Committee identified five goals for the 2000–2001 school year:

■ Improve student performance in reading for understanding and enjoyment.

■ Improve student performance in mathematics in the areas of problem solving, math reasoning, measurement, computation, and concept attainment.

■ Strengthen instructional programs across the district, pre-K–12, to ensure maximum learning across the curriculum.

■ Nurture and support a safe learning environment based on mutual respect, active citizenship, and demonstration of good character.

■ Strengthen communication and collaboration within the school system and with families and the community to support student learning.

These goals form the basis of each school's School Improvement Plan that aligns with the district's goals. Schools also have individual initiatives, based on a school's specific need or interest. New Iowa Schools Development Corporation (NISDC) has worked closely with our district and schools to further enhance our efforts to meet student needs.

Again, the language used here is significant. What is being emphasized in terms of the *district's* response to the state legislation are the importance of standards (albeit locally constructed), assessments aligned with the standards, accountability for high student achievement, interlocking district and building goals (with those at both levels being needs-based data-driven), and, most significantly of all, the district as a school system. There is an important implication here: that Dubuque Community School District has changed from being a system of schools (inferring a loosely coupled conglomeration of schools) to being a school system (that is tighter, more integrated, and more closely packaged for success).

Strengthened Instructional Programs

Petrek singles out the district-wide initiatives and improvements made in elementary reading/language arts, writing, and K–12 social studies and the work to produce revised standards. As she acknowledges:

> A second edition of district standards and benchmarks has been printed and distributed to schools for all staff. Revisions recommended by a variety of individuals and groups have been incorporated in an attempt to make the standards more clearly specify the learning expectations in most content areas. These standards are used to guide teaching and assessment of student performance.

This is an important statement, if not a rallying cry for the locally constructed content area standards. Iowa, in its insistence on the local construction of standards and benchmarks, is the exception nationally. It has to be remembered, however, that in the construction process, local educators used exactly the same foundational materials (reports from national subject panels, e.g., the NCTM standards, and the MCREL "compendium" of examples of standards and benchmarks from around the country), but garnered the additional benefits of local ownership of and commitment to these internally produced expectations for student performance in the major content areas.

Leadership Change and Organizational Restructuring

According to Petrek:

> There has been a change in leadership and a restructuring of the organization. This restructuring eliminated certain positions and redefined others. The underlying philosophy for these changes was to provide more effective and efficient service to our students, teachers, parents, and administrators. At the core of each division is service: Human Resource Services, Educational Program Services, Finance and Business Services, and School and Community Services.

Technology, itself a reinforcer of a more systems-based approach, is also singled out for comment by Petrek:

> Last year was a landmark year as we completed construction of the data infrastructure and connected 1,500 computers to the network. We have Internet access to our desktops....This year we will have the DSCD website up and running along with each school's website. This will allow us to better communicate with the community and parents. A Technology Advisory Council will be in place in order to guide the expanded use of technology in instructional programs as well as operations related to data management....[And] the standards and benchmarks for

technology provide important tools for learning and offer many options for our students, particularly in areas of research and multi-media presentations of their work.

Both Bradley and Petrek were witnessing and, indeed, were instrumental in the transition from the second to the third stage of development. As a consequence:

- Schools (and the teachers within them) were changing from being independent contractors to being members of an organic, integrated school system.

- Site-based shared decision making was being replaced by shared decision making.

- Independence and decentralization were transitioning into interdependence at the local level as part of a "layered" state system.

- High autonomy and low accountability were giving way to relative autonomy and high accountability.

- Differential, inconsistent performance across buildings was being jettisoned in favor of more consistently high performance across the entire system.

- Local ownership and commitment remained intact.

In other words, in order to develop to the next stage of growth, the real strengths of Stage Two are being retained and the weaknesses strengthened. None of this was happening, however, as part of any grand plan. Stage One deficiencies produced the desire for Stage Two and, in turn, Stage Two deficiencies—and their remediation—gave rise to Stage Three. Each stage represents an attempt to compensate for the shortcomings of the previous stage. Two other factors contribute to this stage theory of growth in Dubuque schools over time.

1. The leadership style exhibited at each stage both determines and reflects the nature of the stage. In the early 1990s, for instance, the development of Stage Two was triggered and accelerated by Superintendent Diana Lam. She was able to use her authority position to act as a major catalyst for change. According to Nancy Bradley:

   > [Lam] opened the floodgates of site-based decision-making and the decentralization of school improvement efforts. She moved us from an organization that was using school improvement to refine the status quo to decentralizing the organization in support of a school-based model for school improvement. Schools were more for kids. In some cases, she directed it—for example, when the Junior Highs were directed to become Middle Schools.

Now, in 2003, the leadership style is more collaborative, more systemic, more "service-oriented."

2. The seeds of one stage of growth are always sown during the previous stage. For example, when Pat Dolan led site-based decision-making training workshops in Dubuque in the early 1990s, his guidance not only substantiated the development of Stage Two but also pre-figured (and most probably triggered) what would become characteristics of Stage Three. He emphasized the importance of using a "systems approach" to school improvement. Such an approach, he argued, should

- recognize that the whole system is composed of deeply interconnected sub-systems

- aim to be organic, not mechanistic

- embrace both content and process

- plan to reap the benefits of both short-term quantitative and long-term qualitative gains

The systems approach should also be used to overcome what Dolan saw as four pathological, dysfunctional elements in organizations that are run on the lines of the "traditional, organizational pyramid" (which he describes as top-down, authoritarian, layered in hierarchy, gridded into silos, and restrictive of the flow of information and autonomy. Dolan(1994) describes such an organization as follows:

- It is a non-listening system that cannot retrieve its own data nor learn from it. There is no information flow.

- It is a nonintegrated system in which groups work in specialized teams. These silos then compete for power, position, authority, and resources.

- It is driven by short-term, quantitative measurements that lead to dangerous miscalculations of the actual situation because they do not take into account the qualitative aspects of performance. Improvement efforts that are governed by a short-term quantitative bias (which Alfred North Whitehead referred to as the "fallacy of misplaced concreteness") are characterized by short-mindedness.

- It cannot, by its very nature, sustain the energy, talent, and commitment of those who actually do the work. Staff morale is undermined and the energy, talent, and commitment of those involved become dissipated.

Indeed, when discussing various reports of school improvement efforts, Dolan (1994) issues a major warning:

The overriding lesson of all of these stories is that the remedies look dangerously like the dysfunctions that they are meant to heal. They are almost always imposed from above, driven in isolated and unintegrated fashion, focused on short-term quantitative results, and seldom if ever involve the people who do the work. The net result is often dysfunction and deeper anger and frustration.

In his 1994 book, Dolan reflects on his experiences in Iowa:

A look at one 1991 case in Iowa gives an inkling of what the key elements of education restructuring might be. The Business Roundtable, a group of well meaning private corporations, commissioned a $400,000 study of public education in the state.

After the state board establishes schools and school districts' performance goals and assessment processes in Iowa, this type of recommendation follows:

> 'In evaluating the performance by a school, I recommend that you establish a threshold level of performance that will be deemed satisfactory....In schools in which the proportion of successful students actually declined but by less than 5%, the school staff would lose both one year of longevity pay and one cost-of-living increment.' (Hornbeck, D. *First Draft of Recommendations on the Iowa Initiative for World Class Schools.*)

The various key actors, including the teacher's union, the Iowa State Education Association, the School Administrators of Iowa, the Iowa Department of Education and others, were not significantly involved in developing this plan. Therefore, they were able to forestall a good deal of its thrust. As a matter of fact, these groups began their own collaborative learning model (the same NISDC referred to by participants in Dubuque), based on listening to schools and districts as they started the long restructuring process.

From the beginning, the problem with legislated reform has been that no one reflects on the state of the present system. It is as though it makes no difference whether a district is rural, suburban, or urban; if adversarial relationships exist; what types of resources are available; and how a district or a state system is affected by community special interest groups and pressure groups that make day-to-day functioning an adventure at best. Too often, legislatures simply demand required improvements in test scores, add some carrot/stick language, involve none of the major actors, and wait for something to happen. It will be a long wait.

And from the wings, there increasingly is another voice that says, 'Walk away from the whole system and its failures and use the resources to do it some other way. Trust a good competitive model from the private sector.'

Written ten years prior to the onrush of *NCLB*, this is a most prescient passage. Adding another layer of complexity to an already dense scenario, Dolan (1994) reminds us that we, the participants, are the problem and the solution:

> All the people in this system know a good deal about the problems and don't like the results. Yet they will resist the change. The system is us. We will resist the change we dream of and desperately pursue. It is the deep paradox of system-change at the personal <u>or</u> organizational level. To design reform successfully, strategists must design *against* the pathology, and heal the system as it restructures itself.

Whereas we can all act as "externalizers" (looking to blame others for all our misfortunes, resisting even changes we have asked for, and siting the locus for change outside ourselves), for real change to become "seated," we have to become "internalizers" by accepting the responsibilities and accountabilities of internal control. What Dolan (1994) is emphasizing is that even the *way* that change occurs can convince us of the reality of the former, and thus, prevent us from accepting the reality of the latter. As a consequence, the *way* we go about change can further incapacitate "systems" (both personal and organizational) that are already deeply dysfunctional and lacking in capacity. Indeed, this is a theme explored in Workbook One: *Conceptualizing a New Path*. Just as schools and school districts need to work on both academic and social/climate issues, when it comes to school improvement, both content and process are required (one of the themes examined in Workbook Two: *Creating a Process*).

From Stage Two to Stage Three in Dubuque

Dolan's work with Dubuque, therefore, not only substantiated the process of site-based development (so typical of Stage Two) but also heralded—and laid the groundwork for—the advance of Stage Three. Several other factors contributed to these developments.

1. System-wide (content) expectations were established.

For instance, following a DCSD Community Needs Assessment (3/92), twelve Life-Long Learning Competencies were established:

As a result of their total experience as students in the Dubuque Community School District, our graduates will be able [to]:

- Locate and use information effectively.

- Exhibit civic involvement.

- Display global awareness and multicultural understanding.

- Achieve goals by working cooperatively with others.

- Communicate effectively in a variety of ways.

- Think critically and creatively.

- Apply technology.

- Demonstrate life management and social skills.

- Demonstrate a commitment to personal wellness.

- Anticipate and constructively react to change.

- Solve problems independently and cooperatively.

- Demonstrate an appreciation of the fine arts.

These "Essential Learnings" (tantamount to graduation requirements) were reinforced by the generation of the five **district improvement goals** (as listed by Jane Petrek previously in this chapter). These goals have recently been updated (2003) in response to the district's Strategic Plan and in readiness for the implementation of *NCLB*.

2. System-wide process expectations ("Principles of Procedure for Comprehensive School Improvement Planning") were also agreed upon.

As part of the Data Coach training sessions begun in 2000, participants agreed to—indeed, contributed to—the following statements:

- Student learning is the focus ("keeping our eyes on the prize").

- School improvement is continuous, involving annual revisions of the long-term (five-year) plan.

- Annual revisions are to be needs-based and data-driven (and not "a good idea at the time").

- The annual process is as streamlined, integrated, and user-friendly as possible; school improvement planning should never be allowed to interfere with the very things that are being improved, especially student learning.

- As much as possible there is predictability in terms of the process and paperwork used.

- District/school/classroom improvement efforts are aligned, connected, and mutually supportive.

- A school's capacity for ongoing data use is enhanced by the deployment of trained data coaches.

It was also recognized that data use is the central process activity:

- Data collection is not a one-time-only activity; it is a continuous and continuing concern.

- In a five-year planning sequence any changes in the plan should be reflective of any changes in the data.

- Data collection, therefore, is not going away; it's not a temporary fad. It's an organic part of our way of life in schools and districts.

- Some of the data collected will speak directly to the progress being made on school and district goals; the other data not directly related to current goals may well flag the existence of new, emerging areas of need.

- The best way to honor the central role of data is to build a School Profile.

More specifically, during the training sessions, Data Coaches were advised to return to their schools and do the following:

- Encourage the use of a school improvement/data collection annual calendar.

- Encourage the ongoing collection of up-close data in order to allow colleagues to—in the words of one participating principal—"gather around the data."

- Play a central role in directing/coordinating a school's improvement efforts—by being linked to the Site Council and the staff in general. An updated version of how Data Coaches are situated within the leadership structure of a school is included in the following diagram.

- Encourage more recording/progress reviewing/reporting on the part of action team members and, therefore, more process accountability.

- Advocate for the selection of goals/priorities that are needs-based and data-driven and not "interest-based."

■ Use the ideas from Data Coach training to produce other reports or profiles, e.g., NCA or Title I.

Core Team and Site Council

Principal

Work with Data School Plan to Take to the Site Council for Feedback

Teacher

Core Team
Principal
Date Coaches
Forum Liaison

Community

Support Staff

Business Partners

Provide Feedback on Draft of School Plans

The District
Task 2: Autonomy and Accountability

<u>Purpose:</u> To discuss whether autonomy and accountability are compatible concepts.

<u>Grouping:</u> Work with your Learning Team.

<u>Directions:</u> With your own professional experiences very much in mind, discuss in small groups whether you think it is possible to have both autonomy and accountability at the same time in local school districts. Provide some specific examples to support your point of view.

Autonomy *and* Accountability

Iowa's uniqueness lies in its very real attempt to embrace both local control and relative autonomy of local school systems and demands for accountability, while at the same time building a local and state internal infrastructure to meet the demands of external mandates. These arrangements are embedded in the state's own accountability law (House File #2272) passed in 1997.

To clarify the new situation for participants in Dubuque, John Burgart (now Superintendent), in his former role as Director of Curriculum and Assessment, produced a useful guide to the new legislation to guide district and school improvement planning. A diagram of the improvement planning process follows.

Iowa Department of Education

General Accreditation Standards for Schools

District/School Improvement Planning Process— Dubuque Community School District

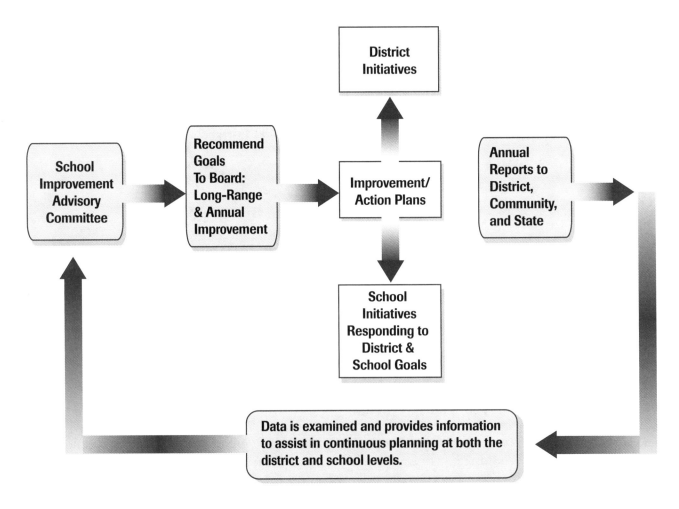

This guide—and others like it in schools and districts across Iowa—changed the face and language of school improvement. Comprehensive School Improvement Plans (CSIPs), Annual Progress Reports (APRs), School Improvement Advisory Committees (SIACs), annual and long-range goals, and multiple assessments became the lexicon of school improvement in Iowa's schools and school districts. It has been the source of much local pride in Dubuque that its award-winning Annual Progress Report has received so much favorable attention. Moreover, while the emphasis is still on the exercise of these responsibilities by those at the local level, the State Department's Team Visitations are geared to the monitoring of these arrangements. In fact, Dubuque's next visit is slated for February 2004.

The increased emphasis on student achievement in specific curriculum areas—reading, mathematics, and science—has resulted in a sequenced massive overhaul of these subjects in Dubuque. The language arts initiative came first and mathematics is currently enjoying the same level of attention. Each of these major initiatives has been data-driven (and informed by both external and internal data) and purposefully linked to the school improvement cycle of development. Thus, the current mathematics initiative has followed three distinct phases of development as depicted on the following diagram.

Mathematics Initiative: Three Phases

District 2001–2002

Mathematics Study

External Data (Research on Best Practices)

Internal Data
- ITBS Results
- Criterion-Referenced Assessments
- District Averages/ School Scores

School 2002–2003

CSIP

School Goal: Mathematics e.g., Problem Solving
- S=School Study (Defining, Planning, and Exploring)
- E=Early Implementation
- I=Implementation
- M=Maintenance

Classroom 2003–2004

Classroom

Action Research— individual teacher, team and whole school application, and monitoring of implementation strategies

The coming school year (2003-2004) will be the major year for school and classroom implementation, following two years of study, planning, and development at the district level involving many mathematics teachers from across the district. As part of this developmental process, the standards and benchmarks for mathematics were overhauled and criteria developed for evaluating new math programs that were then applied—by the members of the elementary mathematics study committee, for example. They used the following criteria to evaluate twelve programs and make their recommendation for the program most suited to the needs of the district.

Criteria for Evaluating Mathematics Programs

<u>Criterion 1:</u> The program's learning goals are challenging, clear, and appropriate for the intended student population.

<u>Criterion 2:</u> The program's content is aligned with its learning goals, and is accurate and appropriate for the intended student population.

<u>Criterion 3:</u> The program's instructional design is appropriate, engaging, and motivating for the intended student population.

<u>Criterion 4:</u> The program's system of assessment is multi-faceted and designed to inform students of their learning and to guide teachers' instructional decisions.

<u>Criterion 5:</u> The program's instructional materials are easy for teachers to access for each lesson and provide strategies for classroom management including ideas for differentiated instruction.

<u>Criterion 6:</u> The publisher provides adequate resources and support for its program.

In selecting a program, these criteria were applied thoroughly and consistently. The stakes are now too high to make a poor decision. Given the emphasis on increasing student achievement in mathematics and the shrinkage of available resources, this is one decision to get absolutely right.

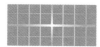

The District
Task 3: District Accountability Before *NCLB*

<u>Purpose:</u> To provide an opportunity for group members to reflect on the degree of accountability for school improvement experienced in their school district(s) prior to *No Child Left Behind*.

<u>Grouping:</u> Work on your own and then meet with your Learning Team.

<u>Directions:</u> Reflect upon and respond to the following questions: Given that school improvement planning was a state-mandated process in Iowa prior to *NCLB*, what was the situation in your own state and school district(s)? How much accountability was already being demanded of your district prior to the new federal legislation? In what ways (be specific) has the legislation impacted school improvement planning in your district? Use the following space to record your thoughts in preparation for meeting with your team to discuss your responses to these questions.

Meeting the Challenges of *No Child Left Behind*

With much foundational work already laid, the Data Coach training sessions in the 2002–2003 school year became the vehicle for understanding the implications and beginning the rise to the challenges of the *NCLB* legislation. During the sessions, co-trainers Peter Holly and Nancy Bradley provided the context for *No Child Left Behind*. They explained the motivations and aspirations behind the new federal law and emphasized that the new demands called for increased

- accountability on the part of states, districts, schools, and classrooms

- scrutiny of data, especially <u>student achievement data</u> concerning the accomplishment of <u>grade-level expectations</u> (as aligned with standards and benchmarks) by various <u>subpopulations of students</u> as evidenced by <u>multiple assessments</u> that display <u>technical adequacy</u>

- attention to the progress made in each classroom and by each and every student

- need to demonstrate improvement toward the goal of 100% of the students achieving proficiency by 2013–2014

The trainers also explained several other fundamental points about the groundbreaking legislation:

- Starting in the 2005–2006 year, all schools in the USA will be required to test students annually in reading and mathematics from grades three through eight, and at least once in grades ten through twelve (grade eleven in Iowa). In Iowa, science will also be tested and reported on.

- Penalties will be in force for low or declining performance in these tests.

- States and school districts must produce annual report cards of students' progress toward meeting state standards, graduation rates, names of schools that need improvement, qualifications of teachers, and percentages of students not tested.

- States and school districts are required to develop plans that indicate how the goals and requirements of the federal law are being met. As a consequence, Iowa's CSIPs and APRs will remain very much in force and be amended to comply with the letter of the new federal law.

- State and local norm-referenced and criterion-referenced assessments will be used to meet the new testing requirements. Such assessments, however, have to be capable of being disaggregated for student subpopulations and have to be aligned with the grade level expectations which, in turn, have to be aligned with standards and benchmarks. In Iowa, where all standards and benchmarks have been generated locally (albeit using the same national standards documents and compendiums as used elsewhere), this task of alignment is somewhat more complicated and is being covered by what is known as the ITAP Project.

The Role of ITBS

The Iowa Test of Basic Skills (ITBS) and the Iowa Test of Educational Development (ITED) are used in the vast majority of schools in Iowa, so it was inevitable that Iowa's application for *NCLB* membership would be heavily reliant on these standardized assessments. It was also inevitable, therefore, that, in the Data Coach training sessions, participants would be helped to get the best out of these tried and tested assessments. Indeed, it was a surprise to the trainers just how much educators did not know about the tests themselves and the uses to which they could (and could not) be put.

Making the best use of ITBS data, argued the trainers, entails using the test results for the following:

- conferencing with individual students (and their parents/guardians) concerning their scores, and their strengths and weaknesses as a prerequisite for personal goal setting

- item analysis to help classroom teachers make informed instructional decisions

- disaggregation of the data to identify those students (and student subgroups) achieving proficiency or not using their percentile scores

- providing trend-line data concerning, for example, fourth grade results across several years

- comparing grade-level results year by year (using grade equivalents) in order to show the kind of growth achieved from, for example, grade three to grade four every year and comparing it to the kind of growth achieved between other grades

- tracking the growth of the same cohort of students across the grades

Participants in the Data Coach training sessions were provided with some useful definitions for ITBS analysis and some guidance concerning the disaggregation of data for student subpopulations.

In the Data Coach training sessions during the 2002–2003 school year, ITBS/ITED data were used for four other major purposes as follow:

1. District scores from 1997–2002 were analyzed to identify trend lines. The results for each building for the same time period were also analyzed and compared with the district averages.

2. District and building trajectories (showing the amount of growth required annually in order for all students to be proficient by 2013–2014 according to the Iowa formula) were also computed and examined.

3. ITBS scores were inputted on to the new Elementary Electronic Student Database, established by a joint district and school task force in the fall of 2002. Full details of this electronic database, which contains almost one hundred "fields," are provided in Appendix C.

4. Participants were also shown how the same data, such as ITBS, could be used for decision making at various levels of the local system: the individual student, the classroom, the school, and the district as illustrated on the following diagram.

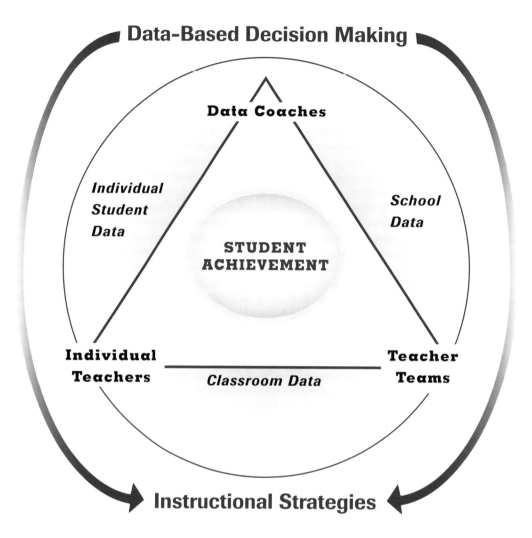

Data-Based Decision Making

Data Coaches

Individual Student Data

School Data

STUDENT ACHIEVEMENT

Individual Teachers

Classroom Data

Teacher Teams

Instructional Strategies

The District
Task 4: Using Assessment Data to Inform Decisions

Purpose: To provide an opportunity for participants to reflect on how standardized assessment data guide decision making in their school district(s).

Grouping: Work on your own and then meet with your Learning Team.

Directions: Respond individually and then in teams to the following question: In what ways are student assessment data—including standardized test results—used to inform decision making at various system levels in your local school district? Give specific examples.

Data Coach Training: Participants' Responses

According to David Olson, principal of Hempstead High School in Dubuque:

> Data Coach Training cannot be considered in isolation from all the other learning events in my life, so I have integrated my ongoing experiences as a principal, including Data Coach Training, the High Schools Project [another project initiated by NISDC], and the AEA Reading Strategies Workshop that I have attended. I also must include the many conversations that I have had in Chapter 12 meetings and other discussions I have had with Nancy Bradley....This is what has happened to my thinking.

> **Data collection as a school is important, but data collection by teachers about their students is more important to improving student learning.** Tracking all the massive data about each student will yield much impressive information, but I am concerned about the action that may follow. I believe now that if a teacher is held accountable to collect his or her own data and report about it, there can be much more student progress. I like what several of the DCSD elementary schools are doing in that regard.

> **Staff development must relate directly to the classroom.** The more I think about staff development experiences I have had, and the more I read, the more I believe that professional growth is a personal experience. Each teacher must be personally inspired to grow. Data that is specific and relevant to the teacher's work is the most powerful. When I observe teachers through the evaluation process, I try to collect data to share with them that can impact their teaching. A common example is when I have collected information on how often a teacher involves or engages all students, not just a few vocal students. This data has changed teacher practice.

> **Ways must be found to include parents and students.** In the process of refining our systems to collect and report data, parents and students are critical. They have a very different point of view and value school issues uniquely. Our Site Council and Action Teams that include parents and students seem to yield better results. We must not only report information to our public, we must include them in the identification of important data and the analysis. When our parents looked at the Zoomerang [on-line survey] results and reacted, their interpretation really helped to shape my thinking.

School planning will continue to evolve and grow (and it must).
Just remembering back to the first SET (School Effectiveness
Teams) when I was a Forum staff person on the Fulton Elementary
Team, and then leading the team at Central Alternative High
School as the principal makes me know how much we've grown.
During my eight years as the Central principal, the Site Councils
were created—which later were called School Improvement
Teams. Now at Hempstead, I look at school plans and I am
amazed at how focused and purposeful we have become. Nancy
says that 'we don't push around lint anymore' and she is right.
The process must also keep growing. The recent Chapter 12 meeting
inspired me to know that we still haven't got it right, that we still
have more to do to link the district plan and planning process to the
school plans. Our data-driven focus will keep us evolving.

**In order to set the vision, and hold on to it, links must be made
among all the new things we try in DCSD.** School improvement
planning, Charlotte Danielson's framework for teacher evaluation,
Track I and II, the teacher mentor program, staff development
planning and use of time, etc., must all be tied together. Remember
in our Site Council meeting how we used the 'weaving' analogy?
At Hempstead I understand that the communication process
is complex so I have created structures that meet the challenge
with neighborhoods and seminars, and department chairpeople,
and layers of ways people receive and transmit information.
Sometimes the complexity becomes humorous to explain, but it is
essential for the entire learning community to be involved and
engaged. We must weave our district efforts also. The Data Coach
Training has been a critical part of the fabric we are creating,
maybe it is even the loom.

David Olson's insightful reflections remind us of the importance of connecting all the
pieces of school improvement. Data Coach Training has become the vehicle for this
integrative process in four powerful ways.

1. For the last three years, Data Coach Training has provided the platform for arguing
   the importance of establishing a Data Profile at each of the four levels of the local
   system: District, School, Classroom, and Student (as laid out in Workbook Five:
   Creating a Data-Driven System). Of all the districts in which the author has worked,
   Dubuque is the nearest to accomplishing this vital task. Provided on the following
   chart is an early picture of what this four-dimensional model might look like and
   the outcomes that might accrue at each of the system levels. In terms of the four
   levels, whether we are talking about profiles or portfolios in Dubuque, the Student,
   Classroom, and School Data Profiles are in what can be described as an advanced
   state of preparedness, while the District Data Profile is still being laced together—a
   process that has certainly been accelerated by the onrush of *No Child Left Behind*.

DUBUQUE COMPREHENSIVE IMPROVEMENT PLAN

Four System Levels

Data Coach Training		Classroom Action Research Workshop	
District Profile	**School Profile**	**Classroom Profile**	**Student Profile**
1. Progress review of current DCSD goals	1. Progress review of current school goals	1. Progress review of current classroom/teacher goals	1. Progress review of current student goals
2. District database	2. School database	2. Classroom database	2. My individual database
■ Unique local insights	■ Unique local insights	■ Unique classroom insights	■ Unique individual insights
■ Stakeholder feedback	■ Follow-up of former students	■ Stakeholder feedback	■ Stakeholder feedback
■ Existing district data	■ Existing school data	■ Existing classroom data (*Me*—Knowing myself as a teacher, *My Kids*—My knowledge of them through assessment, *My Teaching*—My instructional methods or strategies)—*Danielson framework*	■ Existing individual data
3. District improvement process survey	3. School improvement process summary	3. Classroom improvement process summary	3. Individual improvement process summary
Outcomes Comprehensive District Improvement Plan	**Outcomes Comprehensive School Improvement Plan**	**Outcomes Classroom Improvement Plans**	**Outcomes Individual Learning Plans (e.g., IEP, Problem Solving, PEP)**
■ The District Profile will become a building block for continuous improvement at the district level.	■ The School Profile will become a building block for continuous improvement at the school level.	■ Links will have been made in the district's teacher evaluation and professional growth initiatives, including wider use of the Danielson framework (going beyond the mentoring stage).	■ After one year, a representative district committee will make recommendations to the Chapter 12 Committee covering the recommended format for a student profile.
■ The Profile will be continually updated and studied to reassess needs (needs assessment will no longer be seen as a once-and-for-all activity).	■ The Profile will be continually updated and studied to reassess needs (needs assessment will no longer be seen as a once-and-for-all activity).	■ Links will have been made with the teacher compensation package.	■ After implementation, there will be increased student ownership, involvement, motivation, and engagement in their own learning, leading to increased student achievement.
■ Annual goal setting will be made easier and have more clarity.	■ Annual goal setting will be made easier and have clarity.	■ There will be increased teacher reflection, which, according to recent research, is vital to their professional development.	■ The process will capitalize on previous work on student portfolios across the district.
■ The relevant district committee will play a pivotal role in the development, maintenance, and application of the district profile.	■ The Site Council will recognize and accept a new role for itself as the keeper of the school profile (adding to, maintaining, and learning from it).	■ In the spirit of student outcomes, there will be produced rich classroom data that will speak to the implementation of school and district goals.	■ Once fully implemented, the student portfolios will provide rich data for the other three levels (classroom, school, and district).
■ The District's Annual Progress Report (APR) will be an automatic outcome of the updating and maintenance of the profile.	■ Schools will further develop their data-driven school cultures.	■ Activity at this level will help to implement school improvement in the classroom and in the minds and hearts of teachers.	
■ The district level will provide a model for school, classroom, and student profiling.		■ There will be increased alignment of classroom activities (instruction and assessment) with district standards and benchmarks.	

2. For the past three years in Dubuque, the District's Comprehensive School Improvement Plan (CSIP) has been dovetailed with the building-level school improvement plans. Each spring, an updated district plan is distributed to each school and the building leadership teams work to integrate their own projected activities with those of the district. In the spring of 2002, for instance, each building in Dubuque received some guidance materials for developing the Comprehensive School Improvement Plan.

3. During Data Coach Training in 2002–2003 increased efforts were made to show how the many pieces of the school improvement pie actually connect. Building on the idea that a district is a multi-leveled system and incorporating the QIC-Decide model for data-based decision making provided during state-level training sessions, it became possible to complete a map of all the activities that are a part of system-wide, data-driven, continuous improvement in DCSD. According to this two-dimensional model, the QIC-Decide model forms the same four (horizontal) processes that lie at the heart of all the major (vertical) district initiatives (see the following diagram). Whether talking about problem solving on behalf of students, classroom action research, teacher evaluation and mentoring, the comprehensive school improvement process, or the new Iowa Professional Development model, the same four steps of QIC-Decide apply.

	QIC DECIDE MODEL					
	System-Wide Data-Driven Continuous Improvement in DCSD					
	Iowa Teacher Quality Program	**Problem-solving (Student)**	**Action Research (Classroom)**	**Professional Mentoring Program (Teacher)**	**Teacher Evaluation Professional Growth Plan (Teacher)**	**CSIP Process (School, District)**	**Iowa Professional Development Model (School, District)**
Goal: Intended Student Achievement Results	**Q Question** (*Specify a question or decision that data are going to be used to make.*)	■ Define the learner need based on available data.	■ Select the instructional focus area for improvement based on a sense of the available data.	■ Plan	■ Select the focus for self-improvement area(s) based on available data.	■ Select the academic/ student achievement focus area(s) for school/ district improvement based on a sense of internal and external data.	■ Define the adult learner need(s) based on available student achievement data.
	I Information (*Identify specific information that will be needed to address the question or decision.*)	■ Collect additional information about the student (RIOT) and the learning need.	■ Gather data to further define the problem.	■ Teach	■ Review student achievement data and/or self-assessment data in the Iowa Teaching Standards and/or Framework.	■ Review current data about the school/district.	■ Collect additional information about what adult learners need to know and be able to do to improve student achievement in the identified area(s) of concern.
	C Collection (*Collect and summarize information to address the question or decision at hand.*)	■ Review possible interventions (instructional and/or behavioral).	■ Analyze and interpret the data.	■ Reflect	■ Select the goal(s) for self-improvement.	■ Identify needs. ■ Set goals.	■ Collect, analyze, and summarize data to refine targeted needs.
	D Decide (*Use the summarized data to answer the original question or make the decision.*)	■ Select and implement the intervention(s). ■ Monitor and evaluate the results.	■ Develop and implement the action plan. ■ Monitor and evaluate the results.	■ Apply	■ Develop and implement the Professional Growth Plan. ■ Monitor and evaluate the results.	■ Develop and implement the CSIP action plan. ■ Monitor and evaluate the results.	■ Develop and implement a professional development plan. ■ Monitor and evaluate the results.

Outcome: Actual Student Achievement Results

This diagram also positively links two initiatives that had previously been somewhat unconnected—teacher evaluation and school improvement. While Dubuque was one of the first districts nationally to use the ETS PATHWISE®: Induction Program, and to introduce a professional mentoring program and the work of Charlotte Danielson and Thomas McGreal to restructure its teacher evaluation scheme into a three-track Professional Staff Evaluation System (see below and the following page), these activities had remained intertwined with each other, but separated from school improvement planning.

DCSD Professional Mentoring and Staff Evaluation Programs

Overview

DCSD Professional Mentoring Program

- Level 1: Orientation
- Level 2: Training Sessions and Connections with Other New Colleagues
- Level 3: Instructional Focus with Feedback

Components of Professional Practice— A Framework for Effective Teaching

DCSD Professional Staff Evaluation System

- Track I: New DCSD Employees
- Track II: Professional Growth Planning
- Track III: Staff Assistance

Dubuque Community School District
Professional Staff Evaluation System
Overview

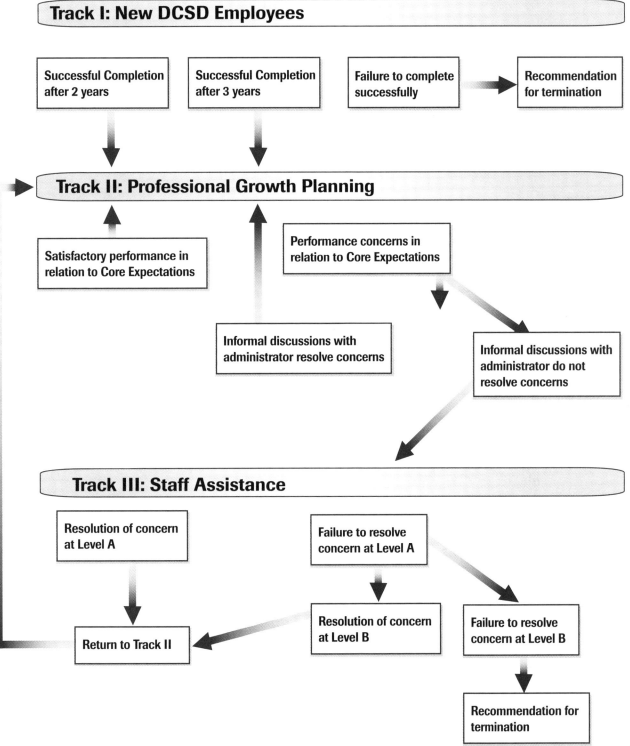

4. As with the State Department's new Professional Development model and its connectivity with school improvement, what is being recognized here is that there is no school improvement without teacher improvement, there are no increases in student achievement without advances in the quality of instruction. Professional growth is key to school improvement. In fact, at best, they are one and the same. This understanding has been recently honored in Dubuque in several other ways.

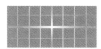 ## The District ■ Task 5: Aligning Teacher Evaluation With School Improvement

Purpose: To discuss whether professional evaluation approaches have been aligned with school improvement goals and initiatives in the participants' schools and school districts.

Grouping: Work with your Learning Team.

Direction: It is often claimed that teacher evaluation is always one of the final strands to be integrated with other school improvement initiatives. Working in district teams, respond to these questions:

1. In terms of this charge, why do you think this is so often the case?

2. Has alignment between teacher evaluation and school improvement been achieved in your district?

   If *yes*, discuss specifically what has made this alignment possible and the sequence of steps to get to this point. What have been the effects of this alignment, both positive and negative?

   If *no*, discuss why not and the steps that need to be taken toward such an alignment.

Focusing on Instruction

The improvement of instruction is a constant preoccupation in Dubuque. Currently, in fact, all roads lead to instructional improvement.

1. Arising from Data Coach Training and responding to *NCLB*, administrators in Dubuque have anticipated the future by instigating their own "Internal Alert" system. This early warning system is intended to identify potential school failure prior to the designation of "in need of assistance" status and launch, through self-evaluation, remedial interventions from the inside rather than the outside. This is a prime example of internally generated accountability—accountability being provided within a relatively autonomous school system.

   As the author commented to participants in Data Coach Training, it's tantamount to "keeping it in the family, but still meeting the central issues head-on." Even more significantly, however, in terms of the required response to "Internal Alert" status, is the reliance on the application of effective instruction. In schools on "Internal Alert," once the needs of individual low-performing students have been identified and the students enter into the problem-solving process, the effectiveness of current instruction is analyzed, necessary changes in instruction earmarked, and professional development opportunities—aligned with the identified needs—provided. This system is clearly an attempt to adopt what has worked well at Bryant on a district-wide basis. The DCSD plan for monitoring student achievement is contained in Appendix D.

2. Another interrelated development is the introduction and deployment of Instructional Strategists in elementary schools. This important role is currently being discussed and a pilot program designed for the school year 2003–2004. The role of an elementary instructional strategist is described in Appendix E.

   Such teacher leaders are intended to support their colleagues by providing best practices in instruction and assessments, suggesting instructional interventions and strategies based on regular student data analysis and interpretation, and having expertise in such related areas as action research, problem solving, student behavior management, and study skills. What is also recognized is that in order to effectively support the professional development of their colleagues, they will need continuing access to professional development opportunities themselves. The goal is to embed instructional effectiveness in schools and classrooms across the district—again, very much in the Bryant mold. Understandably, Chris McCarron has been invited to be the team leader of the first group of Instructional Strategists. As she observes in the following quotation, she is facing a new challenge:

   > As I look at my role not only at Bryant, but the greater Dubuque Community School District, I am less certain of my path. As an instructional strategist, I now work in many of the schools...I

know that gaining the trust of Bryant staff through consistent involvement with them has enabled me to help them on the 'data journey.' They were willing to be pushed a little further with each adventure because we had mutual trust, and I understood where their fears and concerns were based. As I work with others outside of Bryant, they have no trust level with me, and I find myself struggling to help others to work through their data. I have been vocal in my belief that the district should not have common [student data] profiles, but as I try to work across buildings, I'm beginning to challenge my own thoughts. Perhaps, like in most scenarios, a compromise would be the best solution. We may need common fields across schools and then school-specific fields could be added.

In this important set of observations, McCarron raises two vital issues:

- First is the importance of relationships and the trust level required for staff to accept the support of an instructional strategist. Such trust has to be earned—over time—and, with schools other than Bryant, she has to start anew.

- Second, in a school system such as Dubuque, what is often required is a delicate balance of consistent district-wide arrangements and individual (school) initiative and difference. The art is knowing when to emphasize the one or the other. What is required are integration *and* differentiation (Csikszentmihalyi, 1990) or, in Charles Handy's (1989) words, simultaneous loose-tight properties.

Instructional Strategist...A Progressive Conversation With Teachers

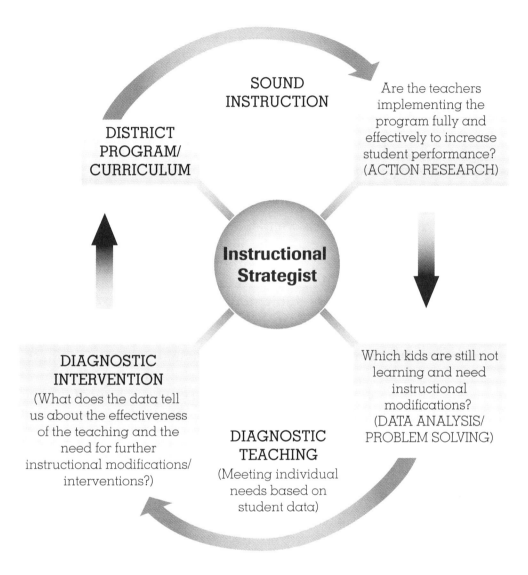

SOUND
INSTRUCTION

DISTRICT
PROGRAM/
CURRICULUM

Are the teachers
implementing the
program fully and
effectively to increase
student performance?
(ACTION RESEARCH)

**Instructional
Strategist**

DIAGNOSTIC
INTERVENTION
(What does the data tell
us about the effectiveness
of the teaching and the
need for further
instructional modifications/
interventions?)

Which kids are still not
learning and need
instructional
modifications?
(DATA ANALYSIS/
PROBLEM SOLVING)

DIAGNOSTIC
TEACHING
(Meeting individual
needs based on
student data)

In her reflections concerning Data Coach Training, Cynthia Oldenkamp, associate principal at Hempstead High School, underlines the importance of relationships when working with data in association with the other vital components of school improvement and professional development activities—content and process.

> The CPR Model for Continuous Improvement organizes the staff's efforts into three components—content, process, and relationships— for the improvement of student learning. Our activities and discussion about **content** stress the need to accurately assess the goals of our school plan. Do they focus on students? Are they important, rigorous, and worthwhile? I find that the goals of the Hempstead SIP (School Improvement Plan) need to be more specific and student-based and the success indicators more focused on student learning. The goals need to lead to implementation strategies and success indicators that are quantifiable. The **process** component of the CPR model involves the use of data to make informed decisions at Hempstead. Analysis, interpretation, and reporting of the data should be an integral part of the SIP. Hempstead's SIP goals, implementation strategies, and success indicators should lead to classroom application and teacher data collection. The classroom teacher should be collecting, analyzing, and using data to improve student learning. Our plan does not require teachers to use data to evaluate teaching and learning. The **relationships** component of the CPR model should lead us to evaluate our communication and interactions with all stakeholders. We find that many staff at Hempstead don't even know or understand the components of the SIP. We need to personalize our plan.

The CPR model is a frame for thinking about, and planning for, continuous improvement in schools and school districts, as illustrated in the following diagram.

CPR Model for Continuous Improvement

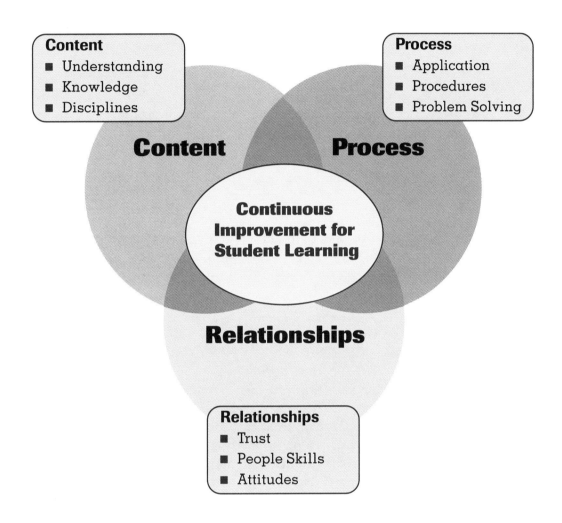

Content
- Understanding
- Knowledge
- Disciplines

Process
- Application
- Procedures
- Problem Solving

Content

Process

Continuous Improvement for Student Learning

Relationships

Relationships
- Trust
- People Skills
- Attitudes

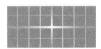

The District
Task 6: Content, Process, and Relationships

<u>Purpose:</u> To use the CPR model for reflecting on school improvement efforts.

<u>Grouping:</u> Work with your Learning Team.

<u>Directions:</u> In small groups, you are invited to reflect on your experiences with school improvement in terms of whether content, process, and relationships have been part of the equation. Then, respond to these trigger questions:

1. Which component has been the dominant one?

2. Which component has been the one most underplayed?

3. Thinking about your responses to the first two questions, provide some specific examples of how school improvement has been affected by what has or has not been emphasized.

2003: Taking Stock

At the time of writing this case study, Dubuque CSD, regarding its school improvement efforts, is well into its third stage of development. The site-based independence of Stage Two has transitioned into the kind of system-wide interdependence that characterizes Stage Three. Each building "doing its own thing" in terms of curriculum development has been replaced by far more curriculum alignment and articulation. School-based collaboration and site-based decision making are now part of a more sophisticated system of shared decision making. The potential power of building-based initiative has been enhanced by the harnessing of "value-addedness" in the form of district-level coordination and support.

Joyce, Wolf, and Calhoun (1993) are three authors who have commented on these same developments relative to their conception of a self-renewing school:

> During the beginning stages of a self-renewing school's improvement efforts, people in all spheres pay a great deal of attention to creating integrative relationships both among people and among previously separated spheres.

District offices need to provide nurturing environments for the school renewal process. Their personnel should make it obvious, from what they pay attention to and from what they find, that the pursuit of instructional effectiveness is valued (Blum and Kneidek, 1991). In fact, we think that every district office professional should participate as an active member in one school's change process. Clear policies, expectations for improvement, and a strong system of support all help schools and districts become stronger organizations. Acknowledging joint responsibility for school renewal—at individual, school, and district levels—is a major first step in changing the culture of our workplace.

Levine (1991), summarizing findings and implications from research on effective schools, succinctly describes this joint collaboration: 'The success of an effective school program depends on a judicious mixture of autonomy for participating faculties and control from the central office, a kind of "directed autonomy"' (p. 392). In a reciprocal way, the schools do not behave as if they were separate school systems, but call on the cadre [district-level coordinating team] for support for their school-based initiatives and cooperate with district initiatives.

Put simply, initiative can emerge at any level of the local system. Whereas Stage One is all about the district-level and Stage Two all about the school-level, Stage Three represents a combination of the two, thus reflecting the reinstatement of what the district-level has to offer, but in a shared, team-based and local change scenario. As the same authors conclude:

> In the self-renewing organization as we can conceive it at present, central office personnel coordinate initiatives, help the generic cadre interface with the schools, generate initiatives specific to the character and needs of the district, and maintain the focus on student learning and collective inquiry.

In Stage Three, the district's role in school improvement returns to legitimacy, but not total control. A more complex, sophisticated balance of power is involved. Indeed, the system invoked in Stage Three is more complex because it is more organic and integrated. According to Joyce et al. (1993):

> The three spheres of the organization—the teacher, the school, and the district—are responsible for improving instruction and supporting one another. The self-renewing organization is integrated, and its work is integrative.

Thus, the idea that curriculum can be 'controlled' by district office personnel is given up, as are notions that school improvement is solely 'site based' and that teachers as individuals are the ultimate decision makers regarding innovation. All of these positions have been more common in the literature than has the idea of an integrated organization. Many change efforts have been oriented to bridge gulfs between the spheres that should not have existed in the first place. In fact, without the other spheres, each is impotent with respect to innovation. We must break the centrifugal force of habit that impels and binds each sphere in role-prescriptive paths of interaction. As the district becomes a center of inquiry, everyone 'on site' in the district becomes responsible for student and collegial learning. Teamwork becomes reality: from team teaching, to interdisciplinary units, to seminars and workshops led by students, teachers, administrators, and community members.

Some types of proposals for 'site-based' management have accentuated the divisions between spheres, advocating virtual autonomy for schools, with the assumption that central office personnel only inhibit the creativity and synergy of the schools. Recent studies of innovation and change have come to a far different conclusion—that, without support from the district office personnel, few schools successfully engage in school improvement (Huberman and Miles, 1984, 1986; Louis and Miles, 1990; Fullan and Miles, 1991). Even where school faculties identify curricular and instructional initiatives, schoolwide implementation is virtually impossible without facilitation and support from the district.

The three spheres are mutually interdependent. The self-renewing school or district lives as a cooperative venture—all members of the organization share the raw responsibility of educating thousands of young people. Without broad cooperation, faculties and central offices are equally impotent when it comes to making significant changes. Faculties not supported by administrators, trainers, and organizers have great difficulty, with rare exceptions, overcoming the alienation produced by the extreme autonomy of the workplace. District offices not closely connected to teachers and schools are unable to create the conditions to support change.

What this case study adds to these arguments is the developmental, dialectical nature of the three stages of growth. The first stage is the original "thesis"; the second stage represents the "antithesis"; and the third stage is very much the synthesis of the strengths of the other two. As mentioned in the beginning of this chapter, the author (1998) described the same three stages of growth of school improvement efforts in another of Iowa's river towns as follows:

> During the first stage [this district] was in a very centralized, top-down mode of operation. The superintendent was seen as a strong, directive and authoritarian administrator who, according to a colleague, "got the job done and accomplished many things." Some of the achievements for which he was recognized were the implementation of both an instructional and a curriculum model, the closure of a school that had a declining student population, and the raising of teacher salaries. Along with the successes of this take-charge leader came the requirement that all employees had to conform to district (i.e., central office) decisions and directives. For example, all decisions regarding textbook adoptions were uniformly imposed throughout the district and the budgeting process was firmly in the hands of those in the central office. This was a stage, then, when the school district was directed by a paternalistic, centralist regime at the local level. All changes were imposed and centrally controlled from the district office. 'Local mandation' might sound a contradiction in terms but, in such a decentralized situation as Iowa, it was (and still can be) a prevalent style of change leadership.
>
> When the superintendent left the district in 1990, the assistant superintendent was promoted to succeed him. Here was a leader with a style in sharp contrast to that of her predecessor. She had been a long-time district employee who had come up through the ranks as teacher, guidance counselor, principal, and assistant superintendent. A strong advocate of teacher empowerment and site-based decision making, this new superintendent believed that the people closest to the problem are always in the best position to come up with the solution. Under her leadership, say those involved, trust and staff morale soared to an all-time high. Building staffs were given a considerable degree of autonomy; for example, building budgeting was introduced. Textbook adoptions became a building decision and faculty members were encouraged to find new initiatives and pilot programs. Schools no longer had to be in lock step with the rest of the district. Building diversity became the new norm within this increasingly decentralized regime....According to those involved, what happened was that the buildings 'fanned out' and developed different projects and different ways of doing things. Moreover, many of the building participants not only relished their newly won freedom but also considered themselves to have won a

power struggle; site-based decision making became teacher-based decision making. Inside each building, personal differences surfaced. Soon, said another observer, individual teachers were allowed to select their own curriculum materials; so much so, in fact, that fourth grade teachers throughout the district might be using nine different reading programs and several different mathematics schemes. The district had atomized.

Indeed, just as the tightness of the previous regime had become unpopular, now the looseness of the current approach was beginning to attract its critics. Curriculum and instructional consistency and continuity, it was claimed, were the main casualties. Given the demographics of the district—many of the students come from transient families and there is regular 'slippage' from building to building—this could be a real problem. When students transferred from school to school, the variety of instructional programs and practices (even at the same grade level) served to exacerbate the disruption. In addition, parents quickly became confused. They became aware of the differences between the schools and thought that it all seemed very fragmented and disjointed. Many teachers were beginning to feel the same way. In 1995, therefore, a third stage of development began. Again, the arrival of a new superintendent initiated—or reflected—a change of heart in terms of how the local system was organized. It was widely recognized that the fragmentation of recent times had to be reversed—thus returning to the system-wide coherence and rationality of the earlier stage—while retaining the enthusiasm, ownership, and commitment of the building-based improvement work. Two moves typified the new direction being taken. First, the new superintendent encouraged the establishment of a district-wide school improvement committee (known as the Transformation Now Team or TNT) and, second, he was instrumental in setting up school improvement training for building level teams. TNT was established as an oversight committee representing all the various 'anchor' groups—teachers, administrators, support staff, parents, business people, and community members. During the 1995–1996 school year the TNT committee met regularly and identified four goals to be accomplished at the district level:

- To continue to support school improvement efforts across the district.

- To create a shared vision for the district.

- To facilitate communication, both internally and externally.

- To support the creation of school-business partnerships.

In addition, during the same school year, several members of TNT, including the new superintendent, attended district leadership training in Des Moines, provided by consultants from the New Iowa Schools Development Corporation (NISDC). New Iowa Schools, in operation since 1994, was set up by a partnership of several stakeholding educational organizations (including the teachers' association, the state department, and state-wide administrator, parent, and school board groups) in order to act as a catalyst for school improvement at the local level. Denied federal funding (in the form of a NASDC grant), the Iowa legislature stepped in and, with the Governor's active support, uniquely agreed to provide the necessary funding to establish NISDC as a support agency for school improvement....[As in Dubuque] during the following school year, building-level teams began receiving on-site school improvement leadership training—again, facilitated by NISDC consultants.

'School improvement' in this district, however, is not just building-based work. Indeed, it is the blending of and reciprocity between building-based and district-based efforts that is so characteristic of the third stage of development. At the district level, twin emphases emerged: setting the system expectations and then finding the resources and supports to enable those in the buildings to meet the expectations. The first expectations established at the district level were for each building to establish a school improvement team and to formulate a school improvement plan, a first draft of which had to be handed in by May 1997.

Reflecting on these activities, the district's Director of Educational Services declared: 'The coordinated efforts of all buildings toward school improvement have brought about a sense of continuity and cohesiveness that had previously been lacking. **Our approach now is neither top-down nor bottom-up, but rather a combination of both.** Good ideas and initiatives flow up and down the system. What we have developed is a crystal clear focus for our district-school improvement. We are leading systemic change through focused, durable, system-wide improvement in student learning.'

This new cohesion (borrowed from the top-down rationality of the first stage of development) and the enthusiasm and commitment of participants (taken from the second stage) were combined in the more focused, more coordinated, and more integrated approach of Levine's (1991) "directed autonomy"—the third stage of development.

As in Dubuque, four characteristic elements of the third stage were soon to emerge from the work.

- All buildings developed their school improvement plans along much the same process lines. The plans were needs-based data-driven—they were grounded in both external and internal data—and contained focused priority areas based on this information.

- Many of these priorities were common across the buildings. These common themes included boosting reading achievement, integrating technology, increasing parent involvement, and improving communication.

- Those involved were committed enough to the implementation of these goals that their minds were shifting to results and how to assess them. This district was one of the first in the state to issue an annual report to the local community showing the progress made toward district goals and targets. While the district indicators of success used to show progress may not have been selected by the teachers generally, the more those in the schools saw the relevance of these criteria to their building goals and what they were trying to do in their classrooms, the more they bought into the idea of system accountability and the significance of the annual report as being "our" way of speaking to "our" community. To substantiate this investment in results, this district was also one of the first in Iowa to invite experts from the Iowa Testing Program to help principals and teachers understand how to better utilize ITBS and ITED results as part of their analysis of student achievement data. This emphasis on item analysis was typical of the growing awareness of the importance of data and its central role in informed decision making.

- In order to support and sustain their school improvement efforts over time, those in the district became more proactive yet more selective in finding appropriate external supports. Knowing their local needs made them more discerning and more demanding consumers of professional development opportunities. They expected more of a return on their investments.

- Another distinctive feature of the third stage of development in this district was the style of leadership being encouraged and modeled at both building and district levels. While teacher leadership and the formation of study groups and action teams were encouraged, none of this would have been possible without the leadership style of the new superintendent. From the outset he tried to practice "transformational leadership" by ensuring that expectations were created and clearly communicated and then empowering all those around him to rise to the challenge. He took on the personal responsibilities of nurturing community partnerships and championing the need for more assessment and accountability. In his leadership style he married openness with determination, approachability with perseverance, and understanding with the setting of high expectations. He was prepared to ask the tough questions but then consistently demonstrated his readiness to roll up his sleeves and join with his colleagues at whatever level of the local system in collaborative problem solving. Above all, he understood his role as "system-keeper." Knowing the power of systemic alignment, he marshaled all the forces of the district behind the improvement of student learning.

This description of the school improvement efforts in another district in Iowa (similar to Dubuque) not only includes additional information concerning the three stages of development, but also enhances our understanding of the nature of the third, most recent and most advanced stage. Indeed, five characteristics or elements lie at the heart of Stage Three. They include

- Element One: Managing Complexity

- Element Two: Differentiation

- Element Three: Data-Based Decision Making

- Element Four: Mentoring

- Element Five: Leadership for Change

Each of these elements will be discussed in the following section of this chapter.

The Essence of Stage Three: Five Elements

Element One: Managing Complexity

Stage Three involves a district and its schools becoming a more developed, more organic, more complex system. Charles Handy (1989), the British organizational theorist who has charted the growth of various new kinds of organizations, describes this stage as being tantamount to federalism. According to Handy: "Federalism is, in my view, a necessary development in the evolution of organizations."

In his 1989 book *The Age of Unreason*, he distinguishes between the autocratic rule of a monarchy (similar to the regimes popular during Stage One), decentralization (Stage Two), and federalism (Stage Three). According to Handy:

> Federalism implies a variety of individual groups allied together under a common flag with some shared identity. **Federalism seeks to make it big by keeping it small, or at least independent, by combining autonomy with cooperation....It is the method**

which businesses are slowly, and painfully, evolving for getting the best of both worlds—the size which gives them clout in the market place and the financial centers, as well as some economies of scale, and the small unit size which gives them the flexibility which they need, as well as the sense of community for which individuals increasingly hanker.

Handy continues by drawing an important distinction between federalism and decentralization:

> Decentralization implies that the center delegates certain tasks or duties to the outlying bits while the center remains in overall control. The center does the delegating, and initiates and directs. Thus it is that we have that most consistent of organizational findings, the more an organization decentralizes its operations the greater the flow of information to and from the center. The center may not be doing the work in a decentralized organization, but it makes sure that it knows how the work is going....Federalism is different. In federal countries, states are the original founding groups, coming together because there are some things which they can do better jointly (defense is the obvious example) than individually. The center's powers are given to it by the outlying groups, in a sort of reverse delegation. The center, therefore, does not direct or control as much as coordinate, advise, influence, and suggest.

Handy (1989) makes four further points relative to federalism—all of which are relevant to a discussion of Stage Three characteristics as follow:

- Handy calls federal organizations "reverse thrust organizations" with the initiative, drive, and energy coming mainly from the outlying parts—the center acting as an influencing force with a relatively low profile.

- Federal organizations, he says, are tight-loose organizations: "The center holds some decisions very tight to itself, usually and crucially, the choice of how to spend new money and where to place the new people. This gives them the means to shape the long-term strategy and to influence its execution through the key executives." Such small centers, he argues, are responsible for making the big decisions that constitute global strategies to link the semi-autonomous parts.

- This is no job for a monarch ("someone with an overriding authority and a liking for autocratic government") Handy argues. The center has to be a place of persuasion, of argument leading to consensus; it has to be leadership through ideas, not personality.

■ Echoing Richard Elmore (2000), Handy reminds us of the term "subsidiarity" and its central importance in federal organizations. Subsidiarity is an unfamiliar term to most, but not to adherents of the Roman Catholic Church. First enunciated by Pope Leo X, but later recalled in the papal encyclical, "Quadragesimo Anno," in 1947, the principle holds that it is an injustice, a grave evil, and a disturbance of right order for a large and higher organization to arrogate to itself functions which can be performed efficiently by smaller and lower bodies.

Put simply, says Handy, stealing other people's rightful decisions is wrong—a sense of immorality is implied. The more people feel trusted to make decisions, the more they feel a sense of responsibility, and the less likely they are to make mistakes. Subsidiarity, Handy reminds us, involves lots of leaders all over the place (and not just in the center). As a consequence, federal organizations tend to be flat organizations with only four or five levels.

They may be flatter organizations, but they are certainly more complex. The best metaphor for Stage Three organizational life is the lattice, which involves vertical and horizontal dimensions working together in a complex, layered, interwoven pattern. By having the interconnectedness of warp and weft, the lattice—or matrix—is the way to embrace seeming dichotomies and opposing forces. Vertical expectations and horizontal relationships, tightness and looseness, large and small are all brought into productive, meaningful working relationships. Indeed, and most importantly of all, the lattice is the means of blending the consistency, uniformity, and verticality of common expectations ("standards") with the horizontality of differentiation—the honoring of difference.

Element Two: Differentiation

Differentiation is another vital ingredient of Stage Three change and learning. The concept implies that there is accommodation of choice and difference within the application of consistent expectations: while different routes are used to get there, the destination remains the same. It sounds very much like "directed autonomy," involving tightness of overall direction and accountability and looseness in terms of implementation. It also suggests a new definition of equity: that different people with different needs are helped in different ways to arrive at the same place. Such an approach, therefore, has to be needs-based data-driven.

In Stage Three school improvement efforts, differentiation figures crucially in two related ways:

Differentiated Instruction

As the Bryant experience testifies, classrooms today have to be based around differentiated instruction (i.e., the teacher helping different students with different needs meet the same standards by using different learning routes and a basinful of different learning strategies). By adopting many of the approaches first used with special education students (like differentiated instruction and progress monitoring) for regular education classrooms, schools like Bryant can now show which interventions have been used with which students for how long and with what success. Chris McCarron has said recently: "Problem solving and differentiated instruction—I can't see a difference any more." Problem solving at Bryant involves—and triggers—differentiated instruction to such an extent that they become one and the same.

Differentiated instruction also involves the application of the business concept of "just-in-time" (JIT) delivery to student learning. In commerce, JIT involves the delivery of new stock just at the point of the sale, thus drastically reducing warehousing bills. It is the principle, as Denis Doyle (2003) points out, that Wal-Mart has used so effectively to beat off competition. It is also a principle that translates wonderfully well to the world of classrooms. In classrooms, just-in-time support and delivery suggests the following:

- There is more effective alignment of the delivery of instruction with learning (and learner) needs.

- Progress monitoring and data-based decision making are used to identify and target the specific learning needs of each and every student within the ongoing, "layering" approach used at Bryant.

- Informal, rapid response mechanisms are in place. JIT applied to the classroom implies responsiveness, flexibility, the quick-fire delivery of learning support at the point of need, and, as the title suggests, just-in-time applications.

- Delays (in responding to learning needs) are avoided—thus preventing the problems becoming compounded over time. Early intervention is key. As one Dubuque principal remarked to the author concerning her school's response to *NCLB*:

> We're doing everything we can with data—and if we fail, we'll feel okay about ourselves; we will have made a good faith effort. We've brought the kids along more than we ever have. We don't want to send them on unprepared. We've built an integrated and rigorous instructional program and scientifically valid, research-based curriculum with interventions based upon assessment results.

- Down-to-earth approaches are applied to students' multiple learning problems. Using what special educators refer to as "functional assessment," the identification of data-driven needs is never allowed to unrealistically extend the problem-solving process. As the same principal commented: "Call it what it is. If it looks like a duck, walks like a duck, quacks like a duck, then it's probably a duck."

What is definitely to be avoided is analysis paralysis in the interests of getting to the point of trying interventions with students and seeing if they work.

■ Just-in-time delivery of instructional interventions is the antithesis of a one-size-fits-all approach to student learning. It demands a very specific fit between the identified individual learning needs and the selected intervention.

■ It also demands a new approach to professional development for the instructors. Just-in-time delivery of instructional interventions to match specific learning needs of individual students demands the just-in-time delivery of professional development supports for both individual and groups of teachers. Again, it is the antithesis of the one-size-fits-all approach to professional development. It also negates the need to "warehouse" and stockpile scores of instructional interventions just in case they are required on some future occasion. What is required is much more fleetness-of-foot.

Differentiated Professional Development

The second type of differentiation related to school improvement is the differentiation of professional development for teachers. The just-in-time delivery of professional development supports for teachers to enable them to provide just-in-time learning support for their students will revolutionize professional development. In three recent articles, we are shown glimpses of this brave new world.

In an article entitled "Targeted Training," Jane Sanborn (2002) describes how the teachers in Pella, Iowa customize their instruction to the data-based learning needs of their students and, concomitantly, how the local Area Education Agency (AEA) staff provide targeted, specific support for the teachers in their areas of instructional need. In two very recent articles, both contained in a special section of the June 2003 *Phi Delta Kappan* entitled "Professional Development That Works," Thomas Guskey and James Kelleher explore much the same territory.

In his article titled "What Makes Professional Development Effective?" Guskey points out that professional development should involve the enhancement of teachers' content and pedagogical knowledge, while providing opportunities (that are well organized, carefully constructed and purposefully directed) to deepen understanding, analyze students' work and develop new instructional approaches. Another important task, he says, is to gather regular formative information to guide improvement efforts. Less than half of the studies consulted by Guskey in his meta-analysis of writings about effective professional development, however, mention the importance of using analyses of student learning data to guide professional development activities and, somewhat surprisingly, only four lists stress that professional development should be based on the best available research evidence. "This is particularly striking," he says, "given the long-standing criticism of professional development that focuses on fads and bandwagon movements rather than on solid evidence of what works with students." Guskey (2003) also points out that *context* is key when it comes to determining the success of professional development activities. He states:

> Nearly all professional development takes place in real world contexts. The complexities of these varied contexts introduce a web of factors that influence whether or not a particular characteristic or practice will produce the desired results. These nuances of context are difficult to recognize and even more difficult to take into account within the confines of a single program. Thus programs that appear quite similar may produce different results for subtle and unanticipated reasons....The characteristics that influence the effectiveness of professional development are multiple and highly complex.
>
> Take, for example, professional development specifically designed to enhance teachers' content and pedagogical knowledge. Schools in economically depressed areas that have trouble attracting and keeping well-qualified teachers and, as a result, have many teachers teaching outside their area of certification, may benefit greatly from such programs. Schools in more affluent communities, on the other hand, that have sufficient resources to attract and retain well-qualified teachers with advanced training in the subject areas they teach, may see little improvement from similar programs. These real-world contextual differences profoundly influence the effectiveness of professional development endeavors....Within the unique context of nearly every school, there are teachers who have found ways to help students learn well. Identifying the practices and strategies of these teachers might provide a basis for highly effective professional development *within that context*.

While Guskey stops short of embracing the JIT approach to professional development, he certainly identifies some of the reasons for using it. Indeed, one of the biggest contextual factors facing any school is the students and their types of learning problems. In addition, Guskey helps us understand what is required to make JIT professional development successful. In typical Stage Three style, he cautions against using a solely school-or site-based approach:

> A recent review by the Consortium for Policy Research in Education...found that when decisions about professional development were primarily school-based, staff members paid

only lip service to research and were more interested in programs similar to what they were already doing than in those producing results. In such instances the decentralization of decision-making appeared to be undermining the use of knowledge rather than promoting it. A carefully organized collaboration between site-based educators, who are keenly aware of critical contextual characteristics, and district-level personnel, who have broader perspectives on problems, seems essential to optimize the effectiveness of professional development.

This is exactly why Dubuque CSD is establishing a cadre of instructional strategists to support JIT approaches to student learning in the schools. These strategists will have ample opportunities to study the external research literature and to pool the strategies that are known to work in similar settings and easy access to work side-by-side with teachers on their classroom issues. Just as Chris McCarron has supported her colleagues at Bryant, now her team will do the same for teachers across the district.

James Kelleher, in his *PDK* article entitled "A Model for Assessment-Driven Professional Development," gets even closer to endorsing JIT than Guskey. He emphasizes that professional development activities have three main responsibilities: to help teachers translate new learning into classroom instruction; to use data to set specific, measurable targets for student learning that are tied to SMART (Specific, Measurable, Attainable, Results-oriented, and Time-bound) goals and not based on whim or caprice; and to use assessment measures to measure the results of professional development. The six-stage process outlined by Kelleher is very similar to the problem-solving model practiced in Dubuque with specific, targeted professional development support activities added to the mix.

As the following chart indicates, taken together, differentiated instruction for both students and their teachers is a powerful package—mainly because it is so intensively needs-based data-driven.

Differentiated Instruction

Students

- Problem Solving
- Identifying individual students' learning needs

- Learner Expectations
  - Standards and Benchmarks
  - Grade-Level Expectations

Internal Data

Differentiated Instruction

External Data

- Diagnostic Teaching
- DBDM at classroom level
- Target Training/Professional Development

- Research-Based Instructional Strategies
- Scientifically-Based Research

Teachers

Element Three: Data-Based Decision Making

At the third stage of school improvement, data-based decision making is suffused throughout the local system. Not only are the same data used to guide decision making at the various levels (see Workbook Five: *Creating a Data-Driven System*) but also, as Kelleher (2003) points out, the net result is the nesting of teacher, department, school, and district goals.

In terms of Dubuque's chief data users, it is fascinating to watch Chris McCarron's continuing journey. While her own description of her early career (at Bryant and at other schools in Dubuque) is presented earlier in this workbook, it is her current work that is of interest here. From being one of Bryant's data coaches and the problem-solving strategist, she has now moved to the Central Office where she will act as the team leader of the district's cadre of instructional strategists. Her work is also receiving attention at the state level and she was recently asked to speak about her work at the ICASE state-wide conference for special education administrators. Looking at a copy of her speech, it is fascinating to read her description of the work that is currently under way in Dubuque. Given the relevance of her speech, extracts are included as follows.

Dubuque's Data-Based Decision Making in General Education

This morning I will be talking about how data is being used in general education. I will share how the following initiatives all come together for improved student performance. I am going to review the model that Dubuque is using to assist in making data-based decisions to improve the instruction of all students. We are fortunate because many of these structures were in place prior to *NCLB* and now we are able to use these structures to help us to address the mandates that are associated with *NCLB*.

- Data Coach Teams

- No Child Left Behind

- District Intervention Plan

- Electronic Student Database

- Standard-Referenced Progress Report

- Problem Solving

Four years ago, our district created what we call data coach teams in each school. The teams consist of teacher leaders from the school, the principal, and a liaison from the district's central office. The liaison helps to provide the bridge between district-level initiatives and the individual schools. These teams come together two to three times per year for intensive in-services on the use of data in the schools. Peter Holly and Mary Lange have served as resources to our district and have helped us to learn the types of data available to the school, and how to utilize the data to understand the needs of the school and to help to plan for improved instruction. One of the greatest advantages to this model is that it provides a common knowledge base to all the schools and creates an 'in-house' data team. The team has the opportunity to participate in the training sessions and then immediately determine the implications for their own particular school.

- Each school in the district has a data coach team.

- Intensive in-servicing has been provided to the teams over the past four years.

- The in-servicing provides a common knowledge base about how to utilize the school data to help determine school goals.

What we have seen happen is that the comprehensive school plans have moved from being interest-based plans to being data-based plans. Previously many of the

continued

school initiatives were based on what staff of the school thought would be helpful, or new initiatives that they thought were interesting. After thoroughly examining the school data, many schools changed their goals to match their identified area of need.

During each of the past four years, there has been an increased alignment between our district's standards and benchmarks, the district improvement plan, and the comprehensive school improvement plans. Teachers are beginning to see how the pieces fit together in the big picture.

- School goals in each comprehensive school improvement plan have moved from being interest-based to being data-based.

- Care has been taken to see that there is alignment among the district's standards and benchmarks, the district improvement plan, and the school improvement plans.

As I stated, Data Coach Teams were in place before the dawning of *NCLB*. As we all know, *NCLB* has caused us all to find ways to address the increased accountability that accompanies the legislation. In Dubuque, we are using the Data Coach Teams as one of the main avenues to disseminate information to the schools and to provide support to the schools as they meet the *NCLB* demands. As a district we have tried to shed a positive light on this seemingly ominous creature called *NCLB*. We continually try to emphasize that this just confirms the direction that the district has been heading—that of using data to improve instruction. We try to emphasize that it is our opportunity to drive change.

No Child Left Behind

- Increased accountability

- Opportunity to drive change

At the same time that *NCLB* is increasing accountability, changes in special education have also altered the face of general education. As the entitlement criteria for special education are being tightened, some of the students who once may have received services are not scoring below the 12th percentile and, therefore, are not qualifying for special education. Meeting their needs has become the responsibility of the general education teacher. In addition, even students who are identified to receive special education services are expected to remain in the general education classroom for greater portions of their instructional day.

All of these factors, working in combination, have increased the interest on the part of general education teachers for more interventions. Teachers are seeking ways to increase their 'bag of tricks.' We are seeing an increase in the number of general education teachers who want to be in-serviced on strategies that previously only special education teachers tended to be interested in.

Special Education Changes

- 12th percentile entitlement

- Greater emphasis on least restrictive environment

- Increased interest in the need for more interventions within general education

Given all these factors, the task of meeting expectations for increased student performance is quite daunting. Consequently, we felt that we needed a measurement tool to monitor our progress. Our method that was created was the District Intervention Plan.

We all know the unpleasant ramifications that come when a building is cited as a low performing school. The reality is that if we are monitoring our own progress data, we really do not need an outside source to tell us when there are concerns about student achievement. We can see them for ourselves. Dubuque took that perspective when it created its internal alert system. This outlines the data indicators that would place a school on internal alert. In addition, and more importantly, it also describes what actions must be taken to address the area of concern.

- Internal Alert

- Describes the responsibility at the district level, school level, and classroom level for monitoring student achievement

Two additional initiatives are being implemented that place an increased spotlight on the use of data: an electronic student database and this year we piloted a new elementary school progress report.

To aid in the manipulation of data and to make data more easily accessible to staff working with students, an electronic student database was created. This database was created using Excel. First, a core template was created. This identified all the data that was required to be kept on each child in the district. This provided a common record across schools and aided in the transfer of information between schools. This year, all schools entered the data and were given basic training on how to use the database. Next year, the focus of the training will be on using the database to inform instruction.

continued

The other initiative that increased our use of data was the pilot of our new standards-referenced progress report. The report compares the child's progress against a grade-level standard. It is determined whether a student is exceeding the standard, meeting the standard, nearing the standard, or is below the standard. To make this determination, a rubric was created for each standard.

Two Additional Initiatives

The Electronic Student Database	Standards-Referenced Progress Report
■ A core template for the elementary level has been created. ■ All schools have implemented it.	■ The progress report has been aligned with the standards. ■ A rubric for marking each area of the report card requires data from the teacher to support the mark. ■ All children being marked "below grade-level" are required to be placed in problem solving.

All of the initiatives that I have spoken about thus far have acted as a sort of data funnel. First, our district and school plans became more data-based; then *NCLB* and changes in special education increased our accountability for a wider range of students in general education. We determined what we knew about individual students with the electronic student database and then assessed them against the standards on the new report card. And if, through any of these initiatives, a child was determined to be performing below grade-level standards, we determined that problem solving was the process that would be used to address those individual concerns.

We have expanded the notion of problem solving from a 'path to entitlement' to a process to address and document the progress of students who are not meeting expectations for whatever reason. We re-established problem solving as a general education initiative. A two-hour in-service was held in each elementary school and the junior high and high schools are currently trying to redefine what the process will look like at the secondary level.

Problem Solving

■ Problem solving is the primary avenue used to meet the needs of students scoring below the 40th percentile

■ Problem solving is being re-established as a general education initiative

One School Example: Bryant

- Three years ago this elementary school made a concerted effort to place all students who were not meeting grade-level expectations into problem solving.

- Teams of teachers met in bi-weekly meetings.

- The spotlight was placed on problem solving.

- Sharing sessions occurred at staff meetings during which staff members shared the successes they were having with students by using the problem-solving process. They also shared the experience of a student with whom they were struggling. In doing so, they put their data in a public forum.

Summary of the School's Results

- More children were placed into the problem-solving process.

- The number of academic concerns increased while the number of behavioral concerns decreased.

- Many of the concerns were resolved.

- While many children met success in problem solving, the intervention needed to be continued over time. However, such children did not need to enter special education.

- Entitlement for special education decreased.

- The number of students scoring below the 40th percentile on ITBS decreased during this period, even though the number of students on free and reduced lunches increased by almost 20%.

Some Reflections

- Collecting and understanding the data does not lead to improved instruction for children.

- The power is not in data-based decision making, but rather it is in <u>data-based action</u>! If we just look at the data, or it remains a collection of facts and figures, we will have little impact upon the lives of our teachers and students.

- It is our hope that by utilizing data to improve our instruction, the result will be improved performance by all children.

As Chris McCarron emphasizes in her presentation, Data Coach Training for the school teams has become *the* vehicle for communicating, digesting, and beginning to respond to such major initiatives as *No Child Left Behind*. In each of the three sessions held during the 2002-2003 school year, *NCLB* updates were provided by means of computerized presentations. Question and answer sessions followed concerning the implications of *NCLB*. Time was also provided for team processing and planning. Discussion also occurred concerning the district's pathfinding response to the kind of demands promulgated by *NCLB*—its own internal alert system. It should be emphasized that this in-house early warning system endorses Bryant's approach to problem solving as the remedial process to follow as the basis of a school's Student Achievement Intervention Plan.

Element Four: Mentoring

Data feedback, peer coaching, mentoring, and collegial sharing are closely related activities. Such practices greatly boost the implementation of school improvement efforts, as Joyce, Wolf, and Calhoun (1993) conclude:

> Thus, before training, teachers need to organize themselves into study groups who will share plans, discuss their experiences, and develop a sense of community as they struggle to bring about change. Observation is very helpful, for it enables members of study groups to pick up ideas from one another.

Charles Handy (1989), in describing the importance of what he refers to as "incidental learning" (learning that is built around real-life incidents), argues that such learning needs to be facilitated not by a boss or supervisor, but by a neutral mentor or coach from inside, or often, from outside the organization. Consequently, Handy concludes:

> The mentor role will become increasingly important....Properly selfish individuals, will, if they are wise, look for their own mentors. Organizations could make this easier by maintaining a list of approved, and paid for, mentors, inside and outside. They will not always be people in great authority, those mentors, and will seldom be one's immediate superior. Mentoring is a skill on its own. Quiet people have it more than loud people; for mentors are able to live vicariously, getting pleasure from the success of others; they are interpreters not theorists, nor action men, best perhaps in the reflective stage of learning, people who are attracted by influence not power.

Mentoring is deeply embedded within Dubuque's current school improvement efforts on at least two levels.

Dubuque CSD's Professional Mentoring Program

As mentioned earlier, Dubuque was one of the first districts to establish a professional mentoring program. Along with the three-track professional staff evaluation system (designed according to the ideas of Danielson and McGreal, 2000), the mentoring program was introduced in the fall of 1999. Both programs shared a common purpose (enhanced teaching and learning for improved student achievement) and incorporated Danielson's framework for effective teaching (1996). In addition, the mentoring program was built around the ETS PATHWISE®: Induction Program. The program was introduced to participants as follows:

Connecting Professionals—
DCSD Professional Mentoring Program

Purpose/Philosophy

The Dubuque Community School District (DCSD) has established the Professional Mentoring Program to support teachers, nurses, and counselors who are new to the district to function more effectively and to grow professionally. This non-evaluative program provides a transition for professionals who are either experienced or inexperienced to become successful members of the DCSD.

Beliefs

- Professionals new to the DCSD deserve to be supported in their efforts to meet the high expectations of the district and to meet the educational needs of all students.

- In order to understand the complexity of our school system, professionals new to the district need information regarding the traditions, common practices, rules, regulations, expectations, values and core beliefs, and mission and vision of the district.

- This program provides growth opportunities for both the mentor and the professional new to the district.

- Providing a sound mentoring program will lead not only to greater retention of new professionals, but will also result in higher quality instruction for our students.

---

continued

Rationale

One of the hallmarks of an effective school system is its ability to attract and retain quality professionals. The following factors indicate a need for a professional mentoring program:

- Retirement rates will increase significantly in the next decade.

- Nationally, nearly 50% of beginning teachers leave within the first four years of their careers.

- Local, state, and federal mandates have resulted in increased expectations for professionals in education.

- Due to the structure of our educational system, educators often work in isolation from their peers, and are often reluctant to ask for assistance for fear of appearing incompetent.

In light of these factors, the DCSD's Professional Mentoring Program will provide guidance and support for educators new to the district. The ultimate aim is to increase retention of those professionals and to provide greater consistency and quality of instruction for our students, thus resulting in increased student achievement.

Goals

- To provide a positive and successful transition of professionals to the Dubuque Community School District.

- To promote the personal and professional well being of professionals new to the district.

- To provide ongoing guidance, support, and reinforcement to professionals new to the district through an organized, well-defined program.

- To promote excellence in instruction to improve student performance.

- To build awareness of the culture of the community, district, and school.

- To increase mutual respect and collaboration through collegial activities.

- To increase retention of professionals new to the district.

Definitions

<u>Instructional Mentor:</u> an educator with a minimum of five years of experience who has been trained in the DCSD's Professional Mentoring Program and who is assigned to provide support to a teacher, nurse, or counselor new to DCSD.

<u>New Professional:</u> any teacher, nurse, or counselor who is new to DCSD.

<u>ETS (Educational Testing Service) PATHWISE Induction Program:</u> a reflective, support process adopted and adapted by the DCSD to assist teachers, nurses, and counselors new to DCSD.

Professional Mentoring Components

The Dubuque Community School District's Professional Mentoring Program is designed to deliver support to new teachers, counselors, and nurses in a three-leveled program.

<u>Level 1: Orientation</u>

This level provides a welcome and collaborative support in the form of orientation activities for New Professionals from individually assigned Instructional Mentors. The New Professional and the Instructional Mentor will meet as arranged in August and September for the purpose of acquainting the New Professional to the school and readying him/her for the approaching school year.

<u>Level 2: Training Sessions</u>

This level provides district-required adult learning opportunities for Dubuque Community School District (DCSD) New Professionals. Sample topics are Behavior Management, Cooperative Learning, Working with Parents and Community, Assessment, School Improvement, and Equity and Diversity. This level also sponsors optional social opportunities for New Professionals to be together.

<u>Level 3: Instructional Focus With Feedback</u>

This level provides for an in-depth collegial examination of teaching and learning between an Instructional Mentor and New Professional through a program called PATHWISE: Induction Program (ETS) adopted and adapted by DCSD. Based on the components of professional practice as identified in *Enhancing Professional Practice: A Framework for Teaching* (Danielson, 1996) and following the developmental cycle of PLAN-TEACH-REFLECT-APPLY, this level provides a series of inquiries, observations, and conversations that facilitate the identification of each New Professionals' teaching strengths and areas for growth.

The Professional Mentoring Program in Dubuque is just ending its fourth successful year of operation. According to the Program's coordinator, Jeff Johll, the successes have included the following:

- Of the 130 New Professionals who have experienced the program, well over 90% are still with Dubuque Schools and 99% are still in teaching elsewhere.

- The level of conversations about good instruction has increased considerably—from which the students undoubtedly benefit.

- Instructional Mentors have provided the New Professionals with emotional support and a level of disclosure. "Take classroom accommodations," says Johll. "It is so reassuring to hear that an experienced professional is still trying to figure this out. It tells me that I'm not a bad teacher; I just have some things to learn."

  Anecdotally, Johll can provide plenty of evidence of good, but uncertain, professionals who have been "saved" for teaching. As one New Professional said this year: "If it hadn't been for my mentor, I would have quit at Christmas time."

- The district climate is more supportive and more collaborative, with educators being more comfortable about sharing ideas concerning their profession—teaching and learning. This also includes the district being less hierarchical as the mentoring relationships are two-way: both sides share ideas and both learn from the exchange. The spirit of mentoring has changed the way the district does its business and, as a consequence, the culture of teaching and learning in Dubuque is so much more positive and supportive. Moreover, given the links among the mentoring program and so many other professional development and school improvement activities, it is possible to argue that mentoring—and everything it stands for—goes to the heart of what Dubuque stands for today.

Critical Friend Feedback

The other level of mentoring occurs at the organizational level. For several years, the author has acted as the district's critical friend and, as such, has visited all buildings and the district office on a regular—at least annual—basis to review the school improvement planning efforts (in terms of content, process, and relationships) and consequently provided constructive feedback on the quality of Dubuque's efforts. His reports have included feedback to district personnel and to those leading the improvement process in each school. Intentionally, the reports have identified strengths (endorsements) and growth points (challenges). Two examples of such reports follow.

<u>Example 1:</u>

Dubuque CSD: Comprehensive School Improvement Planning

Some General Comments

Having read all the building plans for 1999–2000, there are several strengths to mention that are worthy of endorsement:

1. With the State Department's implementation of HF #2272, in a very real sense the rest of Iowa now has to play catch-up with what is already established practice in Dubuque.

2. There is a growing tradition in Dubuque of district-level expectations being in correspondence.

3. Indeed, the district-level "umbrella of expectations" has provided useful guidance for building-level planning. In particular, the learning Competencies, the DCSD Goals (High Student Achievement, Character Development/ Citizenship, and Collaboration/Teamwork), and the district-wide areas of focus (Reading; Technology; Respect, Responsibility and Student Discipline; and Parent and Community Involvement) have acted as planning parameters.

4. It is useful to start each building plan with a profile (containing the school's mission, Site Council membership, and review of current progress).

5. Particularly noteworthy is the growing alignment across the sections of the action plans: goals, supporting activities, success criteria, time-lines, budget, and staff development are all in correspondence.

6. Another strong feature is the local custom of building multi-year plans and then committing to reviewing, updating, and reporting these plans on an annual basis.

7. Two related strengths are the strong emphasis on character and citizenship (the territory of the state-wide initiative known as Success4) and the concomitant understanding that, when it comes to student success, the cognitive and affective domains are so closely intertwined.

8. With the growing emphasis on student achievement and assessment measures, Dubuque Schools are well placed to demonstrate the intelligent use of ITBS/ITED scores as a form of trend-line data.

Besides the strengths listed above, there are various challenges to meet:

1. What has happened to "less is more"? The building plans often contain too many goals and run to too many pages. There needs to be a concerted effort to lessen

continued

the load in order to achieve more. The production of school improvement plans should never become so onerous that it interferes with what the plans are trying to accomplish, i.e., improved teaching and learning.

2. The inclusion of a school profile is still inconsistent across all the building plans.

3. In the action plans there is still some confusion in terms of what is a goal, what is a strategy, and what is a success criterion. Goals are the "ends" and the long-term purposes (e.g., improving reading comprehension); programs, strategies, and activities are the "means" or what we use to achieve our goals (e.g., Guided Reading); and success criteria are the indicators we use to provide evidence that success has been achieved (e.g., increased test scores for reading comprehension).

4. Success criteria do require some attention. They should be more about results than about the processes used to achieve those results. Attendance at a staff development workshop, therefore, is not a success criterion. What happens as a result of this attendance—for instance, changed instructional behavior—gets us to the success criterion of improved student learning. The impact on student learning is the big idea to emphasize. Like curriculum benchmarks, success criteria are the "what" have to be achieved in order to be successful. In turn, data collection methods are the "how" to check that success has occurred.

5. In more consolidated, integrated planning, how can the various funding streams (Title I, Technology, At-Risk, etc.) be identified?

6. HF #2272 challenges us in four new ways:

    ■ There are now three kinds of goals: Student Learning Goals (Essential Learnings/Learner Competencies), Long-Range (Five Year) Goals, and Annual Improvement Goals.

    ■ Also required are multiple, district-wide assessments that are valid and reliable.

    ■ In addition, in Iowa, three proficiency levels are being used (as in ITBS/ITED) to group students achieving below or above the 40th percentile and those scoring above the 90th percentile.

    ■ Five year plans are now required, along with annual updates and reports.

<u>Example 2:</u>

Comprehensive School Improvement
Planning in Dubuque CSD

Introduction

This general report was compiled by NISDC consultants, Peter Holly and Mary Lange, following their visit to Dubuque CSD, March 27–31, 2000. They visited each building and met with Site Council members. The purpose of these meetings was to provide three things: feedback on the quality of the school improvement plans currently in operation, up-to-date information concerning the format to be used for the new plans, and advice concerning how to strengthen the Site Council planning process. As a follow-up to the meetings each building is now receiving an individual report plus this general overview report. This may well be a first for Iowa: critical friends responding to what they have learned and offering suggestions for improvement at both building and district levels. The role of critical friend is an interesting one. According to a poster in one of the buildings visited, such a 'friend is the one who knows your deepest needs, who shares your greatest joys, who helps you reach your highest dreams.' These words speak to the intent of this report.

General Comments

1. Dubuque CSD has been investing in school improvement planning for several years and the investment is paying off. Following the original training sessions, Site Councils have become used to developing annual plans and submitting these to the district. While this is the first time that feedback on the plans has been provided, the ongoing emphasis on school improvement planning is clearly paying rich dividends. Hopefully, this feedback will serve to further strengthen the plans and the planning process.

2. The recent legislation concerning Comprehensive School Improvement (initiated by House File #2272) is asking of districts across Iowa what is already established practice in Dubuque. A 'Chapter 12 Committee' has been meeting since last summer to coordinate the work, a community-based School Improvement Advisory Committee (SIAC) has met (as decreed by the legislation), and a district section of the Comprehensive School Improvement Plan has already been written and distributed to all principals. Building-level planning teams are now being encouraged to write their contributions by extending—in the light of their school data—what has already been presented under the five district goals.

3. Because of the hard work that has gone into school improvement plans in Dubuque Schools over a period of several years, the level of conversation is more sophisticated than generally found elsewhere and, therefore, the degree of

continued

challenge presented by the consultants could be that much more intense. Indeed, the consultants were keenly aware of this issue and continually emphasized that what they were asking of Site Council members would be currently beyond the grasp of many other districts.

4. Comprehensive School Improvement in Dubuque is being tackled comprehensively. The work is characterized by the principles of systemic alignment; it is more connected, more integrated, and more balanced in that it is neither predominantly top-down nor bottom-up. According to a paper written recently by consultant Peter Holly, it represents an advanced stage of development of school improvement. Indeed, his research on school improvement efforts across Iowa has led him to delineate three developmental stages. The first stage is characterized by top-down, authoritarian leadership and tightly controlled procedures at the local level; the second stage is typified by the fragmentation that comes with the autonomy of site-based decision making, and the third by the systemic connectivity that is generated by shared decision making. It is this third stage of development that is currently being explored in Dubuque CSD. It is in this stage that leadership (in the form of collaborative, empowering leadership) becomes more important, not less.

5. All the school improvement efforts in Dubuque are characterized by another essential element: they are increasingly needs-based and data-driven. Each building is developing a school profile/portfolio from which can be extracted on an ongoing basis information to guide school improvement decision making. In the interests of systemic alignment, however, the time is now right to develop a district-level databank (hopefully, soon to be computerized) from which disaggregated data for each building could be extracted. This would still allow each building to make appropriately "local," data-based decisions without having to spend precious time having to create its own database. In its new role as "system hub," this is a vital role for the district level operation.

6. The recent building visits provided a timely opportunity for "improving school improvement." The consultants were able to remind participants of the importance of continuing to apply first principles when planning school improvement efforts. First among the first principles is 'less is more.' Some of the building plans—for all sorts of good reasons—had become bloated and, in the apt phrase of the week, needed 'to be put on a diet.' The point is that school improvement plans are meant to be practical guides for action not epitaphs for wasted effort. Streamlining, then, has to be the order of the day. The intent is to create plans that inform—and trigger—practice that is deeper, more focused, and more likely to be sustained over time.

Thankfully, district personnel are willing partners in this endeavor. They are encouraging the kind of brevity and conciseness that is required in focused and aligned improvement plans. They are doing so in five ways. First, the building contribution to the overall plan doesn't need to repeat anything already included in the district section—these activities can be taken "as read." Second, the district section models the very conciseness that is recommended. Third, a new section of the building plan has been created in which all those changes needing ongoing maintenance (as opposed to the intense attention of early implementation) can be listed. Commonly referred to as 'the parking lot,' this new section provides buildings with the opportunity to really prune and prioritize what is finally placed in the main body of what is essentially an <u>implementation plan</u>. Fourth, buildings are being encouraged to list in their plans only those items (strategies/ interventions) that are essential and most likely to lead to success. Fifth, while five system goals have been identified, each building has the choice of selecting one of the first three goals, thus allowing for some flexibility in terms of building-level goal setting. Experience tells us that if there are too many goals, then the whole plan is inclined to 'fatness.' Those in the buildings were advised to not only resist the temptation to try and get everything in their plans ("Bigger doesn't mean better—it's not a competition," they were told), but also aim to produce pared down, 'leaner, meaner plans, tied more closely to the district goals.' It's a question of being packaged for success.

7. Success-mindedness is the key to good planning. The visits enabled the consultants to remind the participants of the wisdom of outcomes-based planning. As Covey (1989) reminds us, it's always best to start with the end in mind. Drawing on his experience with applying the "1,4,5,2,3 Technique" for action planning [see Workbook Two: *Creating a Process*], Peter Holly stressed the importance of asking key questions to trigger the planning process. Such questions included: 'In the goal area, what do we want to accomplish and what would success look like?' (thereby generating success criteria, i.e., indicators of success); 'How are we going to show evidence of success?' (Which assessment/data collection methods are we going to use to monitor our implementation efforts over time?); and 'What do we need to do in order to get there?' (Which strategies are we going to use and what staff development opportunities will we need to support us?)

8. During the building visits, particular emphasis was placed on how to craft effective success criteria. It is always best, participants were told, to write success criteria directly from the goal statement (and not from the supporting activities) and, when writing them, keep three questions in mind: 'What are the results we want to achieve?' 'What would these results look like in terms of impact on student learning?' and 'In terms of the degree of student achievement to be accomplished, what should this impact be in numerical terms?' Participants were also advised to revisit the columns on their planning sheets and do some spring cleaning. This might entail discarding some extraneous items, adding some items to the parking lot, transferring some items from one column to another, etc.

9. In order to track whether success is indeed being achieved, Site Council members were encouraged to be more data-minded as an ongoing preoccupation. Even if the district profile/data bank becomes a reality, when it comes to the effective use of the disaggregated data to inform building decisions,

continued

Data Coach Training for building personnel will be required. This should ensure the best use of the available data at the building level. This, however, still leaves the classroom level. What is needed here is data-based decision making regarding everyday teaching and learning issues. Classroom Action Research is the best vehicle for this kind of activity. What then becomes possible is a data-processing system in which each level of activity feeds into and from the next: the classroom level interacts with the building (Site Council) level and the building level interacts with the district level. Another advantage of training teachers to be action researchers in their classrooms is the connectedness it affords with the work of building-level action teams and the ground-level implementation of district programs such as the Literacy Initiative, Success4, Expeditionary Learning (EL), Problem Solving, etc. This approach to creating and using data at multiple local levels could become the cornerstone of the kind of district-as-system that succeeds in interweaving the horizontal and the vertical, shared responsibility for development and accountability, and building-level and district-level initiative.

Not only is it gratifying for this author to read back over this report and see how many of the recommendations have been put into effect, but also the report—and the extent to which it has been acted upon—is a very good reminder of how much *Dubuque as a learning system* is open to and accepting of critical friend feedback. As Charles Handy (1989) emphasizes, coaching and mentoring are essential ingredients of a learning organization and can be provided from those inside or outside the organization. In the interests of continuing the organizational learning process and given that there is always room for improvement, Data Coach Training for the 2003-2004 school year in Dubuque has been planned to include these five next challenges:

- More emphasis on **peer coaching** and its connections with classroom implementation, action research, and professional development.

- More emphasis on how Track Two of the Professional Evaluation System can connect with and reinforce working on action teams specifically and school improvement generally.

- A renewed conversation about a district-level Data Profile. The original district profile—now renamed the electronic student database—didn't exactly work out as originally intended; it's become more of a school profile constructed according to a district format and is playing a crucial role in school-level decision making. There is still, however, a vital place for a district-level profile from which the progress of district-level initiatives can be tracked and school-level data disaggregated.

- Now that the schools are working far more in collaboration (the competition that is so typical of Stage Two has been replaced by far more readiness to work as a system and provide mutual support across buildings), the time is ripe for learning from each others' successes—and failures—in what are being referred to as "showcase" sessions.

■ The fifth—and greatest challenge—is to build on everything that has gone before, in the name of school improvement, in Dubuque to rise to meet the challenges of *No Child Left Behind*. This conversation began as part of the spring 2003 school visits (see the following agenda of questions used).

School Visits, Spring 2003

Questions

1. Site Council Process

   ■ Regularity/frequency of meetings (when/how often?)

   ■ Membership (who?)

   ■ Function (what is the purpose/what gets done?)

   ■ Team process (how are meetings processed?)

   ■ Communication (how are colleagues kept informed?)

   ■ Role of data coaches (how are they used in the Site Council process?)

2. Emerging Content Areas for the CSIP

   ■ How are teams reporting on the progress made?

   ■ What are the greatest achievements?

   ■ What issues are emerging from your data?

   ■ What will be your focus areas/goals for next year and longer term?

   ■ How are you intending to accommodate AYP goals?

3. *No Child Left Behind*

   ■ Have you informed colleagues, Site Council, and parents about *NCLB* and its implications?

   ■ What will be its greatest challenges for you?

   ■ How will you use existing processes (e.g., data coaching, problem solving) to meet these challenges?

   ■ To what extent have you analyzed your ITBS/ITED data?

   ■ Which student subpopulations will apply to you?

In her January 2002 report to the school board, Nancy Bradley, Dubuque's Director of School Improvement and Staff Development, summarized many of the initiatives mentioned above. This summary can be found in Appendix F.

Element Five: Leadership for Change

None of what has been described above could have been achieved without the encouragement and support that come with collaborative leadership and collaborative leaders. The descriptor "collaborative," however, does not do justice to the definition of a Stage Three leader. First, while being more than prepared to lead, a Stage Three leader encourages leadership throughout the organization. As Joyce, Wolf, and Calhoun (1993) explain: "In self-renewing schools, vigorous, integrative leadership, supportive and exhortative in appropriate measures, is generated at all levels."

Leadership, they say, should be distributed throughout the organization, which is the principle of "subsidiarity" recommended by Elmore and Handy. Joyce et al. also acknowledge, however, that administrators with broad responsibility for overseeing the health of the organization, making and coordinating initiatives, and leading the district-wide improvement cadre are also required. They then offer an important caution:

> The most effective leadership is not embodied in a 'strong man or woman' who manipulates others, but in the ability to generate a democratic framework and process that binds the organization productively....The most effective leaders do not simply follow established formulas for getting things done, but are effective diagnosticians, problem solvers, and leaders of others to find needs and create solutions.

Each of the three stages of school improvement described in this workbook is characterized by a particular leadership style. Take charge, autocratic leaders dominate Stage One; "hands-off," empowering leadership is typical of Stage Two; and in Stage Three, leaders capable of thriving within the complexity of <u>lattice organizations</u> come into their own. According to Richard DuFour (2003), contemporary superintendents, for instance, have to be capable of living with complexity that, in turn, involves bridging paradox and dichotomy.

- ■ Dufour asks if a superintendent should be a forceful leader who **implements his or her personal vision** of how a school district and its individuals should operate or **embraces site-based management** and encourages the staff of each school to identify and pursue the issues most relevant to them. DuFour's answer is that a superintendent should do both.

- ■ Dufour asks if the desire for equity and equal opportunity should lead a superintendent to **champion uniformity and consistency** throughout the district or should the realization that change occurs one school at a time lead a superintendent to **support the freedom and autonomy** of each school? Again, DuFour's answer is that a superintendent should do both.

Such leaders have to embrace both the "either" and the "or" (even when they are seemingly contradictory) and be capable of melding the vertical with the horizontal. In other words, there are elements of Stage One and Stage Two leadership in Stage Three leadership, but the mix is far subtler and far more organic. As DuFour (2003) concludes:

> For system leaders, it means allowing autonomy within defined parameters....Superintendents who reject the 'Tyranny of the Or' and embrace the 'Genius of the And' are skillful in demonstrating 'loose-tight leadership' or 'directed autonomy.' They focus on identifying and articulating both the fundamental purpose of the organization and a few 'big ideas' that will help the district improve in its capacity to achieve that purpose. They are tight on purpose and big ideas—insisting that those within the organization act in ways consistent with those concepts and demanding that the district align all of its practices and programs with them.
>
> At the same time, however, they encourage individual and organizational autonomy in the day-to-day operations of the various schools and departments. This autonomy is not characterized by random acts of innovation, but rather is guided by carefully defined parameters that give focus and direction to schools and those within them.

DuFour's message is clear: strong leaders are strong because they have the wherewithal to unify and honor difference at one and the same time. His message is echoed in a brace of articles that appeared in the September 2002 edition of *The School Administrator* under the general heading of "Spiritual Leadership." Interestingly, when Dubuque's new superintendent, John Burgart, requested that all school principals read a selection of these articles, Lesley Stephens, principal of Bryant School, responded by feeling both excited and vindicated. As she remarked to the author: "I loved the moral and ethical piece. It's deeper than just educational. It's about *mission*. It's about believing in the worth of every single child that walks in this school."

In one of these articles, entitled "Nurturing Deep Connections," Rachael Kessler (2002) talks about the importance of quality relationships, soul, and deep connections in organizations. Referring to Bob Adams, superintendent in Aurora, Colorado, she says: "By fostering a climate for meaningful connection, his leadership works toward a transformation from within" which he distinguishes from "cosmetic compliance." Kessler continues:

> In a classroom, school, or district where the soul of education is welcome and safe, deep connection allows masks to drop away. Colleagues begin to share the joy and success they once feared would spur competition and jealousy. They share the vulnerability and uncertainty they feared would make them look weak in front of peers and superiors. And they rediscover meaning and purpose in their collective responsibility for the children.

This sounds very much like Jeff Johll talking about what can happen within mentoring relationships. The process of making deeper connections begins, says Kessler, with deep connection to the self: what some administrators in her study called "personal integrity," "resilience in the face of setbacks, criticism, and even misrepresentation" and "the capacity to reflect and create opportunities for silence." It continues by listening to others, empathizing, and the inner suspension of one's own agenda.

Kessler (2002) also lists the five principles that undergird the practical strategies for creating a climate in districts and schools where the inner life becomes safe and welcome and people feel part of a meaningful community.

Principle 1—Personalize: Create opportunities for your team members to reflect on and articulate their own personal goals. At the same time create ground rules to protect them in feeling safe enough to risk revealing their fears, gifts, mistakes, and passions.

Principle 2—Pacing: Move slowly, gently, respectfully. Invite. Offer. Nurture. Affirm. Find a balance by honoring both the study of research/theory (the why) and quick dives into action (the how). Encourage the journey from cooperation, to companionship, to compassion, to communion.

Principle 3—Permission: Provide a "right to pass" and, thereby, create a safety zone. Power struggles occur, says Kessler, when leaders push and the led resist.

Principle 4—Protection: Protect reluctant team members from the pressure to participate by discouraging putdowns and other forms of disrespect such as dominating the conversation.

Principle 5—Paradox: Echoing DuFour, Handy, and Holly (in this workbook), Kessler argues that leaders have to "model the willingness to hold the tension of apparent opposites":

- standards _and_ soul

- privacy _and_ community

- collaboration <u>and</u> authority

- caring <u>and</u> rigor

- uncertainty <u>and</u> direction

In the same edition of *The School Administrator*, Michael Fullan (2002) identifies four crucial aspects of principled behavior in schools and school districts. The first entails making a difference in students' lives. Put simply, the kids come first. The second involves committing to reducing the gap between high and low performers within your school or district, i.e., *all* kids come first. "As assessment literacy evolves," he says, "effective principals disaggregate data to address the needs of all subgroups within the school." The third consists of contributing to reducing the gap in the larger social and moral environment. Indeed, says Fullan, a qualitative shift in what we normally think of as leadership is occurring; school leaders are almost as concerned about the success of other schools in their district as they are of their own. Quoting from his earlier *Educational Leadership* article, Fullan argues:

> Those concerned about the depletion of resources in the physical environment were the first to discuss the issue of sustainability. Our concern is the depletion of resources in the social and moral environment. In the social and moral environment of the school, we need the resources to close the achievement gap between high and low performers, to develop *all* schools in the system, and to connect schools to the strength of democracy in society. Further, if school leaders do not concern themselves with the development of the social and moral environment of the entire district (in addition to the development of the environment within their own school), then not only will the school system deteriorate, but eventually their own schools will also fail.

Such leaders, he says, have to see beyond the sectional interests of their own school. They have to be "coherence-makers" and be capable of connecting to the bigger picture.

The fourth principle is that leaders have to commit to transforming the working (or learning) conditions of others so that growth, commitment, engagement, and the constant spawning of leadership in others is being fostered. You cannot accomplish the previous three levels of leadership, he says, without the transformative powers of creating growth-oriented learning conditions for others in the organization.

Fullan's four principles are all current preoccupations in Dubuque Schools. School principals like Lesley Stephens are determined to put the students and their learning needs first and to ensure that all student subpopulations experience learning prosperity. They have also put the days of competition between schools behind them and are, increasingly, seeing all the students across the district as "theirs." Enough "unlearning" has occurred that the attitude now is that each school gets a portion of the community's children and the staff's successes with these students will be celebrated in every building across the district.

Pride in the system—and its students' achievements—has replaced sectional pride. Moreover, it is widely recognized in Dubuque that any future successes will be dependent on continuing to improve the quality of classroom instruction. And classroom instruction will not continue to improve without high quality professional development and conducive working conditions. In this endeavor, the district has an active partner, the State Department.

The District
Task 7: The Five Elements of Stage Three

<u>Purpose:</u> To provide an opportunity to use the five elements of Stage Three school improvement efforts for local district evaluation.

<u>Grouping:</u> Work on your own and then meet with your Learning Team.

<u>Directions:</u> Review the text covering the five elements of Stage Three, with your own district in mind. As you complete your review, think about where your district's strengths and challenges lie in regard to these five elements. Using this thoughtful reflection as your guide, rate your district on each element using a five-point scale where a "1" rating = Non-Starter up to a "5" = Advanced Practitioner. Next to each element, record your reasons for your rating. Discuss your ratings with your Learning Team.

<u>Rating</u>   <u>Rationale for Rating</u>

_____   Managing Complexity

_____   Differentiation

_____   Data-Based Decision Making

_____   Mentoring

_____   Leadership for Change

Total Score: _____

Stage Four of School Improvement?

The interesting question is what will Stage Four of school improvement look like? The quick answer is: we don't know yet. The best bet, however, is that the most important activity will take place *underneath school improvement*, i.e., in classrooms. As Mike Schmoker (2002) has said: "For all our grand schemes, our systemic reform, our comprehensive improvement programs, we don't engage in simple, teacher-driven processes."

Schmoker's advice is to be simple and to be direct. Being simple does not mean being simplistic. According to Schmoker, being simplistic involves overemphasizing either a single classroom strategy as the new wonder cure for students' learning ills or an elaborate and unwieldy improvement scheme. Results are virtually inevitable, says Schmoker (2002), when teachers working in small teams do the following:

- Focus substantially—though not exclusively—on assessed standards.

- Review simple, readily available achievement data to set a limited number of measurable achievement goals in the lowest scoring subjects or courses and target specific standards where achievement is low within that course or subject area.

- Work regularly and collectively to design, adapt, and assess instructional strategies targeted directly at specific standards of low student performance revealed by the assessment data.

This sounds very much like what schools like Bryant do best: encourage teachers to work together in small problem-solving groups (see Fontana and Perreault, 2001) for the improvement of student learning. It could well be the case that the foundational ingredients of Stage Four are already present within our current school improvement efforts. We just need to be able to see them.

 **The District
Task 8: Stage Four**

<u>Purpose:</u> To brainstorm ideas about how Stage Four will be defined.

<u>Grouping:</u> Meet with your Learning Team. Select a recorder.

Group process strategy: Use a brainstorming technique and create a team list.

Directions: In small groups, brainstorm responses to the question, "What will Stage Four of school improvement look like?" Have your recorder create a team list.

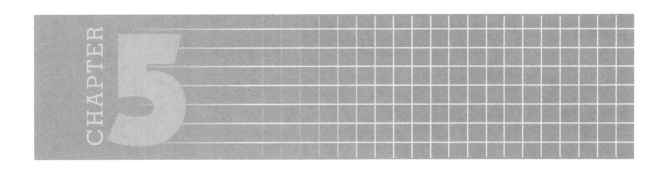

CHAPTER FIVE: THE STATE

Iowa's Uniqueness

Any recent history of American education would reveal that most schools and school districts have been continuously engaged in improvement efforts. Since the clarion calls for reform in the 1980s, however, schools have been increasingly under the gun to either improve more rapidly or be pronounced failures. While the impetus for change in the public schools has come from a number of sources (including federal and state government, the business community, parent and community groups, and from within the schools themselves), the mandates of central government are increasingly believed to provide the most compelling reasons for activating educational change. With the passing of the *NCLB* legislation, the "theory" that individual schools would not change without external regulatory intervention would seem to be the predominant mindset. The experience of school improvement efforts in the state of Iowa, however, would seem to raise some questions concerning this rather pessimistic view of education (and educators). In fact, Iowa provides a rich context in which to examine how educators, relatively—but not entirely—free from governmental intervention, have committed to and undertaken improvement efforts designed to help students learn more and achieve success in a changing world.

Education in Iowa is certainly an interesting case study, partly because schooling in Iowa has certain dissimilarities from the rest of the nation. While test scores always compare favorably with those in other states and Iowa is always in the top tier of states when it comes to student achievement, Iowa has been the only state nationally not to adopt state standards and state assessments. Local control has been the order of the day. Nevertheless, to say that there have been no mandates bearing on schools in Iowa would be untrue. For instance, since 1999, under new accountability laws, school districts have been expected to submit five year Comprehensive School Improvement Plans which have had to show evidence of content standards having been set at the local level and how multiple assessments that are reliable and valid stack up against these same standards and benchmarks. Despite these moves, however, local control of education is still cherished and alive and well in Iowa as the case study of Dubuque CSD amply testifies. Three points are crucial here:

- The previous comments, about district leadership that embraces the vertical and the horizontal and the application of "directed autonomy," apply equally well to the way that the state of Iowa does its educational business. Blending the consistency of system expectations with the ground-level differences of local implementation has become an art form in Iowa.

■ Because of the prevailing culture of local control, educational change in Iowa is a fascinating and "unadulterated" case study of school improvement relatively untrammeled by external regulation and mandates. School improvements in Iowa are still largely founded on local discretion and the extent of the latitude this provides local educators is probably unknown elsewhere in the USA. This is precisely why it has been so intriguing to study developments in school improvement in Iowa over the last ten years. It is also precisely the reason why school improvement efforts at the local level have been "allowed" to travel through the three stages of development outlined in the previous chapter. The argument is that, without the "space" provided by local control, districts like Dubuque would never have reached the more advanced level of Stage Three under their own steam (which, in itself, is part of the secret of Dubuque's success). Nearly all research on school improvement has occurred in situations where there are many confounding variables—mandates included. And when educators feel pressured and under fire, no additional piece of school improvement that comes along is going to be greeted with elation and get their fullest attention.

In such circumstances, school improvement is seen as yet another thing to have to do. Experience shows us that school people, if they feel besieged and constrained by a plethora of change initiatives, will resist any more changes that come along—even if the new changes, if implemented, would work in their interests. Yet there has been little research conducted in places like Iowa, where it has been possible to study what happens when school improvement occurs in relatively uncontaminated conditions. While educators in Iowa may still complain about change overload, there has been enough time spent on the local control of education and educational change that the three stages of school improvement have been able to play themselves out. Districts like Dubuque would not be in such an advanced state as they are today without the comparative freedom of developing school development over the last fifteen years. It could also be argued that Iowa would not be such an advanced state without the accumulated learning that was gained from having to orchestrate local control over the same period of time.

■ Because of its uniqueness, it is easy to misunderstand what goes on in Iowa. For instance, the state continues to achieve low scores in certain types of national surveys. As a consequence, local newspapers on May 6, 2003, carried the following article:

> Although Iowa's testing program scored next to last in accountability in a national study released Monday, education officials say not to worry. The study called "testing the testers" was conducted by the Princeton Review, a for-profit test preparation company. It examines the accountability of school

testing programs, including whether they are consistent, secure, open to public scrutiny and flexible. All 50 states were ranked in the study. Iowa ranked 51st last year, the first year the study was published....An executive vice president for The Princeton Review said Iowa is in its own category when it comes to accountability. 'Our feeling is that Iowa is not a failure so much as it is a conscientious objector,' he said. 'The philosophy has been for a very, very minimal role for the state in setting standards or in enforcing accountability. That's been left to the districts.'

Given that, when it comes to school improvement, Iowa has tended to march to its own drummer, its application for inclusion in *No Child Left Behind* has been an interesting study. Judy Jeffrey, who, as Head of the Division of Early Childhood, Elementary and Secondary Education, is number two to Director, Ted Stilwill, in Iowa's State Department, was responsible for leading these negotiations with the USDE. It could not have been that easy a ride. The problem is that Iowa doesn't fit the required formula. Nevertheless, the protracted negotiations were ultimately successful and, in the midst of the negotiations process, Judy Jeffrey agreed to be interviewed by this author, Peter Holly. Her interview follows:

An Interview with Judy Jeffrey

PJH: Since you've been here, what are you most proud of in terms of the DE's (Department of Education's) work? What do you see as the DE's biggest achievements?

JJ: When I look at the DE's work in the last few years I think that the biggest achievement that I see is the movement of the conversations across the state. You now hear teachers and principals and administrators talking very seriously about student achievement, *talking about the use of data*, and knowing where their kids are—and wanting to make the system better. I think that's just the thing I'm most proud of—that the conversation has changed substantially.

PJH: I liked the story you told the other day about the teacher attending the national certification awards ceremony and turning up with some of her students...

JJ: Isn't that great? Those are the things we run in to all the time. I mean five years ago when we would say to a superintendent or principal, 'Can you tell me how you're fourth graders are doing in reading?' they would look at you and say, 'I can tell you the scores of our football teams but I can't tell you how our kids are doing in reading.' Now they can tell us.

PJH: Even the acceptance of ITBS; when I first came to the state it wasn't widely accepted; in some circles it was even disparaged.

JJ: I mean they gave it, but now it's becoming an important centerpiece of their entire assessment system. They've come to recognize the value of the data; it's important information for them. It's just that whole change, I think, in the whole attitude toward assessment—using the data and making improvements on the strength of it.

PJH: How have you done that?

JJ: We systematically thought about how you change a system. We've worked very hard at aligning that system and, if you think about how the whole system is falling together... I mean we started off with probably *House File #2272 which put accountability into the state*, and then we moved to *AEA accreditation*, and we've changed teacher education programs and administrator preparation programs to prepare people differently and to face a different kind of challenge. We established outcomes for the support system of the AEAs with their standards for accountability. *You really have to take a systems approach and think about where you want to be and how you align the system.*

PJH: What was it like coming from your former position in an LEA?

JJ: It was an eye-opener to find that districts were very different. In Council Bluffs, they're very organized and, when I look back, they were extremely progressive and still are. I had just assumed that the entire state was like that. That was probably the biggest eye-opener—that people had taken school improvement and taken it down very different avenues; they had very different opinions of how you approach school improvement. Some had been very serious about the effort and some had not been quite so serious.

PJH: I guess that's the downside of autonomy—you either do great things with it or it's possible that you do nothing with it.

JJ: That's right, it is, but I still think that it's the best system, because our educators still care about our kids; our communities still care about our kids and giving them the ownership to make the improvements. I still think it creates a sense of independence rather than dependence on an outside system—and we all know that independence and thinking for ourselves is much more rewarding to individuals than having somebody tell you what to do.

PJH: That's a great point. I suspect you've given that answer a few times!

JJ: As a matter of fact, I haven't! I was just processing it in my head as we were talking.

PJH: House File #2272/CSIPs/APRs/District Site visits—looking back, how has that all gone?

JJ: Well, I think in some respects it's gone slower than I had hoped but faster than some people would have said was realistic. When you think about the amount of time since that law was passed and the changes that we see in the school system. It was passed in '97 but we really didn't write the rules until '98. A lot of the districts have only filed one Comprehensive School Improvement Plan. In reality, when you think about the developmental nature of all of this, I think we have moved much faster as a state than a lot of other states. The other piece that's happened is that first, when they filed, I don't think the majority of the people in the district even knew what had been filed. It's now much more integrated in the system; it wasn't real when it started. I think it's becoming more real. And there are still people who think some of the things they have to do are compliance; that's just the nature of bureaucratic organizations.

PJH: How do you deal with that?

JJ: I do what I have to do to meet the mandates and then try to do the right things.

PJH: It sounds like you're the ideal person to have in this position—doing the translation.

JJ: I really work hard at trying to make sense out of it all....I was on the telephone with the USDE this morning trying to make sense of it [*NCLB*]; trying to work on behalf of the school districts and still try to meet the mandates and try not to overwhelm the system. Take the work you were involved in on Monday—looking at the data and analyzing the data. Dr. Showers made the statement to me several times, that, out of all the states she works in, she believes that Iowa is the state that is totally on the right lines because we're doing the right things. We're not spending all our energies on developing a new state test and figuring out how to sanction and punish the schools. We have a huge assessment piece sitting here. We don't have compliance officers and spend a lot of time figuring out how to take over school districts. We don't want to go there; we don't believe it's the right way to go. Besides, Iowans have never responded well to that kind of approach: they don't respond well—they get angry.

PJH: I guess that I'm hoping that Comprehensive School Improvement Plans will still be the basis of where we're going. I say to people, 'You've done them; you've got all that experience locked away.'

JJ: That's absolutely our intent. You've done it—and you've built a really strong foundation—I mean, our Teacher Quality legislation and our Professional Development model. I think we've got all the right things together; the trick is going to be maintaining our resources. When you're poised on the brink of something great and then have the resources pulled....Even then, we have things that are happening in the state. We have some individuals who believe that putting their resources into laptops for 7th and 8th graders is a good move—and not that I disagree with it; it's just, is this the highest priority at this time? Determining your priorities is even more important when resources are limited.

PJH: How does that feel if you've taken on a systems approach and the whole resource question might derail what you've done?

JJ: Sad. You worry a lot about it.

PJH: That's possibly a side of you that not everyone sees. Are you the kind to take your job home or does your job stop here?

JJ: No, it doesn't; but I do try to separate it on weekends. I work hard then to focus on family. It's taking a lot out of Ted [Stilwill] who has worked so hard to build the system. It's hard when you know we could do great things—with the Teacher Quality system—building a very strong foundation, but you need some resources.

PJH: As a state, Iowa would seem to have purposefully invested in data-based decision making?

JJ: We did. When we pulled down the Gates money,[2] I think we were the only state in the nation that said we're going to use this to help people understand data-based decision making better—instead of saying we're going to buy you a Palm™ [Handheld] or we're going to buy you a laptop and teach you how you to use that. We said, we're going to teach you how to fish and then give you the opportunity to fish. And, you know, there were pros and cons of all that too. That was our first experience of going statewide with a consistent approach to the training; we've never done that before and we got absolutely mixed reactions. And one of our dilemmas was [whether], with the autonomy that's been developed in this state, a state-wide training [could be] consistent [and] meet the needs of all individuals. Because we had some districts that really had done a great deal of work and some who had done not much at all. So we had a mixed reaction and we hadn't recruited the trainers well enough to deal with the individual needs of the "students"—in this case the adults that came to the training. It's hard. There's just a huge spread of people who have either been actively involved in this work or who don't have a clue and you're trying to meet the needs of 200 or 400 individuals. That's always a difficult time—if you've got more time to work with the trainers and more time to assess the needs; but, again, at a time of limited resources and limited personnel—we're really hampered.

PJH: Where are you in terms of implementing the Teacher Quality legislation? I know that's one of your favorites.

JJ: We're a lot further, given the limited resources. We don't have the money for the salary increases, but we've implemented teacher and mentoring programs; we turned that around in three months. We implemented at the state-level—again, we've got a real range (from 2s to 10s) in the process, but we continue to work with all those districts—and we're now looking at evaluation programs to see where their weaknesses are and how we can bind them together as a system to harness the best out of the system. So we're working on that and we've done all the evaluator approval. I think we're the only state in the nation that's trained all their evaluators in a year—using consistent training across the state. Danielson and McGreal brought their expertise to the state. We've got the teaching standards in place and every district will be responsible for re-doing their evaluation system. Our intensive assistance program's in place. The pieces that we are not able to implement: we did the pilot of team-based variable pay and really had mixed results on that. I don't know whether that really is the route to go; it was so mixed—the results. We haven't been able to implement the career paths initiative

---

[2] Iowa used grant monies from the Bill Gates Implementation Grant to construct the QIC-Decide model for Data-Based Decision Making (DBDM).

because of limited resources. Frankly, as I mentioned the other day, while I'm disappointed not to have the money to increase teacher pay, I was kind of pleased. Now we've got time to figure it out; what it's going to look like. It's disappointing to the teachers, rightfully so, that the money hasn't flowed to their salaries. But as far as building capacity and building the ability to implement it in the right way; it's given us the time to do that. There are people in the statehouse who say teachers will walk away from this if they don't get paid. We've got two years to get this evaluation in place.

PJH: I must admit—in my work in the schools and districts—I'm not picking up the same level of disappointment and the two years will allow you to get it absolutely right, which should radically reduce any resistance.

JJ: That's what is so refreshing about the state of Iowa—and that's what is so hard to convince some people at the federal level. When you tell them we don't have to impose sanctions to improve the system—they just don't believe us. They don't seem to understand that people really do want to do the right thing. If it's sensible for kids—if you put it in the context of 'this is good educational practice; we know it's hard work but it's right thing for kids,' they usually come along. They're a pretty amazing group.

PJH: Yet that good relationship could be destroyed by over-compliance.

JJ: Absolutely! That's why we didn't make a huge thing about the schools in need of assistance. We didn't need to chastise them; we gave them technical assistance instead.

PJH: Recently you talked about the creation of high performance educational systems. Is that what you're trying to do in Iowa?

JJ: Absolutely. You need a very clear purpose. We were impressed by the Rand[3] study that found that the real difference between church schools and the public schools is the real clear purpose that binds [parochial] schools together. You also have to be standards-based. The crux is knowing what it is that you want kids to know and be able to do. And everyone knows—the kids, the teacher, the parents—they're all tied into that and knowing what it is that's being taught. Do the kids perform? And are we checking? Grade-level expectations—doesn't mean that I don't have a lot more (to teach) but I know what I'm responsible for. Holding ourselves accountable is absolutely crucial. Every student has to hold himself or herself accountable; every teacher has to hold himself or herself accountable, so too the principal—everybody accepts the responsibility that 'I have a job here to do.' I think that's what is neat about this system. The first time we asked the AEAs about whether they thought they were accountable for student achievement, they looked at us like, 'Are you nuts? We don't do that kind of work. We don't teach kids.' But now they accept it. The State Board accepts that they have a responsibility for it; so the entire system is holding itself accountable. Someone has to say, 'Peter, you're not learning; I am responsible for us; I have a job to do to help you learn.' Plus there's the intensive professional development using research-based strategies, knowing what works.

---

[3] Hill, P., Foster, G., Gendler, T. (1990). *High Schools with Character.* Santa Monica, CA: Rand. www.rand.org/publications/

PJH: Talking about intensive professional development, we've learned from something like Every Child Reads that to get it right you have to be so intensive—almost to the exclusion of other things.

JJ: The thing is, it's transferable. Once you learn the process—the intensity of the process it takes and the tracking with data. Given the fact that you can't be implementing all of these strategies at the same time, but given the fact that you know what it takes, and some of the strategies are transferable. I mean, for instance, cooperative learning—we know—has great effects on student achievement. You can use that across any curriculum area. So you pick your most powerful strategies.

PJH: What about the 33 goals in *NCLB*, while we tell people not to have more than one or two major goals?

JJ: Some of them are connected; if you teach kids to read, you reduce your dropouts and you increase your graduation rate. You work on one major initiative and hit several targets.

PJH: You said recently that outsiders (including some at the federal level) don't understand our 'paradigm of local control' in Iowa. What did you mean by that?

JJ: They don't understand it. They understand state-controlled systems. They don't understand how it's possible that a small local community and a small school district can accept the responsibility for student learning—can know what the right things are to teach without somebody telling them. And that they can't know how their children are doing without a state test. Ted (Stilwill) has said this before, 'Maybe if I was the director in another state where the system was broken, I'd think very differently about how to fix the system.' This system is not broken—far from it. Now, can it continue to get better? Absolutely. But the system itself is not broken. We don't have teachers running amok. We don't have teachers who are not licensed; these things don't happen. How do you know they've got good assessments? How do you know they've implemented their standards? How do you know this stuff? You know, we talk to the superintendents—we talk to folks all the time. The AEAs know exactly what's happening in their districts. Everyone knows one another. It's a very small state!

PJH: So is it possible to have both accountability and autonomy in educational systems?

JJ: That's what we're trying to create in our accountability plan—that there's autonomy in the system, but at the same time you're holding them accountable for student results. That's the ideal. It's much harder to create a system like that. I could sit down here and write standards that would be great, you know, but it wouldn't make a difference. We had state curriculum guides. I had them when I was teaching; I never opened them. The things you open and use are the things you create yourself—along with others. Everyone used the McREL [Mid-continent Research for Education and Learning][4] compendium of standards and benchmarks. Many people have used the ITBS interpretative guide and the knowledge and skills embedded in ITBS/ITED.

---

[4] www.mcrel.org

PJH: So is ITBS becoming Iowa's equivalent of a state test?

JJ: It's the voluntary, selective, and common measure across the state. 100% of school districts have been using it for ten years. It's a cheap, well-constructed test and the University of Iowa provides direct technical assistance to school districts.

PJH: So what will happen in Iowa in terms of *No Child Left Behind*? What about the role of ITAP [Iowa Technical Adequacy Project]?

JJ: ITAP is huge for us; it's important not to get off our timeline and the October 15th deadline. I think we'll meet it. People grumbled a little bit at first, but the conversations have turned very substantial. It's the first time that they've had to sit down and examine their standards and benchmarks and say, for example, 'What's that doing there? It makes no sense.' And they've really had to examine what's in ITBS/ITED. We're forcing them into the alignment issue with that. So, they're now developing a better understanding of what's actually taught and they're coming out of the conversation knowing data better and why it's so important to have the alignment. I keep saying, 'I know it's hard work but you'll be better as educators as a result of it.'

PJH: You seem to spend a lot of your time holding the line.

JJ: We made some adjustments [to the ITAP process]. Because the outcry was so great, we showed that we're listening but said, 'This is all about as far as we can go. There are some parameters here.' Yes, I spend a lot of time holding the line between the department and the field and the department and the federal government. I'm the buffer between both sides!

PJH: It must take a lot of patience and skills...

JJ: There's one course I took in my doctoral program on influence and power and how to manage in difficult situations; when to move and when to fall back. I've always had an uncanny sense of that.

PJH: Will there be a continuing role for the AEAs?

JJ: The AEAs? ...without them we're toast. The department does not have the resources to implement the system we envision.

PJH: What's happening about finding research-based strategies in mathematics and science?

JJ: It's coming through the content area networks. We're really ahead of the pack in that regard too. They're operating as we speak; we have approximately 20–30 experts in those content area networks and a really tight protocol has been established for them. They really have to defend the programs and strategies they bring forward and they have to demonstrate standards (1 through 5) to determine whether the strategies really will have an effect on student learning. I think we're going to be really well served; it'll be four years before anything is produced nationally.

PJH: Which brings me to my final question. Ironically, in order to implement *NCLB*, other states might have to come to Iowa to see how it's done. How do you react to this statement?

JJ: I agree. I think it's going to be a couple of years before they realize. It's amazing to me how many experts from across the nation will say to me, 'Hold your course.'

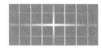

The State
Task 1: Reflecting on School Improvement in Iowa

Purpose: To reflect on the interview with Judy Jeffrey and summarize the ways in which Iowa is different from other states when it comes to school improvement efforts.

Grouping: Work in pairs, then meet as a whole group.

Directions: Working in pairs, list the ways in which Iowa's school improvement efforts are different from those in other states. Use the Jeffrey interview as a reference. Share your list with other team members. Work as a team to identify different themes evolving from your lists.

Unique characteristics of Iowa's school improvement efforts:

Themes for Iowa's school improvement efforts:

Themes for School Improvement

There are eight themes touched on in the Jeffrey interview. They are central to any study of the State Department's role in initiating, pressuring, and supporting school improvement activities across the state while, at the same time, trying to build a system that accommodates both autonomy and accountability. These eight themes include:

1. Comprehensive School Improvement Plans

2. The Establishment of Content Standards and Benchmarks

3. State-Initiated School Improvement Projects and Programs

4. Data-Based Decision Making

5. Professional Growth and Teacher Quality

6. The Role of Area Education Agencies (AEAs)

7. Responding to *No Child Left Behind*

8. A Systems Approach to School Improvement

1. Comprehensive School Improvement Plans (CSIP)

House File 2272, approved in 1998, was *an act requiring the State Board of Education to adopt rules relating to the incorporation of accountability for student achievement into the Education Standards and Accreditation Process.*

The Act also includes the following provisions:

a. Requirements that all school districts and accredited nonpublic schools develop, implement, and file with the department a comprehensive school improvement plan that includes, but is not limited to, demonstrated school, parental, and community involvement in assessing educational needs, establishing local education standards and student achievement levels, and, as applicable, the consolidation of federal and state planning, goal setting, and reporting requirements.

b. A set of core academic indicators in mathematics and reading in grades four, eight, and eleven, a set of core academic indicators in science in grades eight and eleven, and another set of core indicators that includes, but is not limited to, graduation rate, postsecondary education, and successful employment in Iowa. Annually, the department shall report state data for each indicator in the condition of an education report.

c. A requirement that all school districts and accredited nonpublic schools annually report to the department and the local community the district-wide progress made in attaining student achievement goals on the academic and other core indicators and the district-wide progress made in attaining locally established student learning goals. The school districts and accredited nonpublic schools shall demonstrate the use of multiple assessment measures in determining student achievement levels. The school districts and accredited nonpublic schools may report on other locally determined factors influencing student achievement. The school districts and accredited nonpublic schools shall also report to the local community their results by individual attendance center.

Once the rules were developed and adopted (1999), Peter Holly summarized their obligations for schools and school districts.

General Points

- Chapter 12 of the School Rules has been re-written and definitions of the various terms used are provided.

- The old Rules (280.12/18) are subsumed in the new Rules; the last 280 report is due September 1999 and the first Comprehensive School Improvement Plan due September 2000.

- The School Improvement Advisory Committee—containing community representatives—replaces the 280 Committee.

- Comprehensive School Improvement Plans are for increasing student achievement for *all* students (including all subpopulations of students) and have to be submitted to the DE, AEA, and local community.

- They are five-year plans with annual updates. New plans will have to be written after the DE site visits.

- As the DE site visits (to monitor the plans and their implementation) will be undertaken on a rotational cycle, those districts visited in the early years will have to write new plans prior to—in some cases well before—the end of the five-year period.

Components of the CSIP

The following are required components:

- Community involvement in establishing vision, mission, beliefs, and broad learning goals (Essential Learnings)

- Analysis of data to determine needs and strengths

- Annual improvement goals to be set

- Content standards and benchmarks for the required curriculum plus infusion areas

- Action plans to be established containing strategies, timelines, and resources (including staff development plans and the consolidation of funding streams)

- Assessment of student progress using multiple measures, one of which provides for state/national comparisons

- Annual Progress Reports have to be filed with the community, DE, and AEA and show growth against the baseline, the level of performance relative to annual improvement goals, and analysis using multiple measures for each attendance center

- The accreditation visit team will be composed of DE and AEA representatives, and staff from other LEAs scheduled to be visited

2. The Establishment of Content Standards and Benchmarks

While many districts in Iowa had already established standards and benchmarks locally, the new state legislation certainly gave a new impetus to this work. Locally built (by teams of educators), yet externally informed, these standards and benchmarks (sometimes spanning grade "intervals," sometimes specifically grade-related) often covered every major subject area. Moreover, in generating these standards and benchmarks, local educators became more interested in questions of alignment, especially in terms of what was often referred to in Iowa as the Learning Triangle: Curriculum Framework (Standards and Benchmarks), Assessments, and Instructional Strategies (see the following diagram).

The Learning Triangle

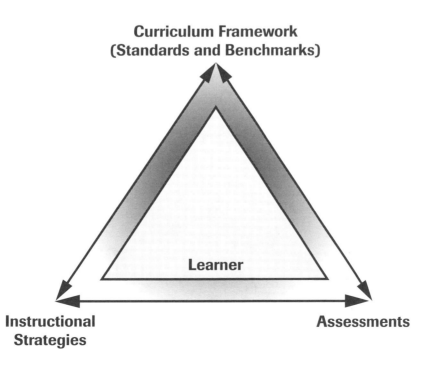

**Curriculum Framework
(Standards and Benchmarks)**

Learner

**Instructional
Strategies**

Assessments

Three interesting documents from the same district in Iowa (Webster City CSD) provide evidence of this learning journey. The first (titled *Progress with Standards and Benchmarks*) maps out the big picture of what will happen over time. The second—specifically written for the high school staff—reminds them of the importance of beginning to use standards and benchmarks for assessment purposes and the third shows how Marzano's (2000) schema for assessing to standards and benchmarks might be adapted for use in this particular district. Indeed, in the fall of 2002, Marzano visited the district and spent a day with the K–12 faculty training them in the alignment of standards and benchmarks, assessments, and instructional strategies (see also Marzano et al., 2001).

In addition, prior to *NCLB*, many districts in Iowa had already begun to amend their standards and benchmarks to be more grade-specific and more articulated developmentally across the grades. In June 2002, for instance, this author worked with the Curriculum Audit Review Team (CART) in Eagle Grove, Iowa to streamline its standards and benchmarks and, in so doing, generate grade-specific objectives. This district had two purposes in mind: to prepare objectives as required by the particular information management system being used and to render standards and benchmarks grade-specific in order to delineate to students, parents, and staff members what the curriculum expectations are for each particular grade level.

The week-long session began with a reminder to participants that the task ahead of them was to write grade-specific objectives aligned with the standards and benchmarks for all subjects—K–12, and which build developmentally and cognitively over time. As a starting point, Bloom's Taxonomy and Ralph Tyler's advice concerning the construction of objectives (contained in his book, *Basic Principles of Curriculum and Instruction*, 1949) were both revisited.

Ralph Tyler's Criteria for Constructing Objectives

Objectives should be

- clearly stated and specific;

- feasible of attainment;

- helpful in selecting learning experiences and in guiding teaching;

- descriptive of the behavioral change(s) expected of the student and what the student is expected to get from the learning experience;

- tied to a particular content area in which the behavior is to operate.

Objectives are inappropriate if they

- describe what the teacher has to do;

- provide a generalized list of topics to be learned;

- describe generalized patterns of behavior not tied specifically to a content area (Essential Learnings).

Having consulted this kind of advice, the participants agreed to apply this list of criteria to their work in the various subject areas.

Our Eagle Grove Objectives, they said, should

- be specific;

- be clearly stated;

- act as indicators and indicate what has to be done for the student(s) to be successful;

- describe what the students will know or be able to do as a result of their learning experiences;

- be aligned with the local standards and benchmarks providing connectivity across the K–12 layers of the educational process;

- link the benchmarks with everyday classroom activities;

- line up against each benchmark—two to five objectives per benchmark;

- be grade-level specific, unlike interval benchmarks which may span various grades;

- be as overt as possible so that their accomplishment can be easily observed or assessed;

- cover the cognitive, affective, and psychomotor domains of knowledge, attitudes, and skills;

- be sensitive to gender, ethnicity, and diversity issues;

- involve an acceptable level of technology in terms of real-life applications.

For each benchmark written, the trainer designed a simple check-off list as follows:

Checklist for each benchmark	No	Not sure	Yes
Is it specific enough?			
Is it clearly stated?			
Is it an indicator of success?			
Does it describe what the student will know or be able to do?			
Is it aligned with a benchmark?			
Does it help to select classroom activities?			
Is it one of a cluster of related objectives?			
Is it grade-level specific?			
Is it easily observed/assessed?			
Does it belong to the cognitive, affective, or psychomotor domains?			
Is it sufficiently sensitive to gender, ethnicity, and diversity issues?			
Does it involve an acceptable level of technology?			

At the end of the workshop session in Eagle Grove, the participants gathered around and reflected upon their work. They agreed upon the following statements:

- The Standards, Benchmarks, and Objectives represent the official District Curriculum: what we should teach to and what the kids should be learning.

- K–12 vertical articulation is vital. Everything should build on everything else; there should be a continuous flow and sequence with no broken links in the chain.

- This district initiative should be embraced equally and consistently by each building. District and building leadership will be a critical ingredient here.

- The IM Series [the district's Information Management System] is not the primary focus; the curriculum is. This work is curriculum-led, not IM Series-led. IM Series is the organizational tool to enhance the curriculum and help with assessment.

- There is an urgent need now to find time to take the CART's [Curriculum, Audit, Review Team's] work to each subject committee for their review.

- There is also a need to embrace accountability. Teaching involves not just instruction but also helping students learn, assessment of their progress, and diagnostic re-teaching in a climate of growth, not blame.

- A time frame is required for linking the objectives with activities within lesson planning.

- Grade-level teams will need to take responsibility for the objectives to be covered at their grade level.

- Everyone needs the big picture (what's coming down the line) and the small picture (what's coming next).

The two examples of local work on Standards and Benchmarks from Webster City and Eagle Grove typify the Iowa approach alluded to by Judy Jeffrey in her interview. It is also worth noting that these two districts are seventeen miles apart, affiliated with the same AEA (Area Education Agency), and are getting to the same destination via somewhat different routes. What is also significant is the amount of local ownership and commitment that is generated, particularly among the ranks of teacher leaders. It is the process inconsistency that outsiders do not seem to understand. Their attitude would seem to be that process inconsistency couldn't possibly lead to product consistency— even if the local sites are working along different avenues to meet the same expectations. What cannot be ignored, however, is the strong sense of local responsibility for development and the sheer local pride that goes into the efforts. Imagine the relief, therefore, when the Eagle Grove folks realized that by completing their task they had also completed—ahead of time—one of the foundational tasks of *NCLB*: the establishment of grade-level expectations for student learning.

Aligning Standards and Benchmarks with Assessments

This is the current preoccupation in districts like Webster City and Eagle Grove and, indeed, all school districts across Iowa. Holly and Lange (2000) created the following exercise to help districts in this process. Taking the idea of Target, Method, Match, Holly and Lange have shown how the right learning **target** (benchmark/objective/grade level expectation) has to be aligned with both the right learning **method** and the right "**match**ed" assessment. The following task represents this three-part exercise.

The State
Task 2: Target, Method, Match

<u>Purpose:</u> To learn by doing: to learn about curriculum alignment by doing the "target, method, match" exercise.

<u>Grouping:</u> Work in pairs or small groups.

Directions: Working in pairs or small groups, the task is to match the Method and Assessment (from the two following lists) with the most appropriate Target (record on the following chart). The first one, Math standards and benchmarks, has been completed for you. (It is probably a good idea to work with a pencil!) Meet with other groups to share and discuss your responses.

Method
a. band practice
b. brainstorming solutions
c. class meetings
d. computation practice
e. cooperative learning
f. hypothesis development
g. identifying and outlining key words
h. interdisciplinary project-based learning
i. lecturing: note-taking
j. line basics
k. practicing basketball drills
l. publicized and implemented school-tardy policy
m. reading and discussion
n. social skills program; empathy training
o. spelling practice and repetition
p. student-led conference
q. using manipulatives

Assessment
a. attitude survey
b. end-of-chapter test
c. ITBS math scores
d. observation
e. oral presentation and exhibition
f. paper-pencil test
g. performance-based assessment
h. recital or concert
i. self-assessment rubric
j. solving 50 math problems
k. student journal
l. student portfolios
m. written student report
n. teacher grading (of notes)
o. tracking discipline referrals
p. tracking tardiness and attendance
q. weekly spelling tests

Target	Method	Assessment
1. Math standards and benchmarks	q	c
2. Employability skills, e.g., teaming		
3. An essential learning, e.g., problem solving		
4. Reading standard: comprehending main ideas		
5. Grade-level expectations		
6. Using the scientific method		
7. Behavioral expectations		
8. Employability skills, e.g., reliability		
9. Tolerance for diversity		
10. Grade-level core spelling words		
11. Understanding key concepts in social studies		
12. Basic mathematics facts		
13. Research skills		
14. Ball control		
15. High quality musical performance		
16. Listening for information		
17. Social skills		

The Iowa Technical Adequacy Project (ITAP)

When it comes to the establishment of standards and benchmarks and matching assessments, local construction is the norm in Iowa. Given that process inconsistency is the first by-product of this arrangement, in preparation for *NCLB*, Judy Jeffrey and her colleagues at the Iowa Department of Education have instigated ITAP [Iowa Technical Adequacy Project]. This has been one of the first real attempts (following on the heels of House File #2272) to inject more process consistency into and across the Iowa system. As Judy Jeffrey mentioned in her interview, by going against the grain of the state system, some early criticism was encountered. This was countered in a memo (dated 02/10/2003) that Jeffrey sent to all districts.

<u>Alignment and Technical Adequacy of the Local
Assessment System</u>

This memo is being sent to you to address recent concerns raised by local school districts. Even though evidence is required this fall for the technical adequacy and alignment, districts will continue to adjust to changing expectations, updating of standards and benchmarks, and new assessment technologies. The department is hopeful that by providing additional time, resources through the assessment funds, and assistance from the ITAP project that this task will seem more manageable.

One goal of a local assessment system is to demonstrate assessment of all standards with at least 5 items per standard in reading and in mathematics for each grade span. Since benchmarks further define the standard it is also expected that at least 75% of benchmarks are measured within each grade span for each reading and mathematics standard through ITBS/ITED and multiple measures.

The submitted evidence for the alignment work within the grade spans will be reviewed for the following criteria:

- At least 75% of a district's benchmarks for each reading and mathematics standard covered within the identified grade span.

- At least a moderate degree of match in cognitive complexity between the assessment content and the benchmarks within the identified grade span.

- At least 5 items are aligned with each reading and mathematics standard within each grade span.

The University of Iowa and the Iowa Testing Program organized this project. A process to deal with the alignment and technical adequacy issues regarding ITBS/ITED and other multiple assessments was designed and taught to district teams in ICN and face-to-face sessions. The expectation was then that the district teams would go back and, involving other colleagues, complete the process and submit their product by October 15, 2003. In Eagle Grove, for instance, members of the original CART team were re-assembled with Peter Holly in early June 2003 and the process, as laid out, undertaken. Other colleagues will be informed of the progress made when the teachers return in August.

3. State-Initiated School Improvement Projects and Programs

Two major statewide and state-initiated school improvement projects have received a great deal of attention—both inside and outside of Iowa.

Success4

In 2000, Peter Holly and Linda Munger visited thirteen local sites and produced a cross-case analysis of their early implementation efforts. In their report, they introduced the project and their research as follow:

> The intent of Success4 as a statewide initiative is to increase the capacities of Iowa schools, families, and communities to meet the social, emotional, intellectual, and behavioral needs of children and youth. The 1998–1999 school year was a planning year in schools and communities across the state of Iowa. The 1999–2000 school year has been the first year of implementation. The purpose of this research project was to study the implementation efforts at a representative sample of sites, complete case study reports for each of the sites, and then write this cross-case analysis.

> Judging by the evidence gathered at the case study sites, Success4 is alive and well at the local level. In fact, it is flourishing. Whether the sites visited are truly representative of what is happening statewide is, of course, another question. What can be said with some authority, however, is that in this somewhat random selection of sites, Success4 is highly valued, is the focus of a great deal of enthusiasm, commitment, and endeavor and is impacting the lives of students, teachers, administrators, parents, and community members in significant ways.

The research team constructed an individual case study of the work of each site and was able to provide constructive feedback information (another purpose of their action research) in the form of an interim report. Their work, therefore, had a formative influence. In their final report, the authors discussed this issue.

A deeply satisfying feature of this case study research project has been its acceptance and impact at the site level. As a result of the first two-day visit, relationships were established which meant that the ensuing 'interim report' received the serious attention of those involved locally. Indeed, when the second visit occurred and the challenges arising from the interim report were discussed, it was gratifyingly noticeable that the sites were already working on the kind of issues addressed in the list of challenges. Sometimes the site members had embarked on this new work under their own volition and sometimes they were directly responding to what they saw as challenges in the original report (Holly and Munger, 2000).

Several major issues emerged from the research and were included in the cross-site summative report.

- The first issue concerned various ingredients of membership: inclusion, consistency, regularity (of meetings), leadership team structure, representation, communication, and process training.

- The second issue—training—focused on the common demand from participants that all training experiences be followed up by planning time and in-house support. In addition, it was found that all sites proved adept at connecting with and including in the school improvement mix the various past and present training opportunities not directly linked with Success4.

- Some participants defined Success4 strictly as a content model (separate from other school improvement efforts), while others defined it in more general process terms as an integrated school improvement effort.

- Community involvement was a major feature of the project work at all the sites.

- Most sites were following the school improvement materials made available to them and were following the process path of shared visioning, followed by needs assessment, goal setting, and action planning.

- All sites had received a great deal of resources, including the grant money, staff collaboration, AEA and NISDC assistance, student and parent involvement, and administrator support.

- When asked: "How would you describe your stage of implementation?" many respondents said: "Mid-course."

- There were also indications that the sites were learning to hone their change management skills. Some sites had learned the wisdom of using different funding streams to support the same goals, while others were committing to data-based decision making to make in-flight adjustments. According to the participants at one site: "Every decision is made with data; we're continually revisiting and being willing to revise as needed." Moreover, another team acknowledged: "The time spent on collaboration, relationship building, and getting everyone on board with the same understanding has definitely paid off."

■ Finally, and crucially, there was a growing awareness that "changing the academic to incorporate the affective" can be accomplished "through the use of new instructional strategies." In other words, getting to academic learning through relationships.

To become a Success4 site, schools and school districts had to apply to their AEA and submit to a competitive RFP (Request for Proposals). The same was also true of Every Child Reads (ECR), the second major statewide initiative. As an aside, sites in Dubuque (other than Bryant) become major players in both projects and their participation is ongoing. Indeed, Prescott Early Learning Center has been identified as a model site for Success4 and Eisenhower School for Every Child Reads.

Every Child Reads

In a handout prepared for educators in Dubuque by colleagues at Eisenhower School, Every Child Reads was explained as follows:

> The purpose of Every Child Reads is to advance literacy among Iowa's children and youth through the establishment of high standards for reading and writing, and the adoption of research-based practices in instruction and assessment.
>
> The focus for the Every Child Reads (K–2) initiative in Dubuque Community Schools will be to
>
> ■ use Action Research as the means of monitoring teaching practices.
>
> ■ implement research-based practices for reading (e.g., using quality nonfiction, read alouds, talk alouds, and think alouds).
>
> ■ participate in collaborative peer coaching.
>
> Teaching will be enhanced by
>
> ■ expanding the teacher's "tool box" of strategies to use with a diverse group of learners.
>
> ■ opportunities to study what is "known" about good instructional practices in the area of reading.

- opportunities to plan lessons and study the effects of the lessons with colleagues.

- providing a disciplined assessment of current practice.

Participants will include the teaching staff, building administrators, central office staff, AEA consultants, and Department of Education personnel.

In terms of time commitment, this is a multi-year professional development opportunity. Plans for the 2000–2001 school year include:

- Meetings before and after school.

- Meetings with Iowa Department of Education personnel.

- Iowa Communications Network (ICN) meetings monthly after school.

The students will benefit in various ways. Students at every grade level will grow in vocabulary development, listening comprehension, listening skills, ability to express self through spoken and written language, and in reading comprehension.

The activities in which we will be engaged in the site-based class include:

- action research

- diagnostic assessment tools

- practice using information from diagnostic assessments to plan students' needs

- demonstrations

- co-planning with peers/peer coaching

- professional readings

- use of non-fiction books with all ages

- view and discuss videotapes of teachers teaching for a specific purpose

- learn about the effective use of read alouds and talk alouds

- practice read alouds, think alouds, and talk alouds with support and feedback

Emily Calhoun has played a major role in the development of the initiative across Iowa. Indeed, in her 2002 article about action research in *Educational Leadership*, she singled out Every Child Reads as an impressive example of a statewide action research initiative.

> Scores of schools across Iowa are involved in an initiative called 'Every Child Reads.' Sponsored by the Iowa State Department of Education, the initiative aimed to change the context in which participants engaged in professional development, help them become more closely connected to scholarship in reading, and support them in generating knowledge and increasing their capacity as learners and leaders. Over a three-year period, participating school facilitation teams (composed of teachers, the principal, and, when possible, district office and intermediate service agency staff responsible for supporting school improvement) became a statewide professional learning community engaged in the study of literacy.
>
> Participants attended 14 days of workshops and received additional technical assistance at their school sites. They studied current practices in their schools and classrooms; examined research related to literacy development; selected and used evaluative instruments to access literacy; organized and used data to make decisions about effectiveness; learned how to implement new practices; and learned to provide staff development to colleagues as they engaged in these same actions.

In the same article, Calhoun describes Katie's story. Katie is a teacher in Iowa and her school is part of the ECR initiative.

> Katie implemented the Picture Word Inductive Model (PWIM), a new teaching strategy for her, and studied her kindergarten students' vocabulary development as part of learning to use this model. The picture word inductive model is an inquiry-oriented language arts approach that uses pictures containing familiar objects and actions to elicit words from students' own vocabularies. Teachers use it to lead their students into inquiry about word properties, adding words to their sight—reading and writing vocabularies, discovering phonetic and structural principles, and using observation and analysis in their study of reading, writing, comprehending, and composing. The picture word cycles (inquiries into pictures) generally take from four to six weeks at the kindergarten level (Calhoun, 1999).

At first, Katie thought the learning tasks might be too demanding for her students. But as she tried the model and studied what her students did in response, she changed her mind. Katie's data collection showed that her students had achieved a mean gain of 16 sight vocabulary words during their PWIM unit (in November), and a mean gain of 27 words in their sixth unit (ending in mid-March). These results confirmed for Katie the effectiveness of the picture word inductive model. Katie also collected detailed data on each student's word knowledge as he or she began the unit and again at the end of the unit. The data allowed her to analyze the word-reading strategies that individual students were using: sight vocabulary, decoding, analogies, common spelling patterns, and context clues (Ehri, 1999). As she analyzed the data for each student and across students, Katie made many instructional decisions, such as which phonics principles needed additional explicit instruction, when more modeling was needed to support using context clues, which students needed small-group work on phonemic analysis, and who needed special attention to encourage independent decoding. Studying specific domains of student performance and her own instructional practice has become a way of life for Katie.

In this same article, Calhoun (2002) provides a description of the comprehensive tool for information management known as the SAR (Schoolwide Action Research) Matrix—described fully in Workbook Three: *Engaging in Action Research*—and concludes by presenting some reflections on the power of organization-wide support.

Katie's use of action research occurred as part of a structured initiative sponsored by a state department of education. This initiative illustrates how education leaders in states, districts, and schools are attempting to make action research a dominant way of doing business—building an organization context that supports inquiry by school staffs working as a whole and by smaller groups and individuals pursuing their particular avenues of study. The development of inquiring communities is what distinguishes action research from school improvement approaches that focus on the implementation of specific initiatives, such as a new curriculum or a new mode of assessment.

Elsewhere, Calhoun (1997), relative to her later work on Every Child Reads, has provided her comprehensive model containing the necessary Components for

Supporting School Improvement for Student Achievement (see the following diagram). This model has been used extensively by participants in ECR project schools in Iowa to plan for and describe their school improvement efforts. It has also proved very influential in the thinking of those at the state level. Student achievement, it is believed, is best accelerated by focusing on curriculum and instruction, providing continuous professional development, and committing to school-wide action research. What is then required in addition are the time to work on all these things, all manner of technical assistance, and other supports including sustained effort over time.

Components for Supporting School Improvement for Student Achievement

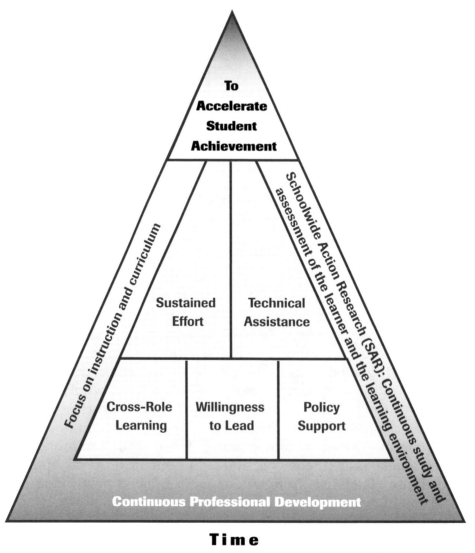

Calhoun (1997)

4. Data-Based Decision Making

As Judy Jeffrey mentions in her interview, Iowa has invested in data-based decision making, specifically in the form of the Bill Gates Implementation Grant monies that were used in Iowa to construct the QIC-Decide model for DBDM. The Iowa Department of Education paper that introduces this approach, entitled *The Origins of the QIC-Decide Data-Based Decision-Making Model*, responds to the questions: "Why data?" and "Why now?"

> Educators are being pushed and pulled to become more data literate and to use data more frequently in their decision-making processes. With the growing accountability movement in education (e.g., Marzano and Kendall, 1996; Thurlow, Elliott and Ysseldyke, 1998; Elementary and Secondary Education Act, 2002), educators increasingly are being pushed to demonstrate with data that their efforts are making a difference in student learning. These requirements have created the need for educators to use data more frequently and in different ways than has been the case historically. Educators are also being pulled to use data through their increasing understanding that data can help them make better teaching decisions to increase student performance.

The paper then acknowledges the two foremost data-based decision making models used in Iowa thus far.

> In Iowa, educators are further expected, in most cases, to use data to help guide their decisions regarding what actions should be taken at a systems level to improve teaching and learning (cf. Chapter 281.12 of the Iowa Administrative Code). This ongoing statewide initiative has become known colloquially as "School Improvement" throughout the state. In efforts to improve the Iowa education system, two major Data-Based Decision-Making (DBDM) models have been advocated by the Iowa Department of Education throughout the past ten years. These include the Action Research Model (Calhoun, 1994) used by the Every Child Reads initiative and the Problem Solving assessment and intervention process that was put into Iowa Rules of Special Education (281.41) in 1995. These models have significant similarities. Indeed, perhaps their most salient difference is the level of the system where the model is applied. Problem solving is applied typically for individual students while action research is applied typically at a group level. Despite these differences, however, their logic sets are very much the same.

In the same paper, following an analysis of the research traditions underlying these two approaches, the argument is made that no matter which approach or model of data-based decision making is used, four thematic steps are present in practitioner thinking:

(1) Determine what **question** is being addressed (or what decision you are being asked to make or what will be done with the data once collected).

(2) Identify what **information** is needed to address this question or decision.

(3) **Collect** and summarize the information.

(4) Make the appropriate **decision**.

Each of these steps has substeps and techniques that need to be applied to guide the thinking process. However, the four steps are the minimum necessary in order to carry out DBDM with accuracy. If any of the four are missed in the decision-making process, something important is missed and the defensibility of the ultimate decisions could be compromised.

The four steps in the QIC-Decide model, therefore, are: **Q**uestion, **I**dentify **I**nformation, **C**ollect and Summarize Information, and **D**ecide. A staff development process was designed—based on these four steps—and each of the modules contains examples of the application of QIC-Decide to common educational decisions. The process is structured in such a way that participants gain experience in applying QIC-Decide to impractical situations, the ultimate objective being for participants to internalize QIC-Decide as a thinking process. Eventually, every school and district administrator will experience this training package, referred to as Data-Driven Leadership (DDL), in order to qualify for his or her evaluator approval license.

The state of Iowa has also invested in data-based decision making in three other ways:

■ Every three years, schools can gain the benefits of being part of the Iowa Youth Survey. The survey is increasing in size all the time. It went from a sample of 26,200 students in 1996 to over 85,000 students in 1999. The school district reports that are issued are designed to help schools and communities identify youth development-related needs, develop relevant programs, and assess the outcomes of those programs. These data can help schools better understand the students and their needs. They can also help to assess the strengths and weaknesses of schools, families, and communities from the students' perspective. According to the reports issued in 2000:

> We are in a new era, with increasing awareness of the interdependence of groups once thought to be autonomous. The questions in the 1999 Iowa Youth Survey reflect this awareness in their focus on home and community, as well as school, influences on students. The Iowa Department of Education and the other agencies funding this study emphasize the crucial role of school-

community collaboration in enhancing life for Iowa's youth and enabling them to become successful adults. It is our expectation that school personnel, parents, youth, and other community members and organizations will come together to study this report and openly discuss what this data says about life for young people in your community. As a result, schools will be well equipped to begin planning programs that better meet students' needs. At the same time, community-based organizations that serve youth will be empowered to develop more effective, needs-based programs.

■ More ambitious again, every year the Iowa Department of Education publishes *The Annual Condition of Education Report*. This is a rich, comprehensive state-level data report. It is a goldmine of information for schools and school districts to use when comparing their progress to that of schools across the state, the nation, and other Midwestern states. It contains all the data that would be in a school or district profile but on a state-wide basis. As such, therefore, the report is the State Profile for Iowa. The report covers pre-kindergarten, elementary, and secondary education and contains sections on Background Demographics, Enrollment, Staff, Program, Student Performance, and Finance. In his introduction to the report, Ted Stilwill makes these comments:

> Having good information for decision making and policy setting has always been important. Today's focus on accountability makes it more important than ever to have appropriate information for decision making and strong information systems. It is very apparent that one of the cornerstones of the new federal *No Child Left Behind* legislation is accountability and providing information to policymakers and community leaders....This 2002 document is the thirteenth edition of *The Annual Condition of Education Report*....As school districts continue to report indicators of progress to parents, students, communities, and state officials, I hope this resource serves to provide useful comparisons. We have provided information regarding trends as well as information by the enrollment size category of districts.

Three highlights of the report made the headlines in the local press. First, 90% of Iowa's ninth graders who began high school in 1997 graduated four years later. Ted Stilwill, however, was quoted as saying that's not enough. While the graduation rate is the third highest in the country, according to Stilwill, there is still room for improvement—especially if the state is to thrive economically.

> The goal for the state ought to be 100%. There's almost an assumption by some people that some students will not be successful in high school or in post-secondary institutions....We need to change that mindset.

Meanwhile, the graduation rate for Iowa's Black and Hispanic students is significantly lower than for White students. One out of three Hispanic ninth graders and three out of ten Black ninth graders, who began in high school in 1997, failed to graduate four years later. One out of ten White ninth graders left school without a diploma.

Second, while 4th, 8th, and 11th graders' reading skills have made a slight improvement, the academic achievement gap between racial and economic groups has widened in several areas. 71.5% of White 4th graders were proficient in reading, compared with 44.6% of Hispanic students in the same grade—an achievement gap of 26.9 percentage points. The same gap a year ago was 24.7. Again, says Stilwill: "That's unacceptable."

Third, the same type of huge investments made in early elementary classrooms are required for middle and high schools so that more students will be able to graduate and move on to two and four year colleges. Currently, 82% of high school seniors plan to go on to higher education and half will graduate.

5. Professional Growth and Teacher Quality

This has been the priority in Iowa over the last couple of years. Grounded in the belief—as an ECR participant put it to the author—that there is no improvement in student achievement without improvement in the quality of instruction, professional development has become the leading cause for those in the Department of Education. Indeed, in a recent speech (May 2003), Judy Jeffrey nicely summarized the reasons for their interest. She mentioned the Teacher Quality legislation (passed in 2001) and the active involvement of the Governor, Thomas Vilsack, during his first term in office. As in her interview, she also mentioned the slowing down of implementation efforts (due to financial cut-backs) but said that, in terms of capacity building, this could well be a good thing. "As it comes down into the system," she said, "we can build leadership at every level; holding individuals to account for results without building capacity is a fruitless exercise." She then summarized the eight elements of high-performance systems:

- They have standards for both content and performance.

- A clear purpose has to be in place, which is then held to by all those involved.

- There has to be a supportive and nurturing climate.

- The organization itself has to hold itself accountable at every level of the system.

- High quality, ongoing professional development—driven by performance data—is essential.

- Resources—even (especially) when in short supply—have to be strategically focused and support high quality practices.

- The organization collects and uses data well.

- There is active, open, substantive, and clear two-way communication across all levels of the organization.

Given that many of these conditions already pertained in Iowa (prior to *NCLB*), she said, it puts the state in alignment with many of the federal expectations. The new professional development program, said Jeffrey, will continue to build capacity in order to move the whole school toward desired results. Pockets of excellence in schools are no longer good enough, she said; the whole faculty has to be involved. Then research-based strategies have to be selected that will really make a difference in terms of bringing all children to their best possible levels of achievement. Alignment, she concluded, is the key ingredient in high performance systems.

As explained in the Iowa Department of Education's introduction to the Iowa Professional Development Model (2002), it was in May of 2001 that the Iowa General Assembly passed the landmark legislation that identified professional development as a key component of school reform in Iowa. The major elements of the legislation (referred to as the *Student Achievement and Teacher Quality Program*) are as follow:

- mentoring and induction programs that provide support for beginning teachers

- professional development designed to directly support best teaching practice

- career paths with compensation levels that strengthen Iowa's ability to recruit and retain teachers

- the eight Iowa teaching standards and supporting criteria which shape the implementation of each aspect of the Teacher Quality Program

- a team-based variable pay program that provides additional compensation when student performance improves

The Iowa Teacher Quality Program also requires each district to submit a career development plan as part of its 2004 Comprehensive School Improvement Plan (CSIP). In addition, the Teacher Quality legislation provides that an individual teacher career development plan will be developed (akin to a professional growth plan), in cooperation with the teacher's supervisor, for each career teacher in the district. An overview of the Teacher Quality Program follows.

TQP: Teacher Quality Program

Overview of the Staff Evaluation and Professional Growth Program

<u>Iowa Teaching Standards</u>
1. Enhancing academic performance/supporting district achievement goals
2. Content knowledge
3. Planning for instruction
4. Delivery of instruction
5. Monitoring student learning
6. Classroom management
7. Professional growth
8. Professional responsibilities

Plan I	Plan II	Plan III
Who:	**Who:**	**Who:**
New beginning teachers New experienced teachers	All tenured teachers demonstrating the specific Iowa Teaching Standards	Teachers in need of professional assistance in identified area(s) of the Iowa Teaching Standards
Purpose:	**Purpose:**	**Purpose:**
■ To insure that the Iowa Teaching Standards are understood, accepted, and demonstrated. ■ To provide support in the implementation of the Standards of Accountability for decisions to continue employment.	■ To enhance professional growth. ■ To focus on district school improvement goals. ■ To focus on continuous implementation of the Iowa Teaching Standards.	■ To enable a tenured teacher the opportunity to seek assistance in meeting any of the Iowa Teaching Standards. ■ To provide a structured process for supporting and directing needed help in any of the Iowa Teaching Standards.
Process:	**Process:**	**Process:**
■ Classroom observation. ■ Collaborative development. ■ Portfolio development. ■ Required Professional Development activities. ■ Regular evaluation reports and feedback.	■ Phases of individual/team professional growth plans. ■ Reflection and feedback on growth plan progress and impact.	■ Awareness and assistance. ■ Development and implementation of a professional assistance plan. ■ Regular evaluation reports and feedback.

There are several elements of the Teacher Quality Program already in place.

<u>The Iowa Teaching Standards</u>

The eight Iowa Teaching Standards, listed above, amend and extend the work of Charlotte Danielson and Thomas McGreal (both of whom have worked with the Iowa State Department). More detailed descriptions of each follow:

1. Demonstrates ability to enhance academic performance and support for and implementation of the school district's student achievement goals.

2. Demonstrates competence in content knowledge appropriate to the teaching position.

3. Demonstrates competence in planning and preparing for instruction.

4. Uses strategies to deliver instruction that meets the multiple learning needs of students.

5. Uses a variety of methods to monitor student learning.

6. Demonstrates competence in classroom management.

7. Engages in professional growth.

8. Fulfills professional responsibilities established by the school district.

Each of the standards is broken down into criteria for effectiveness and, taken together, the standards and criteria form the basis of the Comprehensive Evaluation Summative Evaluation Form which, so far, has to be completed for each Beginning Teacher. In order to be an approved evaluator of a Beginning Teacher, every school administrator in Iowa has had ten days of training: four days of DDL (Data-Driven Leadership) focusing on the QIC-Decide model and six days of evaluator training—the Iowa Evaluator Approval Training Program (IEATP) grounded in the eight standards and how to provide evidence of their accomplishment.

Alongside these developments, every Beginning Teacher in districts in Iowa has to receive mentoring support. In a district like Dubuque, therefore, which had the mentoring program in place and Track One of the Professional Evaluation program was already in existence, only minor shifts in existing practice were necessary. The main tasks were the incorporation of the new Teaching Standards and the ten days of training for all administrators. What this all means, of course, is that Beginning Teachers are now doubly supported through mentoring and teacher evaluation procedures. The same level of support is envisioned for career teachers, but this work has been held up by financial cutbacks.

Working with educators in Eagle Grove, Iowa to overhaul their teacher evaluation system (something that many districts had embarked upon prior to the legislative changes), the author presented a summary of the *New Requirements for Teacher Evaluation*.

■ First and second year new professionals (Beginning Teachers) will be evaluated by an administrator who has been through the ten days of DE/AEA training currently being offered.

■ All first and second year new professionals will receive mentoring.

- At the end of two years, school districts have three options:

  - recommend the new professional for an educational license and offer a contract for the next year;

  - recommend the license but not offer a contract;

  - do not recommend for a license and recommend a third year of "probation."

- Evaluation of Beginning Teachers has to be based on the eight Iowa Teaching Standards and the stipulated use of the evaluation instrument provided by the State Department.

- If a new professional should be terminated at the end of the first year, there is no recourse for that person beyond an appeal to the School Board.

- The career path/professional growth model for the evaluation of all licensed teachers—again, based on the eight Iowa Teaching Standards—is being prepared, but its implementation has been delayed. The plan is for a supervisor to formally evaluate each career teacher every three years, using an evaluation instrument provided by the State Department.

- This evaluation process will be integrated with the Individual Career Development Plans, based on the eight standards, tied to district achievement goals, and jointly developed by the teacher and supervisor.

Iowa Professional Development Model

This model (diagrammed on page 196) has been built with the assistance of Beverly Showers and participants from pilot sites across the state are currently being trained in its use. This model is meant to be data-driven and cyclical (which makes it similar to the model advocated by Kelleher, 2003), and, therefore, supportive of and integrated with the comprehensive school improvement process. Alignment (of goals, action plans, and staff development) is the key concept here. According to the same introduction to *The Iowa Professional Development Model* (2002), professional development activities in Iowa should

- align with the Iowa Teaching Standards;

- focus on research-based instructional strategies aligned with the school district's student achievement needs and the long-range and annual improvement goals established by the district;

- deliver professional development that is targeted at instructional improvement and designed with the following components:

  - student achievement data and analysis

  - theory

- classroom demonstration and practice

- observation and reflection

- teacher collaboration

- integration of instructional technology, if applicable

■ include an evaluation component that documents the improvement in instructional practice and the effect on student learning;

■ support the career development needs of individual teachers.

Iowa Professional Development Model

Student Learning at the Center of School Improvement/Staff Development

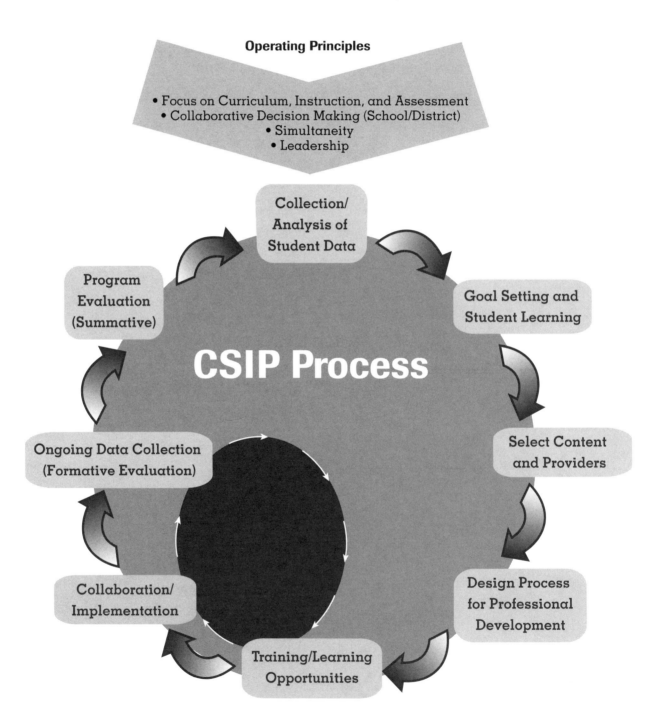

Operating Principles

• Focus on Curriculum, Instruction, and Assessment
• Collaborative Decision Making (School/District)
• Simultaneity
• Leadership

Collection/
Analysis of
Student Data

Program
Evaluation
(Summative)

Goal Setting and
Student Learning

CSIP Process

Ongoing Data Collection
(Formative Evaluation)

Select Content
and Providers

Collaboration/
Implementation

Design Process
for Professional
Development

Training/Learning
Opportunities

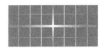

The State
Task 3: Planning a School Improvement Initiative

Purpose: To undertake a major professional development/school improvement planning activity, by using the Iowa Professional Development Model.

Grouping: Work with your Learning Team or other district team configuration.

Directions: Working in teams, use the following planner provided by the Iowa Department of Education to plan a major professional development/school improvement initiative for your school/school district by filling in each of the boxes.

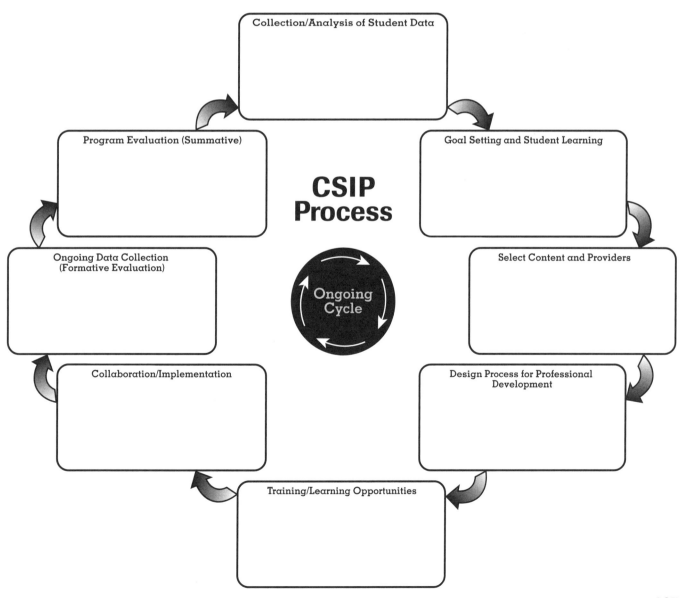

The model is also supported by four operating principles:

- Focus on Curriculum, Instruction, and Assessment

  The primary focus of professional development in the Iowa model is on the classroom: the curriculum students are expected to learn, the instructional strategies that make the curriculum accessible and comprehensible, and the aligned and appropriate assessment measures—the Learning Triangle.

- Participative Decision Making

  To prevent decision-making processes from becoming the focus of change efforts, schools and districts need to decide how they will make decisions and what is required for them to make *binding* decisions prior to embarking on building cohesive and coherent professional development plans.

- Simultaneity

  The **content** of professional development has to be addressed simultaneously with the **context** (climate, relationships, decision-making arrangements, leadership) and **process** (data-based decision making, selection of research-based strategies).

- Leadership

  The leadership of teachers, principals, district administrative staff, and school boards, working interdependently, is critical if the Iowa Professional Development Model is to drive increased achievement for all students.

On the topic of **leadership**, it should be noted that the six Iowa Standards for School Leaders have also been developed (included below) and sample evaluation forms that incorporate these standards produced by the Iowa Association of School Boards (IASB) and the School Administrators of Iowa (SAI) working in tandem.

Iowa Standards for School Leaders

Standard 1: A school administrator is an educational leader who promotes the success of all students facilitating the development, articulation, implementation, and stewardship of a vision of learning that is shared and supported by the school community.

Standard 2: A school administrator is an educational leader who promotes the success of all students by advocating, nurturing, and sustaining a school culture and instructional program conducive to student learning and staff professional development.

Standard 3: A school administrator is an educational leader who promotes the success of all students by ensuring management of the organization, operations, and resources for a safe, efficient, and effective learning environment.

<u>Standard 4:</u> A school administrator is an educational leader who promotes the success of all students by collaborating with families and community members, responding to diverse community interests and needs, and mobilizing community resources.

<u>Standard 5:</u> A school administrator is an educational leader who promotes the success of all students by acting with integrity, fairness, and in an ethical manner.

<u>Standard 6:</u> A school administrator is an educational leader who promotes the success of all students by understanding, responding to, and influencing the larger political, social, economic, legal, and cultural context.

6. The Role of Area Education Agencies

In her interview, when asked about the future of Area Education Agencies (AEAs) in Iowa, Judy Jeffrey responded by saying: "Without them, we'd be toast!" They are so much a part of the state's support system and so much a part of the state's training and implementation plans that, without them, the State Department really would be in dire straits. As a consequence, when during the 2003 legislative session, the future of the AEAs seemed to be in some doubt, Ted Stilwill responded with an impassioned plea:

> One proposal being heavily discussed is a severe reduction in AEA funding and the restructuring of and potential dismantling of Iowa's AEA services. In the nearly 30 years that AEAs have existed, they have developed into an integral part of Iowa's educational network, serving as regional hubs for services such as curriculum development, special education, media and technology services, school and community planning, professional development and leadership training. They are nationally recognized and respected as a model for the states seeking to improve their education systems....We quite simply are doing some things that many other states are not. Our AEAs, for example, are envied by most other states as an asset to support school improvement...Especially now, when every aspect of education is striving to meet new demands, we absolutely need the involvement of every local, regional, and state education partner to work together. Without the regional portion of that network, we will begin failing our children.

Such a negative move, emphasized Stilwill, would "signal the erosion of a quality system." Stilwill also reminded his readers that the AEAs had just been through an extensive, rigorous re-accreditation process (involving, like school districts, the establishment of comprehensive improvement plans and the issuing of annual progress reports). Stilwill continued:

> AEAs also have followed an accreditation process for the past six years, a quality-control measure that assures they are accountable for high standards with meaningful results in improved student learning and teacher instruction....In the annual customer satisfaction survey conducted last year by the DE, 89% of local educators reported they were satisfied or more than satisfied with both the quality of service and the responsiveness of AEAs to meet local needs in a timely manner. As such, AEAs are fulfilling the equity and efficiency goals outlined when legislators began the system in 1974.

The author has worked intensively with one particular AEA—Great River AEA 16, based in Burlington, Iowa—over a period of several years. This working relationship has focused on the creation of a data-driven school system that includes the AEA as a full partner (as depicted in the following matrix) and the operation of three main activities that occur monthly:

- Data Coach Training sessions for leadership teams from districts in the AEA 16 region, much as in Dubuque

- training sessions for AEA staff acting as "liaisons" and facilitators for the district teams

- work with the AEA's Central Data Team—the leadership team that has been responsible for steering the AEA through the accreditation process and is now working on the tracking (in data) of the implementation of the agency's goals over time

DATA - DRIVEN SCHOOL SYSTEM				
Student	**Classroom**	**School**	**District**	**AEA**
Current goals based on previous year's data and vision	Current goals based on previous year's data and vision	Current goals based on previous year's data and vision	Current goals based on previous year's data and vision	Current goals based on previous year's data and vision
Data Profile	**Data Profile**	**Data Profile**	**Data Profile**	**Data Profile**
Reviewing progress on current goal	Reviewing progress on current goal	Reviewing progress on current goal	Reviewing progress on current goal	Reviewing progress on current goal
New goals based on review of profile data and vision and standards and benchmarks	New goals based on review of profile data and vision and standards and benchmarks	New goals based on review of profile data and vision and standards and benchmarks	New goals based on review of profile data and vision and standards and benchmarks	New goals based on review of profile data and vision and standards and benchmarks
Action Plans	**Action Plans**	**Action Plans**	**Action Plans**	**Action Plans**

One major element of all this work has been the CPR model for continuous improvement. First introduced by Peter Holly, the AEA staff members have really made it their own (see the following page). The CPR diagram is on the wall in every room in the AEA and was described to AEA colleagues using an information sheet. The model was also used to come up with diagnostic questions for the AEA liaisons to ask of their sites and a self-assessment fill-in sheet for district personnel.

Great River AEA #16's CPR Model of Continuous Improvement for Student Learning

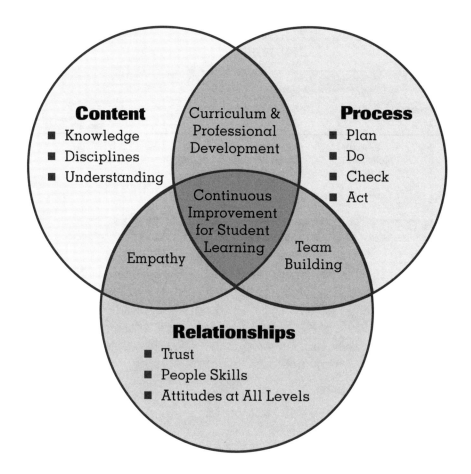

Reporting on Progress

In its *Annual Progress Report to Local School Districts and the Iowa Department of Education*, AEA 16 staff included their Mission Statement, Guiding Principles (including being data-driven and the primacy of the CPR model) and Areas of Service/Organizational Structure (School Improvement, Professional Development, Technology and Data, Special Education, and Instructional Media).

Great River AEA: Goals

The AEA currently has two major goals and three support considerations.

Goal #1: To reduce the achievement gap in reading between students receiving free or reduced lunches and those who do not.

Goal #2: To increase the percentage of schools and school districts that meet their annual improvement goals.

These goals will be supported in three ways: by using research-based practices; by using data-based decision-making; and by ensuring equity and quality of services that support school improvement.

Great River AEA: Data Review

When selecting their goals, AEAs are in an interesting position: they have to look both ways. They have to be aware of two kinds of data: they have to scan their regional data (across the constituent districts) to find common areas of current need and they have to look outside, including to the State Department of Education, to anticipate future needs. When looking at ITBS/ITED results for all the schools in the AEA, for instance, the collective districts' data become the AEA's. The understanding that underpins this process is that the work of the AEA does impact both teacher improvement and, by extension, increases in student achievement. The successes—or failures—of the schools are also those of the AEA. Very careful attention, therefore, is now paid to the assembled data, such as reading proficiency reports. Other data included in the report are regional dropout rates, statistics related to post-secondary success, and the leveled impact of professional development activities.

Integrated Planning

This particular AEA is currently planning the next iteration of data coach training and other related activities. With *NCLB* very much in mind, an ambitious and integrated plan has been formulated that "aims to pack a real punch" in support of reading development. Schools in AEA 16 will develop Implementation Plans (based on local achievement data) that specifically link to one of the following initiatives:

- *NCLB* (national)

- Iowa Comprehensive School Improvement Plans (state)

- Every Child Reads (state)

- Reading First (national/state)

- Reading for Understanding (regional)

- Partnering for Improvement (regional)

Embedded in the work will be *scientifically-based research strategies* and all improvements will be enhanced by the incorporation of technologically-rich applications. The local school improvement *implementation plans* will be linked directly with the Iowa Professional Development Model through the Great River AEA #16's Partnering for Improvement program.

The Partnering for Improvement Program

In a paper prepared by AEA staffers Sally Wood and Pat Shier, the new program is introduced as follows:

> The Partnering for Improvement program is a re-design (in light of *NCLB* and Iowa's accountability needs) of Great River AEA #16's Data Coaching effort of the past three years. Through this effort, the goals have been to improve student achievement and to build capacity of schools/districts to make better decisions based on data and to assist schools with their school improvement planning, annual progress reporting and use of data. In year one and two, the emphasis has been to identify data sources, read and interpret data, develop student learning goals, and report progress toward those goals as per Iowa's CSIP and APR processes. This has been an area-wide school improvement effort with all school districts participating.
>
> Partnering for Improvement will help to assure that school implementation plans are thoughtfully designed, and carefully implemented. AEA Implementation Coaches will help to assure the necessary ongoing and on-site support as per the Iowa Professional Development Model.
>
> National, state, and regional reading initiatives/programs (such as Reading First, Every Child Reads, and Reading for Understanding) will become the content basis for professional development activities. Partnering for Improvement will add to the content base (Ruby Payne's materials) and provide for a team process to thoughtfully design the implementation plan, obtain assistance toward the implementation, integrate technology as appropriate to the implementation, account for data collection and assist with assessing progress and plan evaluation. At the heart of the program remain the goals: to increase student achievement in reading and lessen the achievement gaps between those receiving free and reduced lunch and those who do not.

7. Responding to *No Child Left Behind*

Two points are crucial here.

First, many of the elements of *NCLB* (for example, teacher quality and professional development) were being planned or implemented in Iowa prior to the passing of the federal legislation. Accountability, therefore, is definitely not a new notion to those working in, and in support of, schools and school districts in Iowa.

Second, the somewhat protracted negotiations concerning Iowa's application to join the ranks of *NCLB* were mainly a result of Iowa not matching up to the "cookie-cutter" federal formula. Iowa is different. These differences (not necessarily weaknesses) had to be explained so the Iowa approach could be better understood at the federal level. Those in Iowa also came to better understand what was expected by those at the federal level, and which items were non-negotiables. Eventually, a compromise was agreed upon and, on June 9, 2003, Iowa's entry into *NCLB* was officially announced.

Anticipating Iowa's inclusion in *NCLB*, preparations have been under way for several months at many different levels in the system. From September 2002 onwards, for instance, during Data Coach Training sessions in AEA 16, participants have been discussing the legislation and its implications. Peter Holly introduced these conversations as follows:

NCLB: The Changing Context for Comprehensive School Improvement

Introductory Points

- The data-driven nature of comprehensive school improvement is becoming even more important.

- In the federal legislation of January 2002 (*No Child Left Behind* Act), the focus is on achievement for all students.

- While the DE is clarifying what will be expected of schools and school districts, it makes eminent good sense to be proactive and anticipatory.

- CSIPs and APRs will still be required, but more so.

- While we can only deal in generalities and not specifics at this stage, what is certain is that, in terms of data needs, the legislation should have been called the "No Classroom Left Untouched" Act. With the emphasis on accountability, student progress classroom-by-classroom will be scrutinized like never before.

- The onus, therefore, is on <u>classroom improvement for student achievement</u>.

Some Basic Points

- Starting in the 2005–2006 year, all schools in the USA will be required to test students in reading and mathematics, in grades 3 through 8 and at least once in grades 10 through 12 (in Iowa grade 11). In Iowa, science will remain in force and be extended to the elementary level.

- There will be penalties for low (or declining) performance in these tests.

■ State and local assessments and norm- and criterion-referenced assessments will be used to meet the testing requirements.

■ States and school districts must produce annual report cards of their students' progress toward meeting state standards, graduation rates, names of schools in need of improvement, qualifications of teachers, and percentages of students not tested.

■ States and school districts are required to develop plans that indicate how the goals and requirements of the federal law are being met.

■ Paraprofessionals have to meet new training requirements and all teachers have to be "highly qualified" by 2005–2006.

■ Two new emphases have data implications:

  ■ More disaggregation of student achievement data will be required to show the progress being made by all student subpopulations (gender, ethnicity, ELL, students with IEPs, socioeconomic groups, etc.) and the size of the <u>achievement gaps</u> between the various groups.

  ■ Reporting of progress will be tied to standards and benchmarks but using "grade level expectations" (the equivalent to critical objectives as they are called in AEA 16).

Data Coach teams from AEA 16 school districts then used a Team Task: Self-Assessment (included in Task 4 of this chapter) to begin to plan and prepare for the advent of *NCLB*.

It is interesting to note what was said when Iowa's Accountability Plan for inclusion in *NCLB* was approved by the USDE. The local press in Iowa, in covering the event (06/06/03), remarked that the plan was based on four principles:

■ It supports Iowa's current philosophy of continuous improvement by expecting all school districts and all school buildings to improve student performance.

■ It maintains Iowa's current policy that schools and school districts are the entities primarily accountable for student performance.

■ It continues to support the local district responsibility for the development of content standards and benchmarks.

■ It continues to support the development of local assessment systems that can effectively drive instruction.

In short, the message was "steady as she goes."

 ### The State
Task 4: District *NCLB* Readiness

<u>Purpose:</u> To undertake another major planning activity relative to *NCLB* preparation.

<u>Grouping:</u> Work on your own and then meet with your Learning Team or other district team. Select a team recorder.

<u>Group process strategy:</u> Use a consensus-building strategy for Step 3 (refer to the **Group Process Guide**).

<u>Directions:</u> On your own, complete <u>Step 1: Readiness</u>, rating your school district's level of readiness for the requirements of *NCLB*. Use a five-point scale, with a score of "1" indicating a **low level of readiness**, up to a score of "5" indicating a **high level of readiness**. Also complete <u>Step 2: Prioritizing</u> on your own, and then meet with your team to complete <u>Step 3: Team Consensus</u>.

<u>Step 1: Readiness</u>

Readiness
<u>Rating</u>

_____ Annual testing of students in reading and mathematics, grades 3–8 and 11

_____ Annual testing of students in science, grades 4, 8, and 11

_____ Highly qualified teaching force

_____ Annual report cards reporting:
■ student progress toward state standards
■ graduate rates
■ names of schools needing improvement
■ teachers' qualifications
■ % of students not tested

_____ Norm- and criterion-referenced assessments

_____ Disaggregation of data for all student subpopulations

_____ Intense scrutiny of student performance in every classroom

_____ Classroom improvement

(Step 1: Readiness is continued on the following page.)

_____ Critical objectives that are
- specific and clearly stated
- indicators of what students have to accomplish
- aligned with standards and benchmarks
- grade-level specific
- tied to classroom activities/lessons and unit plans
- used as the basis of regular assessment

_____ School-wide information database (SID) in place

Step 2: Prioritizing

Now, it is time to use your ratings from Step 1 to determine which items are most in need of attention as your district prepares for implementing *NCLB*. Review your readiness ratings, putting an asterisk (*) next to the items that received the lowest ratings. For example, if you rated "Disaggregation of data for all student subpopulations" as a "2," that is an area that your district will probably want to give high priority. Record below the five items that received the lowest readiness ratings. This list now becomes your own priority list for your district. Next to each priority, record your reasons for including this item on your priority list.

Highest Priority   Reasons

1.

2.

3.

4

5.

Step 3: Team Consensus

Now, it is time to meet with your team to develop a team list of the highest priority items. Your team should come to a consensus on the items needing the most focus and the actions and timelines required to move these items to a higher level of *NCLB* readiness. Have your team recorder create a list on poster paper with the following headings. Use the space below for your own notes.

High Priority Items   Action   Timeline

Annual Yearly Progress (AYP) Goals and Trajectories

When the Iowa plan was submitted to the federal authorities in January 2003, it hinged on the twin elements of AYP goals and trajectories. Starting in the summer of 2003, school districts in Iowa will have to compute their expected Annual Yearly Progress gains relative to their "trajectories." The state's trajectory is based on the mean of all the achievement levels of all school districts in Iowa on the ITBS/ITED standardized tests. The key concept, of course, is "proficiency," i.e., the percentage of students scoring above the 40th percentile. The trajectories have been designed in such a way that in several "steps," the achievement levels of all students in Iowa will increase over time to reach the expected 100% proficiency by 2013–2014. Each district in Iowa has its own trajectory to follow (based on its results and matching the state's in terms of its design). Districts scoring below the state's mean, however, will enter the scheme by taking the state's trajectory as their own. In the future, therefore, all annual improvement goals in Iowa districts will take the form of AYP goals (what have to be achieved to stay on trajectory) and every district will have six trajectories—one each for reading and mathematics in grades 4, 8, and 11. An example of a trajectory for grade 4 reading is included on the following page. These samples have been made available to school districts to assist in their goal-setting process. Each sheet already includes the state trajectory and a section to add proficiency scores for various disaggregated groups. A sample AYP Goal reads as follows:

> The percentage of fourth-grade students reading at the proficient level will increase by 1 percent during the 2003–2004 academic year. The percentage of increase for Low SES and Special Education students will be, of necessity, proportionately higher than 1 percent in order for all fourth graders to reach 81.7% in reading by 2004–2005, our first three-year target.

District A: Grade 4 Reading

89% Proficient (All Students)

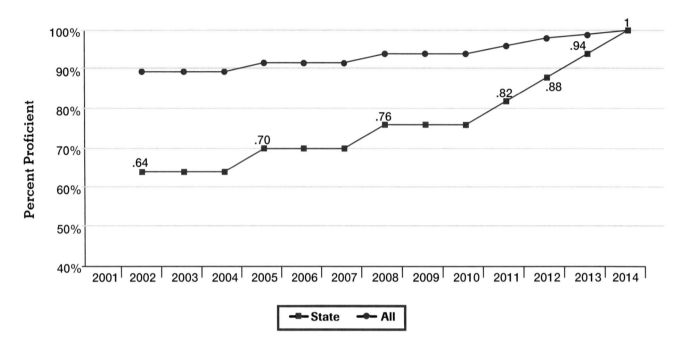

Grade 4 Reading	Proficient	Not Proficient
All Students	89%	11%
White	89%	11%
Low SES	90%	10%

Implications of *NCLB*

Bloomfield and Cooper (2003) have provided an "overview of the most sweeping federal education law since 1965." What no one disputes, they say, is that *NCLB* has completely reshaped federal involvement in American education. They see the new role of federal government from five perspectives:

■ **Federalization** of education under the law. Bloomfield and Cooper state:

It is an 'only-Nixon-could-go-to-China' irony that, despite traditional Republican positions favoring local school autonomy and small government, a Republican president signed into law *NCLB*, which not only increased national regulation of local education, but also meant growth in federal spending of $22.3 billion on schools....The federal government has involved itself in the daily operation of schools as never before, requiring schools to demonstrate that students are making adequate yearly progress (AYP).

■ **Standardization**: moving toward a national standard of education.

■ **Systemization**: the federal government has mandated a large-scale system for creating and maintaining state educational standards, testing, and accountability. According to Bloomfield and Cooper:

> This arrangement extends from the child to subgroups of children to the school, the district, and the state, removing much discretion from the local community and creating a system of control that is quite new to the American education system....The trend toward macro-authority of state and federal mandates, and away from the relatively micro-authority of local governance, has moved much decision making to the state level under strict federal guidelines that demand institutional solutions.

■ **Privatization**: more involvement on the part of the private sector, particularly in providing assistance to failing schools, test construction, and the generation of scientifically-based research.

■ **The Future of Public Education**: does *NCLB* signify a new beginning for public education, ask Bloomfield and Cooper, or the beginning of its end?

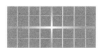

The State
Task 5: Reflecting on the Future of Public Education

Purpose: To reflect on the future of public education in the light of Bloomfield and Cooper's commentary.

Grouping: Work on your own.

<u>Directions:</u> Working reflectively and individually, write down your thoughts in response to Bloomfield and Cooper's question: Is *NCLB* a new beginning for public education or the beginning of the end? Be specific and provide rationales for your point of view.

8. A Systems Approach to School Improvement

As Judy Jeffrey testifies in her interview, the Iowa State Department has made a concerted effort to take a systems approach to the initiation, support, and monitoring of school improvement efforts at the local level. It can be argued, therefore, that what local educators have tried to do in Dubuque is being replicated at the state level. Concepts like alignment, integration, nested-ness, and capacity-building all come into play here. As Karen Hawley Miles (2003) has emphasized recently relative to professional development:

> Good professional development is not the same thing as a good professional development strategy. But a good professional development strategy is the heart of a good district strategy for school improvement....A strategically designed professional development system allocates scarce resources to its most important priorities in ways most likely to improve student performance.

Such a strategy is needs-based data-driven in that resources are provided to those parts of the system which have indicated the greatest needs. Moreover, says Karen Hawley Miles, such a strategy, while requiring tightness of coordination and orchestration, cannot take a "one-size-fits-all" approach. She continues:

> It cannot be one-size-fits-all because it responds to each school, teacher team, and teacher...[It involves] using student performance data to zero in on specific schools, teachers, and students that need improvement.

This is exactly the kind of system that educators in Iowa are trying to create by interlocking the classroom, school, district, regional, and state levels of application in pursuit of system priorities, e.g., reading excellence. Every Child Reads is a good example of this phenomenon. While focused on a statewide priority—reading comprehension—and initiated, sponsored, and supported at the state level, the program incorporates instructional strategies known to work in other contexts in order to meet needs identified at the local level through school-based action research. As previously noted in this workbook, such a systems approach, especially in the context of *NCLB*, involves the effective accommodation of seeming opposites:

- autonomy and accountability

- local control and state mandates

- the vertical and the horizontal

- tightness and looseness

- independence and interdependence

- pressure and support

- internal and external perspectives

- compliance and commitment

- standards and soul

In Iowa, probably more than anywhere else in the nation, "directed autonomy" is both a mission and a hypothesis. It is a set of values and an ongoing action research project. Take the issue of achievement gaps. Closing them has been identified as a major system priority. Given this vertical exhortation and direction, however, forward progress will largely be made horizontally. An external partner, the North Central Regional Educational Laboratory (NCREL) has been identified as having experience working in this important area (see Stewart, 2002) and two of Iowa's larger districts, Sioux City and Waterloo, have been invited to form task forces and work with NCREL to investigate what the problems are and what can be done about them at the local level. No doubt the findings will then be "taken to scale" (see Elmore, 1996) using various systemic strategies. Indeed, Iowa is a good example of what Michael Fullan talks about in his 1996 article, "Turning Systemic Thinking On Its Head." He argues that a system (district or state) is composed of top and bottom halves. What works in one sphere, he says, does not work so well in the other. Although central direction works well in the top half, the bottom half is far "messier" and non-linear and has to be approached in very different ways (i.e., ways that are supportive of and sympathetic to local autonomy). According to Fullan (1996):

- It's a case of achieving system coherence (through alignment and clarity and consistency of policy) *and* greater coherence in the minds and efforts of local educators.

- Being nonlinear and dynamic is part and parcel of the way complex societies *must* evolve.

- What looks like clarity at the top may increase clutter at the bottom.

- It is even more important to achieve clarity at the receiving end than at the delivery end.

- Neither top-down nor bottom-up strategies work by themselves.

What can the top and bottom do in combination, Fullan asks, that will maximize the impact on learning outcomes?

> Assuming that the top has already worked on matters of vision and direction, it would probably have done so in collaboration with various parts of the system. This process would have mobilized only a small percentage of those who need to become involved—probably 5% at most. What strategies, then, are going to be most effective in working with the remaining 95%?

Networking (interestingly Fullan's description of networking sounds very much like the way the Every Child Reads program has operated in Iowa), reculturing, and restructuring are Fullan's solutions to the problem. They are strategies that have the potential to help develop and mobilize conceptions, skills, and motivation in the minds and hearts of scores of educators.

AEAs in Iowa, therefore, are in a very interesting position. They are continually becoming another arm of the State Department (and, as such, are very much part of top-half policy-making and its implementation), yet are "of their constituent districts" and, as such, very much part of bottom half "herding" through such strategies as networking and reculturation. If, however, they lean too far either way, they can quickly lose the support of top-half policy-makers or bottom-half practitioners. This boundary and translation role played by AEAs also explains their crucial importance. Without their "inter-mediation," the system in Iowa would be severely damaged. They represent and translate policy, while activating local response mechanisms. In carrying out the DE's purpose and direction, while enabling local school systems to grow and prosper, they embrace compliance and commitment. They represent the complexity of the mature system that is Iowa. The key activity undertaken by AEAs is negotiation. Charles Handy (1989) nicely explains the importance of their role. In a section entitled "The Theft of Purposes," he argues:

> Proper, responsible selfishness involves a purpose and a goal. It is that goal which pulls out the energy to move the wheel (of learning). Diminish that goal, displace it or, worst of all, disallow

it and we remove all incentive to learn or to change. Proper selfishness, however, recognizes that the goal needs to be tuned to the goals of the group, or the organization, or society, as well as being in line with our own needs and our own talents.

It is tempting to impose our goals on other people, particularly on children or our subordinates. It is tempting for society to try to impose its priorities on everybody. The strategy will however be self-defeating if our goals, or society's goals, do not fit the goals of the others. We may get our way but we don't get their learning. They may have to comply but they will not change. We have pushed out their goals with ours and stolen their purposes. It is a pernicious form of theft, which kills the will to learn. The apathy and disillusion of many people in organizations...is often due to the fact that there is no room for their purposes or goals in our scheme of things. Left goal-less, they comply, drift, or rebel.

In a sensible world the goals are negotiated....Responsible selfishness knows that there are core duties and necessary boundaries but also that there must be room for self-expression. Squeeze it out, as tidy bureaucrats so often do, and we kill any motivation to learn.

Those in AEAs live these tensions daily. Such educators have to learn to live with—and indeed, exploit—the creative tension that comes with having to continually reconcile opposing forces. Rachael Kessler (2002), in her article, "Nurturing Deep Connections," explores this phenomenon. One of her five principles of leadership is living with paradox. She explains:

> Leaders model the willingness to hold the tension of apparent opposites: standards and soul, privacy and community, collaboration and authority, caring and rigor.

Kessler also quotes the work of Robert Johnson, author of *Owning Your Own Shadow* (1993), who speaks of "the art of taking opposites and binding them back together again, surmounting the split that has been causing so much suffering." Consequently, he continues:

> It helps us move from contradiction—that painful condition where things oppose each other—to the realm of paradox, where we are able to entertain simultaneously two contradictory notions and give then equal dignity. Then, and only then, is there the possibility of grace, the spiritual experience of contradictions brought into a coherent whole, giving us a unity greater than either of them.

Reflecting on these words of wisdom, Kessler (2002) concludes that perhaps the most challenging paradox that must be held by a leader today is the tension between standards and soul. She states:

> A school based solely on 'standards' could easily become an arid, numerical, test-driven landscape that cannot nourish true learning, turns teachers into managers and students into robots.
>
> Conversely, a school based exclusively on 'soul' could become lost in the inner world of its students, a pedagogical free-for-all where nothing is required and everything becomes an expression of each person's precious uniqueness.
>
> But when both soul and standards are honored and school leaders ride the paradox, an environment for learning is created that is strong enough to hold all tensions, trends, and turmoil of American life.

When this author asked Lesley Stephens, principal of Bryant School in Dubuque, "What do you need to help you get to the next level?" she looked at him somewhat blankly. "Is there a next level?" she asked. She was making a serious point. After all, those in Bryant School and Dubuque Community School District have climbed their way to Stage Three of school improvement (as, it can be argued, has the State Department in Iowa). Leaders like Lesley Stephens and Judy Jeffrey have learned to harness the power of paradox and the importance of embracing both standards and soul. By arriving at Stage Three, itself, those involved have learned to connect the best of Stage One (direction and consistency) with the best of Stage Two (local initiative and commitment). When Stephen Covey (1989) talks about moving from dependence to independence to interdependence, he is describing exactly the same journey. It sounds a lot like the developmental process of growing up—moving from infancy through adolescence to maturity. If so, what if there is something prescriptive about the sequence of stages involved in the learning journey (i.e., it has to be this way)? It is tempting to hypothesize the following:

- It is not possible to miss any of the stages.

- It is not possible to move from Stage One to Stage Three without experiencing Stage Two; there are no short cuts!

- If Stage Two is not experienced, you will continue to crave it.

- If Stage Two is not experienced, you cannot learn its limitations. No amount of telling is an adequate substitute for experiential learning.

- If Stage Two is not experienced, Stage Three will be a continuation of Stage One (and, therefore, won't be Stage Three at all).

■ Stage Three—the synthesis—not only contains elements of the previous stages, but is synergistically different.

In Stage Three, another level of development is achieved (while not being possible without the experience of the other stages), which constitutes a qualitatively different plane—a much more complex level of development. It is not a case, argues Ackoff (1994), of mere addition. Metaphorically, he contends, an automobile is not the sum of its parts but the product of their interactions. The properties of the whole, he says, are not possessed by any one part. The parts are necessary but not sufficient: it is only through their dynamic interplay that the system emerges.

Ackoff's apt metaphor speaks to developments in Iowa and elsewhere in two ways. First, much of the denunciatory research on site-based decision making (SBDM) was conducted when sites were struggling with the independence that characterizes Stage Two. SBDM was yet to find its true purpose. It is best seen as one contributing ingredient within a wider scheme of things. It is only during Stage Three that the true purpose of SBDM is discovered and it disappears into the mix of ingredients that constitute school improvement.

Returning to Ackoff's metaphor, the critical research on SBDM is the equivalent of blaming a car part for not being a major means of transportation. Second, it is a short step to seeing a community school district in the same light as the car—as a fully functioning, systemic mix of different but complementary parts. This is a very different view of a school district and is certainly a far cry from seeing it as a level in some "command and control" hierarchy of line management (Stage One) or as an irritating interruption during the fragmented, heady, if somewhat hedonistic days of laissez-faire self-expression (Stage Two). The district, in this new interpretation, is an organic system, which is more than the sum of its parts. Each part of the system—including each school building—makes its contribution (a crucial concept in this context) toward the functioning of the whole.

Moreover, in being akin to Maslow's self-motivating, self-regulating, and self-actualizing organism, such a district system accepts the need for internal accountability and reporting. In the absence of mandated state standards, the members of educational communities across Iowa have not only created their own standards, but also have used them to guide and assess their progress. The locally-generated combination of externally-referenced standards and the comprehensive assessment of student learning gives a school district the best of both worlds: objective reality and subjective meaning.

The irony is that scores of school districts across Iowa (i.e., those that have arrived at Stage Three status) are more than ready to deal with the challenges of the same federal legislation that would seem to be treating them as Stage One beginners. They may not take too kindly to this. Another irony is that the more you have top-down, mechanistic accountability, the more incapacitated you become and the less you have the will, capability, and psychological resources (capacity) to act. In other words, as Charles Handy would say, you are unable to learn and, therefore, unable to change.

Another irony, therefore, is that on the same day (06/11/2003) that the *Des Moines Register* carried the announcement of Iowa's successful application to be included in *NCLB* and President Bush's endorsement of those educators who "are embracing a new level of accountability, which is creating a new culture for our nation's schools: a culture of achievement, *a culture of results over process*," in its editorial columns it announced that "Schools have been clipped again. The 2003 [State] Legislature eliminated a $10 million program called Phase III, which provided most of the money the state spends on professional development for teachers."

The federal government may well be correct in its thinking that, too often in the past, process was unintentionally over-emphasized at the expense of results in education. What is necessary to realize, however, is that results *depend* on process. While you can have process without results, you cannot have results without process.

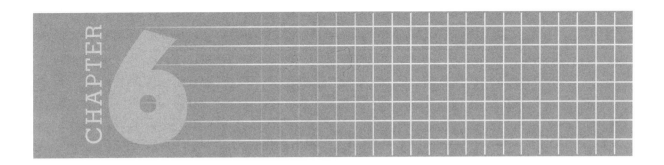

CHAPTER SIX: THE NATION AND BEYOND

The United Kingdom as a Case Study

As Michael Fullan (2001) has remarked, all of us involved in the pursuit of leaving no child behind might want to keep at least one eye on current events in the United Kingdom. Having made a visit to England in April 2003, this author would definitely concur with Fullan's advice.

Given the fact that, traditionally, this is the time for the annual conferences of the three major teacher unions and the hyperbole tends to be heightened, education in the UK seems to be—to put it mildly—in crisis. Indeed, judging by press reports alone, the present system might well be in its death throes. The national curriculum and the national assessment system both seem to be ailing amidst a cacophony of ground level protests and political rhetoric. For those that think that increased centralized control is the only solution to educational improvement, the UK experience would seem to be a salutary one.

Newspapers in the UK are trumpeting the bad news. Student unruliness, angry and frustrated teachers, budget cuts and staff redundancies, threatened union militancy, the continuing debate over assessment—these are all issues that are keeping education in the headlines.

Deteriorating Student Behavior

The issue of student behavior seems to be the touchstone for much of the teacher frustration and resentment. For example, in *The Times* (04/24/03), under the headline, "Classroom Anarchy," education correspondent Sally Morris reports that disruptive behavior is getting worse and that some pupils are "unteachable." Indeed, she says, disruptive pupil behavior in the classroom is now endemic. According to Morris, it is one of the most frequently cited problems facing teachers who feel that they have fewer and fewer options when battling to contain children who have no apparent interest in learning. Quoted in the same article is David Bell, the chief inspector of schools nationwide, who referred in his latest report to a "hard core of pupils with no social skills" whose language is "offensive," who have "little or no understanding of how to behave sensibly," and who are "unteachable." According to the same article:

- Verbal and physical abuse of teachers by students is on the increase.

- Parental control (and interest) is declining.

- The number of disillusioned teachers leaving the profession, now one in three, is rising.

- Some students seem unable to sit still and listen and, perhaps as a result of computer and television habits, expect to be entertained rather than to participate in an education process.

- The problems are particularly severe with boys and are not confined to urban areas.

- Of 2,500 teachers questioned in the latest National Union of Teachers' survey, 80% thought that standards of student behavior had deteriorated during their time in teaching and that even children in nursery schools are now displaying high levels of unacceptable actions ranging from offensive language to abusive comments and threats.

- In the same survey, one in twelve teachers claimed to have been threatened by parents on a regular basis.

Four changes are called for:

1. Teacher training should be made available concerning how to deal with abusive pupils and those that commit low-level, day-after-day disruption, thus damaging the learning of other students. Such training, says Morris, should focus on the psychology of control, including how to introduce incentives and rewards for acceptable behavior.

2. More professional help should be made available for persistent, serious offenders.

3. Parents should be enlisted as allies, although as psychologist Nick Barlow points out in the same article, many children come from over-controlling backgrounds where they are so used to being told off that it has no effect when used by teachers.

4. The Government should implement its plans to invest $700 million over the next three years in a new national behavior and attendance strategy. If it helps teachers to stop being undermined by the behavior of some pupils, concludes Morris, it will be money well spent. If not, she says, anarchy in the classroom will only get worse.

Several other newspaper articles connect the upsurge in student unruliness with policies concerning the inclusion of special needs students in mainstream schools and classrooms. In one article in *The Daily Telegraph* (04/17/03), for instance, under the headline "Increasingly Unruly Students," inclusion is singled out as making the "majority suffer." According to a speaker at one of the Easter teacher union conferences, the inclusion of children with special needs in mainstream classes makes education a lottery for the majority of students. The article continues:

- Classes are continually disrupted while teachers stop to deal with pupils with behavioral problems.

- The inclusion of a minority causes the majority to be neglected.

- Special schools are under threat as LEAs move children with disabilities that cause emotional and behavioral problems, such as autism, into primary schools and secondary comprehensives.

- Many teachers remain silent, afraid that their criticism of inclusion could be seen as a reluctance to embrace all children.

- Because of a shortage of skilled support staff, for most of the week, class teachers are often on their own with a "highly volatile cocktail of children with a huge range of needs."

The drumbeat continues. In the same newspaper (04/23/03), the "failed policy of inclusion through which thousands of children with emotional and behavioral problems have joined mainstream classes" is again singled out as the culprit. It is a no-win situation, says the feature writer. Because the included students do not get the time and attention they need, they become alienated in the mainstream schools that do not have the resources and expertise to help them. And, in the meantime, other children are missing out on their share of education and teachers are imploding because the problems they face are so large and varied. According to a Teacher Union spokesperson:

> We welcome the inclusion of any child with disabilities who can cope and has the potential to learn in the mainstream, provided sufficient resources are available, but we oppose the ideological commitment to include all youngsters without the recognition that at times special provision must be made for those who need the more amenable surroundings of a special school.

Many educators support inclusion in principle, concludes the article, but not at the price that children and their teachers have to pay. Children with challenging behavior are not being educated according to their needs in mainstream classes.

In two other articles, a parent and a teacher join the debate, both arguing that the current system is failing the more able students. In "Crossing the Great Divide" (*The Times*, 04/24/03), Jill Parkin explains why she has reluctantly decided to send her daughter to a private secondary school. In the country's secondary schools, she claims, equality has become synonymous with mediocrity. She comments:

> I wish I had a week's [school] fees for every time I have heard that 'bright children will be fine, wherever they go.' It may be true, but

doing fine is not quite enough. Education should stretch you, meet your needs and show you delights ahead....Without education we are what one of Kipling's short-story characters calls 'the beast without background,' cut adrift from our history and able to consume only the empty calories of the market....While we were told that grammar [selective state] schools formerly failed our less able children, now we are failing the brightest ones, most of all those who live in poorer areas. Yes, we need to value our plumbers as much as our doctors. We need both. But they are different, and need different educations.

According to a secondary teacher, Frances Childs, disruptive children are preventing their well-behaved classmates from reaching their academic potential. In a *Daily Telegraph* article (04/23/03) entitled "Gifted Pupils Have Special Needs, Too", she explains:

Like many others, our school suffers from a shortage of teachers. It is not easy, on a teacher's salary, to have things such as a car and a home of one's own that most professionals see as their right. But, much more than the money, what is driving teachers out of the classroom is the behaviour of pupils with emotional and behavioral difficulties who ought not to be in mainstream schools.

They are there because special schools, staffed by teachers trained to deal with disturbed children, are being shut down. Of course, with their high teacher-pupil ratios, special schools are expensive to run. But the official reason for closing them is that children with severely challenging behaviour should not be made to feel excluded from normal society. Teaching them in special schools, policy makers would have us believe, stigmatizes them. Yet such children cannot cope in mainstream schools, academically and emotionally. They experience only failure and disappointment.

At the same time, well-behaved children are being deprived of their right to a decent education. The time I should be spending with pupils who do not have special needs is being taken up by those who in the past would have been receiving psychiatric help. But they are not. Instead, they are in mainstream schools with staff who do not have the skills either to help or control them.

During the endless meetings about children with special needs, says the same teacher, her mind often turns to those children who have special needs because they are gifted—those, she says, who might have been brilliant.

Resurgent Union Militancy

Faced with the kind of problems outlined above, teacher unions in the UK are increasingly voicing the concerns of their members and in more militant ways. While the Government's education minister has come out fighting and accused the most militant union of "posturing and sloganizing" and questioned whether its members should even be teaching children, the union is contemplating strike action for four main reasons:

- the kind of student behavior issues mentioned above

- funding problems leading to budget cuts and teacher redundancies

- the projected use of unqualified classroom assistants to teach lessons in place of teachers in some circumstances

- national curriculum tests taken by two million students aged 7, 11, and 14

According to *The Observer* newspaper (04/20/03), the industrial action that has been called for over the spending cuts in thousands of schools would be the first major action taken by teachers since 1994. One typical teacher reaction to the budget cuts is this letter to the editor of the *Daily Telegraph* (04/19/03):

> Teachers and assistants at our thriving school spent the last two weeks before the Easter holiday complying with redundancy procedures. We have submitted profiles and CVs [Curriculum Vitaes], and we will be told whose contracts are to be terminated on our return after Easter.
>
> [Our LEA] is being forced to lay off teaching staff. Budgets are already pared to the bone. The national curriculum is delivered at an unrelenting pace. There are constant assessments and endless paperwork.
>
> Many children are ill equipped to concentrate, let alone sit still. Teaching assistants are not a luxury in a class of 30 infants; they are essential. A highly trained workforce is about to be lost.

Beyond the stress caused by cuts and redundancies, two large policy differences are dividing the major teacher unions. In January 2003, the largest union, the National Union of Teachers (NUT), refused to sign the workload agreement with the Government that aims to reduce teachers' hours in return for the use of classroom assistants. For teachers, the intended benefits include fewer overall hours and guaranteed time within the normal school day for planning, preparation, and assessment. The second largest union, the National Association of Schoolmasters and Union of Women Teachers (NASUWT) was a signatory to the workload agreement. A second disputed issue is the threatened NUT boycott of next year's national assessments. In an article entitled "Teacher Unions Split Over Boycotting Tests" (*The Daily Telegraph*, 04/22/03), the NASUWT decision not to join the projected boycott was announced. According to a spokesperson:

> What exactly are they planning to boycott anyway...The tests for 11- and 14-year-olds are set externally and delivered to schools for head teachers to administer and are then marked externally...Does the NUT plan to boycott the teaching which prepares pupils for the tests, in which case it would be a very serious development if they refuse to carry out their contractual obligations to teach children.

This statement is somewhat disingenuous, however, as the NASUWT tends to represent secondary teachers and the NUT teachers in primary schools where there are more on-site responsibilities for test administration. Even the NASUWT members, however, are concerned about examination overload and may campaign for an end to tests for 7- and 14-year-olds, but not those for children aged 11 (which is the age for transferring from primary to secondary schools). In calling for a dialogue about possible alternative methods of assessment, this union would like to see a less formal means of assessment for children part way through their primary and secondary schooling, and possibly one which took into account more than just the three core subjects—English, mathematics, and science. Another of their concerns is how test scores are currently used to construct league tables.

The 200 schools in one LEA, Bradford, found themselves at the bottom of the education league tables and experienced two repercussions. A private company took over the running of the local education authority and improvement targets were established based on results in examinations—the SATs (Standard Assessment Tests) for 7-, 11-, and 14-year-olds and the pre-existing national examinations for 15-year-olds (GCSEs). Now, however, according to a *Daily Telegraph* article (04/19/03), the beleaguered education authority wants to lower the examination and test targets to give the private company running its schools more of a chance to earn $3 million in bonuses. In addition, says the article, Bradford's schools are also having to cut budgets and shed staff, leading to larger as well as mixed-age classes and a heavier burden on the teachers who remain.

Political Capital

As always, education is highly political, so the recent turmoil is clearly providing rich fodder for the opposition Tory party. Damian Green, the Shadow Education Secretary and his party's spokesperson, made the rounds of the Easter conferences, saying that a Tory government would abolish the national targets and questioning the Government's "addiction to centralization" that he claims has met the needs of neither parents nor of teachers. Speaking at the NASUWT conference and reported in *The Times* (04/24/03), he declares:

> If politicians are to allow schools to meet the challenges that they should be meeting, we must spend the coming decade setting them free and giving more choice to all involved in education. The current system is broken, and a sea-change is necessary.

Speaking earlier at the NUT conference and reported in the *Daily Telegraph* (04/22/03), he maintains: "I'm the first aspiring education secretary to say he wants less power not more." Again, he claims that a Conservative government would make a "bonfire of exam targets", arguing:

> The targets in primary schools have actually damaged the opportunities for children to learn, because teachers have been forced to teach towards the tests, not towards the goal of a broad, high-quality education.

Warming to his task, Mr. Green says the root cause of most current problems in education is an approach that says everything must come from the top-down.

> Teachers are disillusioned with the Government's centralized approach, which has turned you into form fillers and worn down your professional autonomy....This culture has transferred decisions that teachers should be making—on the curriculum, on standards, on discipline—to faceless bureaucrats. The effect has been devastating. It's no wonder so many teachers are saying, 'I've had enough.'

Government, he says, should have the role in education of an enabler, not an enforcer.

> I believe that the role of the Government is to give you the tools to perform the job and then let you get on with it, not the other way round.

The Tories would slim down the national curriculum, reduce the exam burden and amount of paperwork, and treat teachers as professionals.

> We will trust your professional judgment and let you do what you do best—teach....I want the school to be the most important institution in the education world, not the Department for Education.

These interesting comments by Damian Green are somewhat disingenuous on two counts. On the one hand, it was a Tory government that introduced the national curriculum and national assessments in the first place and, on the other, according to *The Times* reporter, the Tory rallying cry for more local choice is the precursor to the introduction of an education voucher system. According to the same article, the Tory party is edging closer to advocating a form of education voucher that would enable parents to opt out of failing state schools. In his speech to the NASWUT conference, however, while he announced his party's intention to introduce a scheme to give more power to parents who can't exercise any choice at present, Damian Green shied away from describing the scheme as a voucher, declaring that the scheme was intended to provide choice for parents who could not afford to move to areas that had better schools. Clearly, "choice" is a central issue in these debates.

Given this current amount of educational turmoil in the UK, what are its immediate antecedents?

According to Mike Baker, education correspondent for BBC News in the UK, England's recent educational history is a "Cautionary Tale for the Bush Education Reforms." Writing in *Education Week* (10/31/01), he describes the steps that were taken to reform the education system in the UK.

1. Just over a decade ago, Margaret Thatcher's government introduced mandatory testing in English, mathematics, and science for students at ages 7, 11, 14, and 16. The move, says Baker, arose from a sense of public crisis over student achievement similar to that felt by Americans. As a consequence, however:

   > Just as in the United States, the English reforms were opposed by the teachers' unions and seen as a threat to the autonomy of schools and local school districts. Parents worried their children would be burdened by excessive testing and liberal educators warned that regularly weighing the pig would do nothing to add to its weight.

   > But this opposition was briskly swept aside as Mrs. Thatcher set her laser-beam gaze on school reform. The changes were sweeping. Centralizing powers, the like of which no U.S. president could even dream of, were taken by national government.

Indeed, just as it is easier in the United States for a Republican president to extend federal powers over schools, similarly, only a Conservative administration in Britain could have achieved this. Critics would have denounced such reforms as creeping socialism if they had come from a left-of-center government.

2. The Thatcher administration then established national standards in all main academic subjects and, in so doing, created a national curriculum that details precisely what each child should learn in each grade.

3. The next move was to align the national tests with the national curriculum. In Baker's evocative language, he describes:

> England's mandatory testing was designed as a form of handcuffs, chaining teachers to the national curriculum. Only this way could policymakers be sure the national standards were being followed.

4. The effective nationalization of England's schools was maintained, even accelerated, under Tony Blair's Labour Party administration. Indeed, says Baker, the Blair government's first act after the 1997 election was to "name and shame" England's worst-performing schools. It toughened the penalties for school failure by introducing the so-called "Fresh Start" policy, requiring failing schools to be closed and then reopened with a new name and new staff.

5. Blair's government kept up the pressure by narrowing the national curriculum and increasing the emphasis on mathematics and English in elementary schools. Ambitious national targets were set for the annual test results and schools and school districts were judged against these targets.

6. In Baker's estimation, the most ambitious move yet was the creation of a "literacy hour" and a "numeracy hour." These national templates for daily English and mathematics lessons were set out in unprecedented detail, giving teachers a minute-by-minute structure for lessons and even telling them how to organize the classroom furniture.

7. In order to complete the reform package, regular assessment of teaching quality was instigated. A national department for inspecting schools, the Office for Standards in Education, known as OFSTED, was created, to check on teaching quality. In its early years, says Baker, OFSTED was almost universally hated by teachers, who saw the presence of inspectors in the classroom as threatening and punitive. Yet, while it was sometimes too heavy-handed, the existence of OFSTED meant it was possible to do more than just identify, and penalize, failing schools. It was also possible to explain why they were failing.

Michael Fullan, in his 2001 book, *Leading in a Culture of Change*, takes up the story. Fullan was a member of the University of Toronto team that was hired to monitor and assess the entire National Literacy and Numeracy Strategy (NLNS) as it unfolded during the 1998 to 2000 period. As Fullan (2001) acknowledges, this work amounted to a very large case study involving a whole country, 20,000 schools, and 7 million students up to age 11. It was the ambition of the national strategy that clearly impressed Fullan. As he says, when the new government was formed in 1997, Tony Blair, the Prime Minister, declared that his three priorities were "education, education, education."

> We have heard that before, but this government goes further. It says that the initial core goal is to raise the literacy and numeracy achievement of children up to age eleven. The government sets specific targets. The baseline they observe is that the percentage of 11-year-olds scoring 4 or 5 on the test of literacy was 57 percent in 1996 (level 4 being the level at which proficiency standards are met); for numeracy the baseline was 54 percent. The minister announces that the targets for 2002 are 80 percent for literacy (up from 57 percent) and 75 percent for numeracy (up from 54 percent). He makes a commitment that he will resign as secretary of state if those targets are not met (Fullan, 2001).

From the outset, says Fullan, the leaders of the initiative in the Department of Education and Employment were determined to "use the change knowledge base" to design a set of pressure-and-support strategies to accomplish their goal of raising student achievement. Michael Barber (2000), who was appointed to head up the government initiative, has summarized the main elements of what amounts to a comprehensive set of strategies, some of which have already been touched upon in Baker's article. They include

- a nationally prepared project plan for both literacy and numeracy, setting out actions, responsibilities, and deadlines through to 2002;

- a substantial financial investment sustained over at least six years and skewed toward those schools that need most help;

- a project infrastructure involving national direction from the Standards and Effectiveness Unit, fifteen regional directors, and over 300 expert consultants at the local level for each of the two subject areas;

- an expectation that every class will have a daily mathematics lesson and a daily literacy hour;

- a detailed teaching program covering every school year for children from ages five to eleven;

- an emphasis on early intervention and catch up for pupils who fall behind;

- a professional development program designed to enable every primary school teacher to learn to understand and use proven best practices in both curriculum areas;

- the appointment of over 2,000 leading mathematics teachers and hundreds of expert literacy teachers who have the time and skill to model best practices for their peers;

- the provision of "intensive support" to about half of all schools where the most progress is required;

- a major investment in books for schools (over 23 million new books have been put into the system since 1997);

- the removal of barriers to implementation—especially a huge reduction in the prescribed curriculum content outside the core subjects;

- regular monitoring and extensive evaluation by the national inspection agency, OFSTED;

- a national curriculum for initial teacher training requiring all providers to prepare new primary school teachers to teach the daily mathematics lesson and the literacy hour;

- a problem-solving philosophy involving early identification of difficulties as they emerge and the provision of rapid solutions or interventions where necessary;

- the provision of extra after-school, weekend, and holiday booster classes for those who need extra help to reach the standards.

Based on his close association with the project, Fullan (2001) concludes:

> The impact of the strategies on achievement, measured as a percentage of pupils reaching levels 4 or 5, is in many ways astounding (recall that twenty thousand schools are involved). By the year 2000, the whole country had progressively moved from 57 percent proficient achievement in literacy in 1996 to 75 percent; and from 54 percent to 72 percent in numeracy. We have no doubt that the targets of 80 percent and 75 percent will be achieved by 2002, although I do not present it as a problem-free case because a preoccupation with achievement scores can have negative side effects, such as narrowing the curriculum that is taught and burning people out as they relentlessly chase targets.

As it has turned out, Fullan's projections proved incorrect—perhaps for the very factors he cites as problematical. Put simply, Fullan is wrong because he's right. In *The Guardian* newspaper (12/05/02), under the headline "Teacher Training Drive to Lift Results. Minister Says Targets Will Be Hit Next Year," education correspondent Rebecca Smithers reports that the government did not achieve its targets in 2002 as expected to do so. According to Smithers, the target for mathematics was 75% of all eleven-year-olds reaching at least level 4 and, in the event, 73% achieved this target. The target for English was more ambitious (80%), but the achievement rate stayed static at 75%.

A spokesperson said he was confident that the government would hit the 2002 targets the following year, before "more challenging" targets of 85% come into force in 2004. While the government ruled out the prospect of a review of its strategy, it did set out a package of further measures to raise national test results—especially in the lowest-attaining schools. It was announced that 5,000 head teachers and their deputies would be given training to help them improve their school's performance in English and mathematics in the key stage two tests taken by 11-year-olds in their final year of primary school, while teachers would also get extra training in phonics instruction to raise standards in reading. In addition, further work would be done to target poor standards of writing among boys.

Although the education secretary did not have to resign (he had already moved to another government position), the government's strategy would seem to be stalling and, given the furor encountered in April 2003, there would seem to be doubts about its future. Four factors seem to be contributing to the hiatus:

- a crisis of leadership

- too much "noise in the system"

- a failure to create a satisfactory balance between accountability and autonomy at the local level

- many students don't seem to be going along with the program, despite the constant emphasis on student achievement

Leadership

In terms of the leadership question, Fullan (2001) points out that, according to Goleman (2000), there are six leadership styles: coercive (the leader demands compliance); authoritative (the leader mobilizes people toward a vision); affiliative (the leader creates harmony and builds emotional bonds); democratic (the leader forges consensus through participation); pacesetting (the leader sets high standards for performance); and coaching (the leader develops people for the future). According to Goleman's research, two of the six styles adversely affect organizational climate and, in turn, performance and productivity: the coercive style (people resent and resist) and the pacesetting style (people get overwhelmed and burn out). All four other styles positively impact climate and performance. Based on Goleman's findings, therefore, Fullan (2001) comments on the styles employed in the situation in England.

> There can be a fine line between coercive and authoritative leadership. Certainly the strategy in England has elements of coercive as well as pacesetting leadership. Is this degree of pressure required to get large-scale change under way? We don't really know, but I would venture to say that the strategy that moved the English school system from near-chaos to a modicum of success is not the same strategy that is going to create the transformation needed for the system to thrive in the future. For that you need plenty of internal commitment and ingenuity. School systems all over the world, take heed.

While, the national strategy has plenty of moral purpose to justify it (Fullan says that "getting thousands of students to be literate and numerate who otherwise would not be so is not a bad day's work. This is bound to make a difference in many lives."), moral purpose, he says, cannot just be stated, it must be accompanied by strategies for realizing it, and those strategies are the leadership actions that energize people to pursue a desired goal. Moreover, the way leaders lead may have to change during the change process. The pacesetting and coercive/commanding styles, for instance, may work in the short term, but not the long term as, according to Fullan (2002), they serve to demotivate people and do not develop capacity and commitment. Sustainability of initiatives, he says, is very much tied to the application of those leadership styles that do motivate, develop people, and generate their commitment.

Those in charge of the NLNS in England would seem to have received this message. According to Sir Michael Bichard, the permanent secretary at the Department for Education and Employment in England:

> For me leadership is about creating a sense of purpose and direction. It's about getting alignment and it's about inspiring people to achieve....[There is a] need to enthuse staff and encourage a belief in the difference their organization is making—whether it is a school or a government department. We can do a lot by making heroes of the people who deliver. It's important to make people feel part of a success story. That's what they want to be.

Judging by the press reports covered in this chapter, however, this would not seem to be the case. This makes Fullan's (2001) comments all the more prescient. Talking about the possibility of "collateral damage," he reflects:

- Do other subjects like the arts suffer?

- Are schools becoming preoccupied only by the test results?

- Are teachers getting burnt out?

- Will short-term success be followed by deeper failure?

- Is the strategy really inspiring principals and teachers to do better? How deep is their commitment?

- Is it the difference between what Argyris (2000) calls external commitment and internal commitment? Has the former been gained, but not the latter? Is it fallacious to believe that the one can lead to the other? As Fullan (2001) concludes:

> In order to go deeper, for example, to get at the creative ideas and energies of teachers, additional leadership strategies will be needed—strategies that will foster internal commitment (that is, commitment activated by intrinsically rewarding accomplishments).
>
> Unless, of course, it's too late and the gaining of too much external commitment is the very thing that now stands in the way of gaining internal commitment. Maybe both should have been included from the outset. Given what the newspapers are saying, the omens are not good. Maybe, as the saying goes, it's a case of too much water has gone under the bridge.

Disturbance

Fullan (2001), echoing Pascale, Millemann, and Gioja (2000) makes a telling point.

> Living systems cannot be *directed* along a linear path. Unforeseen consequences are inevitable. The challenge is to *disturb* them in a manner that approximates the desired outcome.

Fullan admits, however, that there is productive disturbance and unproductive disturbance and taking on all innovations that come along is not the productive kind. Using the same kind of argument as in Workbook One: *Conceptualizing a New Path*, Fullan (2001) observes:

> In schools, for example, the main problem is not the absence of innovations but the presence of too many disconnected, episodic, piecemeal, superficially adorned projects...schools are suffering the additional burden of having a torrent of unwanted, uncoordinated policies and innovations raining down on them from hierarchical bureaucracies. Many superintendents (of the pacesetter style) compound the problem with relentless "projectitis."

Thomas Hatch (2000) has shown what happens "when multiple innovations collide." As a result of so many reforms and so little time to do them, he says:

> Rather than contributing to substantial improvements, adopting improvement programs may also add to the endless cycle of initiatives that seem to sap the strength and spirit of schools and their communities.

In language very similar to that used in the English newspaper stories quoted in this chapter, Hatch (2000) talks about the frustration and anger of teachers and administrators who feel "we're over our heads" trying desperately to deal with too many affiliations with ill-assorted reform initiatives. In such circumstances, unproductive disturbance is clearly holding sway. Unlike at Bryant School where the inclusion of special education students has enriched the instructional mix, inclusion in the UK is clearly seen as yet another initiative (for which educators are ill-prepared), which is a distraction and undermining factor in terms of the efforts to implement the National Literacy and Numeracy Strategy.

Productive disturbance occurs, according to Fullan (2001), when "guided by moral purpose and when the process creates and channels new tensions while working on a complex problem." Put another way, and this is the genius of Bryant, what are generated are variations on a theme—each variation being used to reinforce, solidify, expand, and strengthen the original theme. It is the process of "layering" (that the Bryant staff apply to student development) applied to school development. Such a process, because of its nonlinear nature, has to be somewhat proactive and planned for, but equally reactive, opportunistic, even exploitative—and definitely, creative.

Accountability and Autonomy

One of the tensions running through the National Literacy and Numeracy Strategy in England is how to reconcile both accountability and local autonomy. Indeed, in his perceptive article entitled "Accountability vs. Autonomy," Mike Baker (2001) explains how the one was promoted above the other to the detriment of the whole initiative. Given the elevation of accountability over autonomy, he says, benefits have accrued.

- Standards of basic literacy and numeracy are undoubtedly higher.

- Failing schools cannot so easily hide poor performance from parents and their communities.

- The examination of what does, and what does not, work in the classroom provides a helpful guide to future growth.

Stemming from the punitive tinge to the reforms, however, the downside has been considerable.

- "Naming and shaming" schools, Baker (2001) says, was a disaster. "It was about as likely to achieve rehabilitation as throwing medieval miscreants in the stocks. It is now recognized that failing schools need more help and more money, not less."

- There are also signs (including many recent examples of "Letters to the Editor" in the British press) that parents feel the expansion of mandatory testing may have gone too far.

  A new government-inspired test for 17-year-olds, introduced in 2000, proved the final straw, provoking an angry reaction from students and parents, who now feel testing is obstructing learning. Once middle-class, suburban parents get restive, governments need to watch out.

  Glenn Frankel (2002) has explained the debacle for American audiences (in an article titled "In Britain, a Grade-A Scandal: Accusations of Result-Tinkering Threaten High School Test"). What is relevant here is not the story itself , which centers on examination rigging affecting university entrance and is a veritable "who-done-it," but the impression that parents are getting: that the government is obsessed with examinations, testing, and the accountability they afford, but at what cost.

- According to Baker (2001), however, the most serious negative aspect is that the reforms have been *done* to, rather than *with*, the teachers. The teaching profession, he says, has not been a stakeholder in the new curriculum or the new teaching methods. This has so demoralized existing teachers and deferred many potential recruits, that the biggest threat to school quality in England is now a shortage of teachers. Indeed, he says, one pattern stands out in countries where accountability measures have undermined teachers' autonomy: there is now a recruitment crisis. Britain's cautionary tale, therefore, is that policymakers must involve teachers in the reform process.

The warning is there. Somewhere along the road of England's school reforms, the policymakers took their eye off the ball. It is as if the football coach had worked out the most careful and detailed theoretical plays only to look up, on the day of the game, to find his players had lost interest and gone home with the ball.

■ Accountability, Baker (2001) concludes, must be balanced by professional autonomy. Formerly, he explains, teachers in England had high autonomy and low accountability; the reforms of the past decade, however, have tilted things to an opposite imbalance and there is now low autonomy and high accountability, resulting in a demoralized, devalued teaching profession and a crisis in teacher recruitment. What is required, he says, is high accountability and high autonomy.

What both the United States and the United Kingdom need is a balance: both high accountability and high autonomy for teachers. Not one or the other, but both.

This is clearly a major theme running through this workbook. What Peter Block (2001 and 2003), Michael Fullan (2001), and Richard Elmore (2000) have all explored comes down to this question: How do you harness both high accountability and high autonomy at the local level? However counter-intuitive the combination may sound, clearly it is what is required and, to its undying credit, it is what has been explored in the state of Iowa over the last ten to fifteen years.

Richard DuFour (2003) has drawn our attention to the need for educators to combine seemingly opposing ideas. They err, he says, when they resolve apparent dichotomies by choosing one approach or the other. Citing the work of James Collins and Jerry Porras, co-authors of *Built to Last: Successful Habits of Visionary Companies* (1994), DuFour says that successful organizations embrace the paradox of living with two seemingly contradictory forces at the same time. They reject the "Tyranny of the Or" and embrace the "Genius of the And." Instead of choosing between A and B, says DuFour, these organizations figured out how to have both A and B. DuFour quotes Collins and Porras who argue:

> We are not talking about balance here. Balance implies going to the mid-point, 50-50, half and half....[A] highly visionary company doesn't want to blend yin and yang into a gray, indistinguishable circle that is neither highly yin nor highly yang; it aims to be distinctly yin and distinctly yang, both at the same time, all the time.

For system leaders, concludes DuFour (2003), it means allowing autonomy within defined parameters—autonomy within the accountability that comes with expectations.

> Superintendents [and other educational leaders] who reject the 'Tyranny of the Or' and embrace the 'Genius of the And' are skillful in demonstrating 'loose-tight leadership' or 'directed autonomy.' They focus on identifying and articulating both the fundamental purpose of the organization and a few 'big ideas' that will help the district improve in its capacity to achieve that purpose. They are tight on purpose and big ideas—insisting that those within the organization act in ways consistent with those concepts and demanding that the district align all of its practices and programs with them.
>
> At the same time, however, they encourage individual and organizational autonomy in the day-to-day operations of the various schools and departments. This autonomy is not characterized by random acts of innovation, but rather is guided by carefully defined parameters that give focus and direction to schools and those within them (DuFour, 2003).

While DuFour (2003) largely confines his comments to superintendents and local school districts, the principles at stake here are pertinent to any level of the educational system as Richard Elmore (2000) and Michael Fullan (2001) have both contended. Living with both accountability and autonomy may not, however, be an easy co-existence. While exploring the British press, for example, the author came across this article in the *Daily Telegraph* (04/18/03) that is "slanted" politically and has nothing and everything to do with education. The article is a description of the financial woes of the Royal Mint, which seem to have been partly caused by moves toward "localism" which itself, says the article, is "quite the buzzword in Westminster." According to the article:

> It [localism] is a step short of privatization, whereby control over public services is devolved from Whitehall. It all sounds terribly attractive, as it reduces the power of bureaucrats in London and is supposed to create 'public sector entrepreneurs.' It also, we're told, shifts liabilities off the Treasury's balance sheet.
>
> But localism is potentially a recipe for disaster as the Public Accounts Committee found this week in its investigation into the Royal Mint. In an early experiment in localism, the Royal Mint was given control over its own affairs. But step-by-step, this autonomy also resulted in its accountability being diluted. With the Mint 'localized,' nobody has taken responsibility.

> If the State does not run services directly, it would be better if they were privatized altogether. At least, they would then be accountable to their owners and, hopefully, their customers. The hole in the Royal Mint goes to show that which nobody owns, nobody cares for.

The Piper Alpha disaster provides a similar message. Piper Alpha was an oil platform in the North Sea that caught fire and exploded on July 6, 1988. As an analysis by researchers at Rice University would indicate, it was the worst ever offshore petroleum accident, during which 167 people died and a billion dollar platform was almost totally destroyed. The court of inquiry discovered that a chance combination of factors caused the accident. One factor, however, intrigued the team of investigators. Previously, much reliance had been placed on the auditing efforts of external evaluators. Those on site, however, didn't pay much attention to these inspectors and their recommendations, partly because the external inspections had "robbed" those who were internal to the situation of the will to step up and take responsibility. As Charles Handy would say, the external inspectors had stolen the decisions from those who should be making them.

Peter Senge (1990), with his "limits to growth" theory, helps us understand what is happening in such examples. According to this theory, when any change or set of changes is implemented, there is an initial period of time when a reinforcing and amplifying process is set in motion to produce a desired result. In short, things go well at first. This creates, says Senge, a spiral of success but also creates inadvertent secondary effects (manifested in a balancing process) that eventually serve to slow down the success. Literally, over time, the rot sets in. This principle explains why there is often early growth until the improvement plateaus and maybe even goes into reverse. Senge gives the example of the farmer who increases his yield by adding fertilizer until the crop grows larger than the rainfall of the region can sustain. The initial growth and momentum are very good for participant morale; when the limits to growth are encountered, however, growth mysteriously slows down and levels off and maybe goes in reverse, which is very bad for morale. At this point, explains Senge, people typically react by pushing harder and doing more of the same; after all, doing this worked before. Unfortunately, the more vigorously you push the familiar levers, the more strongly the balancing process resists, and the more futile your efforts become. What you have to do is stop pushing on the growth side and deal with the problems on the limits to growth side. The task is to identify—and remove—the factors limiting growth.

This useful principle helps us understand several phenomena encountered in this workbook.

- ■ It shows us why each of the first two stages of school improvement prospers but then runs out of gas. The first stage becomes too dictatorial and authoritarian and produces a counter reaction; Stage Two, in turn, is popular until it is seen as too permissive and too libertarian. What will happen to Stage Three over time is an interesting question. Will it be able to accommodate the demands of *NCLB* or will *NCLB* produce a new Stage Four?

■ It definitely helps us understand why the momentum of the national changes in England has run out of steam. As Fullan (2002) has concluded:

> In our evaluation of the National Literacy and Numeracy Strategy in England, we found that although literacy and numeracy achievement scores went up in the 1997–2002 period, the morale of teachers, if anything, declined in that same period. Raising achievement scores is one thing, creating a dynamic, engaged teaching profession is another. We are now working with the British to determine what policies would transform the working conditions of teachers.

In addition, those at the Qualifications and Curriculum Authority (QCA), who are responsible for formulating the key stage tests at ages 7, 11, and 14 plus "voluntary" optional tests in between, have realized that their work has helped create an "assessment frenzy." In an interview with the BBC, a QCA spokesperson says that schools are suffering from a culture in which assessment is "an end in itself." He continues:

> I think that the QCA itself probably has fuelled the assessment frenzy by putting so much effort into the optional tests. They may well serve a very useful purpose, but if they're simply used as a training programme for further assessment then they're not fulfilling the fundamental purpose of assessment for learning, which is basically what assessment should be about....We have got to stand back and say there needs to be a proper balance between the time given to teaching and the time given to assessing. And I think at the moment the indications are that we are not giving sufficient time to learning and to preparation at the expense of the examination process.

It is formative learning that's required, the QCA spokesperson concludes, which shouldn't involve "weighing the baby" all the time and spending $350 million annually on testing.

■ In the USA, closer alignment of what is taught (standards and benchmarks) and what is assessed will undoubtedly have an initial impact. Longer term, however, the quality of teaching and student motivation and engagement are much more likely to create the next wave of impact.

The Students

In reading about current educational affairs in the UK, while there are constant references to the ultimate goal of "student achievement," there are precious few references to the students themselves and how they are feeling except in the articles mentioned earlier in this chapter that describe their disruptive behavior and the near-anarchy in the classroom. If the current reforms were being done to rather than *with* teachers, the students would seem to be a further step removed. Indeed, maybe there is some kind of link between this degree of disenfranchisement and the recent reports of bad behavior. If we know anything, we know that the last thing to do to at-risk students is to render them more at-risk by the reforms that we introduce. This is why new (more stringent) attendance policies, block schedules, tighter homework schedules, and increased graduation requirements are all associated with higher dropout rates—especially among the at-risk population. According to psychologist Nick Barlow, who works with this population and is quoted by Sally Morris in her article in *The Times:*

> The children may have problems concentrating in a classroom, but they have no problem concentrating for hours on computer games or the T.V. So perhaps it is that they see no relevance in what they are expected to learn. That is why broad-based policies in schools don't work. The child must be addressed as an individual.

...and as a *whole* individual. It is impossible to separate "academic child" from "social, emotional, and behavioral child." This is why in leaving no child behind, it is the whole child that demands our attention, as the staff at Bryant School would attest.

The very good news from this extended case study is that there are scores of schools across Iowa—*NCLB* notwithstanding—that are valiantly trying to improve the learning of their students. It is fitting, then, to end with this self-assessment from an elementary school in Sioux City, Iowa:

> The staff at Hunt has created a climate of learning for students and adults. Teachers more adeptly use data as a source for decision-making, as they utilize formative and summative data to measure progress and to make instructional decisions. The staff tackles problems collaboratively with a willingness to think outside the box and find creative solutions. With finite blocks of time available, the staff finds ways to work together to carve out opportunities for planning, peer coaching, and practice. Through welcoming colleagues into classrooms and cooperative planning, teachers have created an atmosphere of shared ownership. They view the students as "our" students, not "my" students, and share in celebrating successes.

And they have much to celebrate. This is a school that is making major inroads into the achievement gaps between Low SES students and their counterparts and between the various ethnic groups. This is a school—like Bryant—where increased student achievement is the norm and, as is increasingly the case, not a single child is left behind.

The Nation and Beyond
Task 1: The Impact of Implementing *NCLB*

<u>Purpose:</u> To have an extended opportunity to reflect on events in the British Isles relative to the impact of *NCLB* in the USA.

<u>Grouping:</u> Work with your Learning Team or other small district group.

<u>Directions:</u> Having read about events in the UK in this last chapter, in small groups discuss what might happen in the USA over the next ten years as a result of the implementation of *NCLB*.

About the Author

Peter Holly is the author of the PATHWISE: *Data-Driven School Improvement Series*. Having been a teacher, administrator, researcher, and school improvement consultant in the United Kingdom, since 1990 he has worked solely with schools and school districts in the United States. He was one of the lead consultants for Schools for the Twenty-First Century in Washington State, the National Education Association's (NEA) Learning Lab project, and the New Iowa Schools initiative. Currently, he is an independent school improvement consultant working with school systems mainly in the Midwest. In helping school systems become more change-oriented and data-driven, he uses many of the materials to be found in this workbook.

Notes

242

References

Ackoff, R. (1994). From Mechanistic to Social Systemic Thinking. *The Systems Thinker*. 5(1).

Argyris, C. (2000). *Flawed Advice and the Management Trap*. New York: Oxford University Press.

Armstrong, J. and Anthes, K. (2001). How Data Can Help. *American School Board Journal*. November. Summarized in National Staff Development Council *Results*. (February 2002).

Baker, M. Accountability vs. Autonomy. *Education Week*. 31 October 2001.

Barber, M. (2000). High Expectations and Standards. Unpublished. London: Department of Education and Employment.

Barth, R. (2002). The Culture Builder. *Educational Leadership*. 59(8).

Block, P. (2001). *The Answer to How is Yes*. San Francisco, CA: Berrett-Koehler.

Block, P. (2003). The Answer to 'When?' is 'Now.' *Journal of Staff Development*. 24(2).

Bloomfield, D. and Cooper, B. (2003). NCLB: A New Role for the Federal Government. An Overview of the Most Sweeping Federal Education Law Since 1965. Special Supplement: *Making Sense of NCLB. T.H.E. (Technological Horizons in Education) Journal*. 30(10).

Blum, R. E. and Kneidek, A. W. (1991). Strategic Improvement that Focuses on Student Achievement. *Educational Leadership*. 48(7).

Brimijoin, K., Marquissee, E., and Tomlinson, C. A. (2003). Using Data to Differentiate Instruction. *Educational Leadership*. 60(5).

Burnette, B. (2002). How We Formed Our Community. *Journal of Staff Development*. 23(1).

Calhoun, E. (1994). *How to Use Action Research in the Self-Renewing School*. Alexandria, VA: ASCD.

Calhoun, E. (1997). *Components for Supporting School Improvement for Student Achievement*. Training materials for Every Child Reads. Iowa Department of Education.

Calhoun, E. (1999). *Teaching Beginning Reading and Writing with the Picture Word Inductive Model*. Alexandria, VA: ASCD.

Calhoun, E. (2002). Action Research for School Improvement. *Educational Leadership*. 59(6).

Collins, J. C. and Porras, J. I. (1994). *Built to Last: Successful Habits of Visionary Companies*. New York: Harper Business.

Covey, S. (1989). *Seven Habits of Highly Effective People*. New York: Simon and Schuster.

Csikszentmihalyi, M. (1990). *Flow: The Psychology of Optimal Experience*. New York: Harper and Row.

Danielson, C. (1996). *Enhancing Professional Practice: A Framework for Teaching*. Alexandria, VA: ASCD.

Danielson, C. and McGreal, T. (2000). *Teacher Evaluation to Enhance Professional Practice*. Alexandria, VA: ASCD. Princeton, NJ: Educational Testing Service.

Deojay, T. R. and Pennington, L. L. (2000). Reaching Heather: A Framework for Developing Data-Based Solutions to Student Learning Problems. *Journal of Staff Development. 21*(1).

Dolan, W. P. (1994). *Restructuring Our Schools. A Primer for Systemic Change*. Kansas City, MO: Systems and Organizations.

Doyle, D. (2002). Knowledge-Based Decision-Making. *The School Administrator. 11*(59).

Doyle, D. (2003). Data-Driven Decision-Making. Is It the Mantra of the Month or Does It Have Staying Power? *Making Sense of Data* Special Supplement. *T.H.E. Journal. 30*(10).

Duffy, F. M. (2003). I Think, Therefore I am Resistant to Change. *Journal of Staff Development. 24*(1).

DuFour, R. (2002). Leading Edge. Bring the Whole Staff on Board. *Journal of Staff Development. 23*(3).

DuFour, R. (2003). Building a Professional Learning Community. *The School Administrator. 5*(60).

Ehri, L. C. (1999). Phases of Acquisition in Learning to Read Words and Instructional Implications. Montreal, Canada: Paper presented at the annual meeting of the American Educational Research Association. April.

Elliott, J. (2003). IDEA 2003: Reauthorization or Retrofit? *The School Administrator. 3*(60).

Elmore, R. (1996). Getting to Scale with Good Educational Practice. *Harvard Educational Review. 66*(1).

Elmore, R. (2000). *Building a New Structure for School Leadership*. The Albert Shanker Institute. Winter.

Fontana, L. and Perreault, G. (2001). Problem-Solving Groups. *Journal of Staff Development. 22*(4).

Forsythe, K. and Holly, P. Resilient Students in Resilient Schools (Unpublished).

Frankel, G. In Britain, a Grade-A Scandal: Accusations of Result-Tinkering Threaten High School Test. *Washington Post Foreign Service*. 26 September 2002.

Fullan, M. and Miles, M. B. (1991). Getting Educational Reform Right: What Works, and What Doesn't. *Phi Delta Kappan. 73*(10).

Fullan, M. (1996). Turning Systemic Thinking On Its Head. *Phi Delta Kappan*. February.

Fullan, M. (2001). *Leading in a Culture of Change*. San Francisco, CA: Jossey-Bass.

Fullan, M. (2002). Moral Purpose Writ Large. *The School Administrator*. September.

Fullan, M. (2002). The Change Leader. *Educational Leadership. 59*(8).

Garmston, R. J. (2002). Groupwise. *Journal of Staff Development. 23*(3), 74-75.

Garmston, R. J. and Wellman, B. (1999). *The Adaptive School. A Sourcebook for Developing Collaborative Groups*. Norwood, MA: Christopher Gordon.

Glickman, C. (1990). Pushing School Reform to a New Edge: The Seven Ironies of School Empowerment. *Phi Delta Kappan*. September.

Goleman, D. (2000). Leadership That Gets Results. *Harvard Business Review*. March-April.

Guskey, T. R. (2003). What Makes Professional Development Effective? *Phi Delta Kappan. 84*(10).

Handy, C. (1989). *The Age of Unreason*. London: Hutchinson.

Hatch, T. (2000). *What Happens When Multiple Improvement Initiatives Collide*. Menlo Park, CA: Carnegie Foundation for the Advancement of Teaching.

Hehir, T. (2003). Beyond Inclusion. *The School Administrator. 3*(60).

Holly, P. J. (1991). The Contradictions of School Improvement. Speech given at the Gheens Academy, Louisville, KY.

Holly, P. J. (1998). Three Stages of School Improvement. Unpublished paper, New Iowa Schools Development Corporation (NISDC).

Holly, P. J. (2003). *Data-Driven School Improvement: Conceptualizing a New Path*. Princeton, NJ: Educational Testing Service.

Holly, P. J. and Lange, M. (2000). Classroom assessment training materials. Webster City, IA: The Learning Group.

Holly, P. J. and Munger, L. (2000). *The Implementation of Success4: A Cross-Case Analysis*. Des Moines, IA: Iowa Department of Education.

Huberman, A. M. and Miles, M. B. (1984). *Innovation Up Close: How School Improvement Works*. New York: Plenum Press.

Iowa Department of Education. (2002). *The Annual Condition of Education Report*. Des Moines, IA: Iowa Department of Education.

Johnson, D. and Johnson, F. P. (1999). Effective Staff Development in Cooperative Learning: Training, Transfer, and Long-Term Use. Paper presented at the annual meeting of the American Education Research Association, Montreal, Canada. April.

Johnson, D. and Johnson, F. P. (2000). *Joining Together. Group Theory and Group Skills*. Boston: Allyn and Bacon.

Johnson, R. A. (1993). *Owning Your Own Shadow*. San Francisco, CA: HarperCollins.

Joyce, B., Wolf, J. and Calhoun, E. (1993). *The Self Renewing School*. Alexandria, VA: ASCD.

Keiffer-Barone, S. and Ware, K. (2002). Strategies for Renewal. Organize Teams of Teachers. *Journal of Staff Development*. 23(3).

Kelleher, J. (2003). A Model for Assessment-Driven Professional Development. *Phi Delta Kappan*. 84(10).

Kessler, R. (2002). Nurturing Deep Connections. *The School Administrator*. September.

Lave, J. and Wenger, E. (1991). *Situated Learning: Legitimate Peripheral Participation*. New York: Cambridge University Press.

Levine, D. U. (1991). Creating Effective Schools: Findings and Implications from Research and Practice. *Phi Delta Kappan*. 72(5).

Lewis, A. C. (1998). Student Work. This Focus for Staff Development Leads to Genuine Collaboration. *Journal of Staff Development*. Fall.

Lewis, C. (2002). Everywhere I Looked—Levers and Pendulums. Research Lessons Bring Studies to Life and Energize Teaching. *Journal of Staff Development*. Summer.

Lipsky, D. K. (2003). The Coexistence Of High Standards and Inclusion. *The School Administrator*. 3(60).

Louis, K. S. and Miles, M. B. (1990). *Improving the Urban High School*. New York: Teachers College Press.

Marzano, R. (2000). *Transforming Classroom Grading*. Alexandria, VA: ASCD.

Marzano, R., Pickering, D., and Pollock, J. (2001). *Classroom Instruction that Works: Research-Based Strategies for Increasing Student Achievement*. Alexandria, VA: ASCD.

Miles, K. H. (2003). The Big Picture. *Journal of Staff Development. 24*(3).

National Partnership for Excellence and Accountability in Teaching. (2000). *Characteristics of Effective Professional Development*. Washington DC.

National Staff Development Council. (2001). *Standards for Staff Development*. Oxford, OH: NSDC.

Pascale, R., Millemann, M. and Gioja, L. (2000). *Surfing the Edge of Chaos*. New York: Crown Business Publishing.

Peterson, K. (2002). Positive or Negative. *Journal of Staff Development. 23*(3).

PQ System. (1996). *Pocket Tools for Education*. Miamisburg, OH.

Richardson, J. (2003). The Secrets of 'Can-Do' Schools. NSDC *Results*. February.

Rosenholtz, S. (1986). Organizational Conditions of Teacher Learning. *Teaching and Teacher Education. 2*(2).

Sanborn, J. (2002). Targeted Training. *The School Administrator. 11*(59).

Saphier, J. and King, M. (1985). Good Seeds Grow in Strong Cultures. *Educational Leadership. 42*(6).

Schmoker, M. (2002). Up and Away. Teach, Evaluate, Strategize. That's All It Takes to Turn Performance Around. *Journal of Staff Development. 23*(2).

Schmoker, M. (2003). First Things First: Demystifying Data Analysis. *Educational Leadership. 60*(5).

Schmoker, M. Planning for Failure? *Education Week*. 12 February 2003.

Senge, P. (1990). *The Fifth Discipline*. New York: Doubleday.

Stewart, J. (2002). Closing the Achievement Gap in Suburban and Urban School Communities. *NCREL Policy Issues #13*. December.

Stiggins, R. J. (2002). Assessment Crisis: The Absence of Assessment for Learning. *Phi Delta Kappan. 83*(10).

Stilwill, T. (2003). Iowa Education Leader #11. A Policy and Advocacy Update from the Iowa Department of Education by Director, Ted Stilwill. 18 April.

Supovitz, J. and Watson, S. (2000). Team-Based Schooling in Cincinnati: The Third Year. Philadelphia: Consortium for Policy Research in Education, University of Pennsylvania.

Surber, J. (2003). Flexible Service Delivery. *The School Administrator.* 3(60).

Tomlinson, C. A. (1999). Mapping a Route Toward Differentiated Instruction. *Educational Leadership.* 57(1).

Tomlinson, C. A. and Kalbfleisch, M. L. (1998). Teach Me, Teach My Brain: A Call for Differentiated Classrooms. *Educational Leadership.* 56(3).

Tyler, R. (1949). *Basic Principles of Curriculum and Instruction.* Chicago: University of Chicago Press.

Appendix A

Decision-Making Model

Decision Making

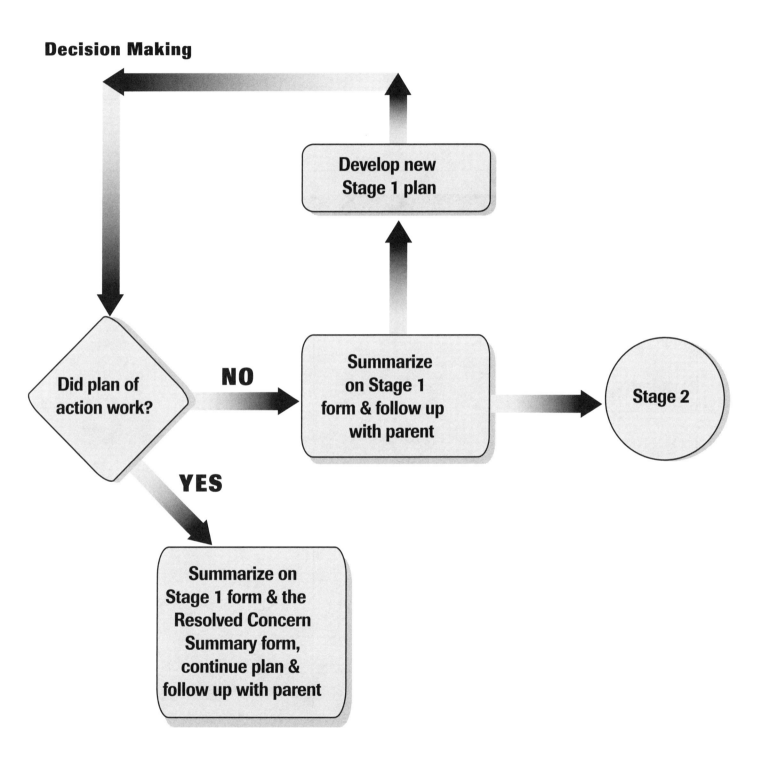

Problem Solving: Stage 1

(Form must be completed prior to problem-solving team involvement.)

Student Name _____ Teacher Name _____ Grade _____

Desired Behavior _____

_____

_____

PLAN OF ACTION	TEAM CONCLUSION AFTER REVIEW OF DATA
Date: Who: Plan:	**How was plan successful/ not successful?** **Be specific.** Next step after interpretation of data by Team: ___ Continue Intervention ___ Move to Stage 2 ___ New Intervention ___ See Attached ___ New Problem ___ Move to Inactive

Date outcomes were reviewed with parent _____ _____

Parent Contact Log

Student Name:

Parent Name:

Home Phone:

Address:

DATE	NOTES	By Phone	By Contact	By Note Home	Initials	Stage

Resolved Concern Summary

Student Name:_____ **School:**_____

Parent Name:_____

Resolved Concern:_____

Person Completing Summary:_____

Please write a brief summary statement including the following:

- Number of interventions
- Brief description of interventions
- Duration of interventions
- Explanation of why student is moved to "inactive" list

Decision-Making Model

Decision Making

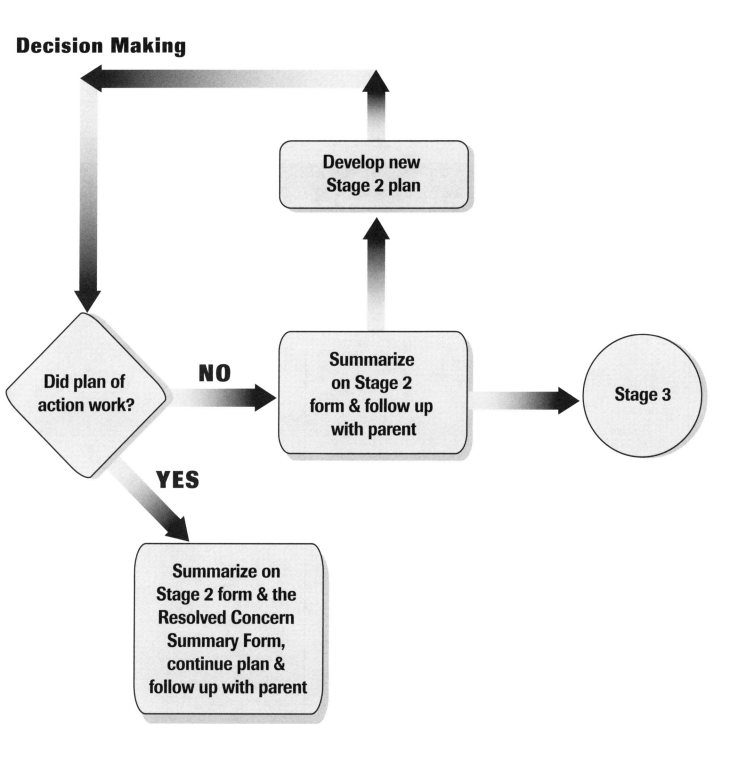

Problem Solving: Stage 2

Student Name _____ Teacher Name _____ Grade _____

Desired Behavior _____

_____

_____

PLAN OF ACTION	TEAM CONCLUSION AFTER REVIEW OF DATA
Date: Review Date: Who: Plan:	How was plan successful/ not successful? (Please attach data documenting success or lack of success with Plan of Action.) Next step after interpretation of data by Team: ___ Continue Intervention ___ Move to Stage 3 ___ New Intervention ___ See Attached ___ New Problem ___ Move to Inactive

Date outcomes were reviewed with parent _____ _____

Decision-Making Model

Decision Making

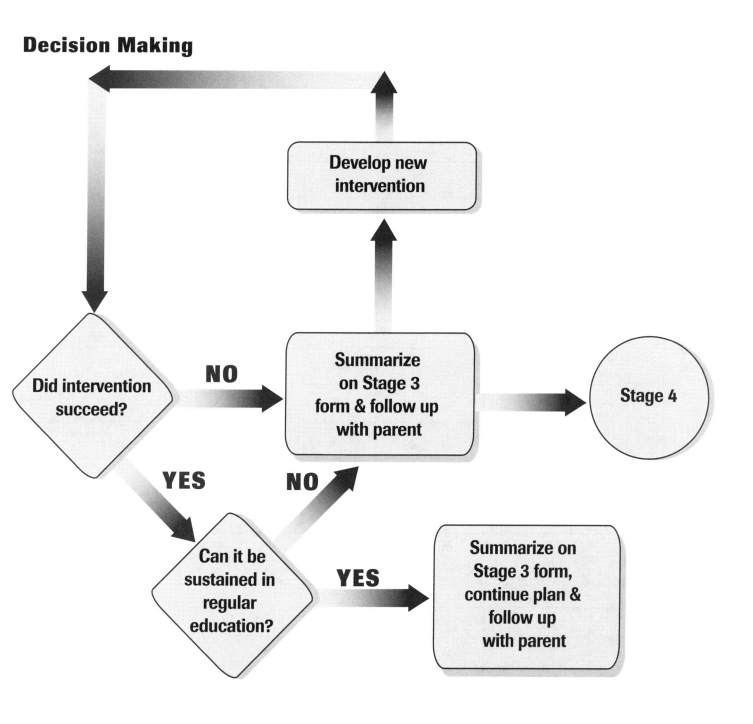

Progress Monitoring Graph

Student Name _____ Teacher Name _____ Date _____

Base-line

Performance Indicator

M   M   M   M   M   M   M   M   M   M   M   M   M   M   M   M   M

M															
T															
W															
Th															
F															

Interpretation of Data/Comments:

Decision-Making Model

Decision Making

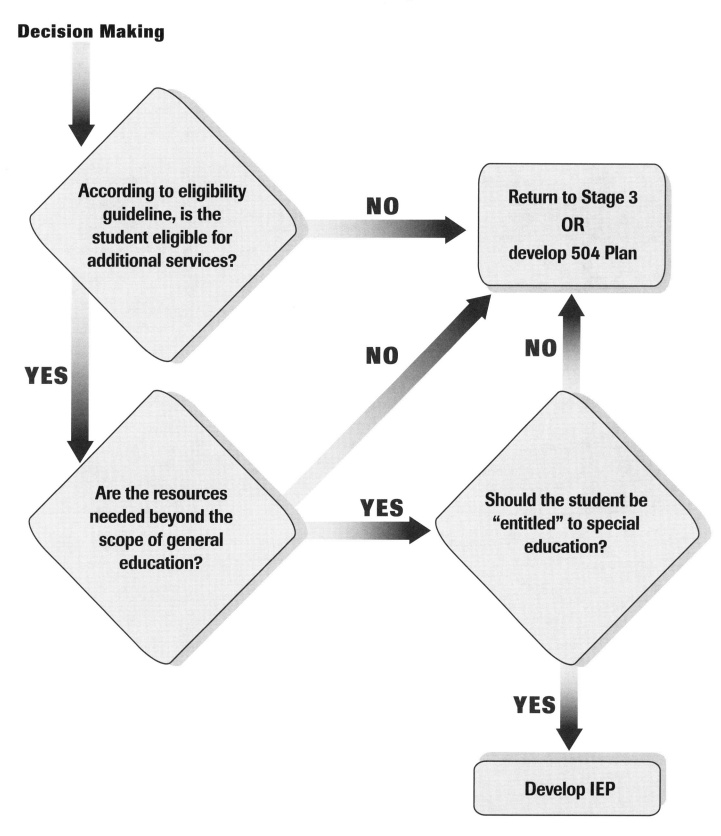

Appendix B

GUIDELINES FOR ACTION TEAM WORK			
Bryant Elementary, Dubuque, Iowa			
School Year	**Writing Action Team Responsibilities**	**Citizenship Action Team Responsibilities**	**Problem-Solving Action Team Responsibilities**
'01–'02 Jan.–May	Study and Planning Year ■ Begin to gather external data/best practices ■ Facilitate group discussions of external data/best practices ■ Arrange for presentations of models of writing instruction ■ Attend workshops related to writing and bring back information to staff	Maintenance Year ■ Review alternative recess option ■ Review and plan for any further implementation of Steps to Success ■ Review and plan for any further implementation of social skill instruction ■ Determine if this action team can put practices in the "parking lot" or if it needs to move to next year to complete plan	Maintenance Year ■ Review current problem-solving procedures ■ Examine how classroom profiles will fit with problem solving ■ Prepare problem-solving procedures to be put in the "parking lot" of the plan ■ **Dissolve Problem-Solving Action Team**
'02–'03	Planning and Early Implementation Year ■ 1st semester—continue to examine best practices ■ Lead staff to consensus on the approaches the building will embrace ■ Possible pilots of interventions ■ Collect baseline on writing	Maintenance Year ■ Complete all of the review of procedures outlined above ■ **Dissolve Citizenship Action Team** **OR** Study and Planning Year ■ Determine the *needs* to support writing in respect to citizenship and character development ■ Develop supporting activities	Study and Planning Year ■ Determine the needs to support writing with respect to communication and collaboration ■ Develop supporting activities

GUIDELINES FOR ACTION TEAM WORK (CONTINUED)

Bryant Elementary, Dubuque, Iowa

School Year	Writing Action Team Responsibilities	Citizenship Action Team Responsibilities	Problem-Solving Action Team Responsibilities
'03–'04	Implementation Year ■ Whole-school implementation of writing best practices/interventions ■ Provide opportunities for staff to share ■ Organize collection of up-close data	Study and Planning Year (see above) **OR** Early Implementation Year ■ Plan for and begin the supporting activities	Early Implementation Year ■ Plan for and begin the supporting activities
'04–'05	Implementation/Modification Year ■ Continue with implementation of writing best practices ■ Make modifications as needed based on up-close data	Implementation Year ■ Implement supporting activities of citizenship and character development to support writing ■ Monitor effects of interventions	Implementation Year ■ Implement supporting activities of communication and collaboration to support writing ■ Monitor effects of interventions
'05–'06	Maintenance Year ■ Examine all data ■ Evaluate ■ Make preparations to become "way of doing business" (parking lot)	Maintenance Year ■ Examine all data ■ Evaluate ■ Make preparations to become "way of doing business" (parking lot)	Maintenance Year ■ Examine all data ■ Evaluate ■ Make preparations to become "way of doing business" (parking lot)

Appendix C

Elementary Electronic Student Database

Dubuque Community School District

The Elementary Electronic Student Database will include the following information:

- Student demographic information

- Curriculum information (basic reading and math assessments)

- Standardized test information (ITBS and CogAt)

- Documentation of specialized services (IEP, PEP, reading support)

- Extra-curricular involvement

Advantages:

- Provides consistency in and among buildings

- Provides a broad look at student performance over time

- Enables one to look at multiple sources of data at one time

- Creates a general perspective of student performance

- Operates as a springboard to more in-depth diagnostic data review

- Allows for calculations on the performance of a variety of subgroups to be made at the school level and district level

- Allows for students in different elementary schools to be compared using the same data

- Allows for individual schools to add to the core database to meet their specific needs

- Accepts data from CIMS for much of the demographic information

Disadvantages:

- Will not provide an in-depth look at any one particular curriculum area (Example: the math and reading cards will still be used to keep track of subtest scores, individual unit scores, etcetera)

- Data for reading will not be able to be electronically transferred directly

- Data entry is very time consuming

- Requires expertise in Excel in each building

Wish List:

- A diagnostic database for each curricular area (reading, math, science, social studies...) could be created that would interface with the general database and report cards so that all data collection could be electronic

Elementary Electronic Student Database

Dubuque Community School District

Implementation Plan: 2002–2003

a. **Bryant, Irving, and Eisenhower Elementary Schools**

Immediate implementation based on previous experience throughout 2001–2002 as pilot sites for the database and as members of the development team for this template

b. **All Other Elementary Schools**

Orientation for elementary principals (*overview, purposes, school issues to be addressed*)	September 11, elementary principals' meeting
Orientation for data coaches, IMS, data entry personnel, database managers, and elementary secretaries	September 25 and 30 from 3:45–4:45pm in the board room (*Participants will attend one of these sessions and will receive hourly pay from district funds*)
Training in Excel (*in data entry and database management*) and use of the database for each school's data entry person and database manager	October–November in groups with substitutes provided plus regular IMS meetings
Training in application of the database: ■ for diagnostic school improvement with principals, data coaches, and site council liaisons ■ for diagnostic teaching with database managers (principals, forum personnel, and others welcome)	December–March data coach training sessions Ongoing throughout 2002–2003 and 2003–2004
Information for the Board of Education	February or March instructional board meeting

Elementary Electronic Student Database

Dubuque Community School District

Issues

1. When will we implement the database?

   - Bryant, Irving, Eisenhower Schools...immediately

   - All other elementary schools...throughout the 2002–2003 school year

2. Who needs to know about it?

   - Principals

   - Forum personnel

   - Board members

   - Teachers and support staff, including secretaries and paraprofessionals involved

   - Keystone special education personnel

3. What training is needed?

   - Excel (*how to use Excel and how to apply Excel to this database*)

   - How to use the database for diagnostic school improvement and diagnostic teaching purposes

4. Issues for the school to address:

   - Who will do the data entry? (*data entry person*)

   - Who will be trained in Excel at each school? (*data entry personnel and database managers*)

   - Who will see that data is submitted for entry?

   - Who will do the data analysis and interpretation?

   - Who will help teachers use the database for teaching and learning?

- Accuracy of data

- Who can access the database? (*file permission vs. read-only*)

- Confidentiality (*staff only*)

- "Vulnerability" of teachers with exposure of individual class/teacher data (*discuss process of self-discovery of strengths and deficiencies—district culture shift*)

- What additional fields, if any, will your school choose to add to the database?

5. Strong link to Track II Professional Growth Plans

6. Who will do the training?

- Orientation to the database (*purpose, structure, issues*)—district task force representatives

- Teacher training in Excel and its application to the database—J. Lagen

- Diagnostic use of the database for effective school improvement—P. Holly, N. Bradley

- Diagnostic use of the database for effective instruction—Educational Programs Services directors, coordinators, supervisors, and strategists, plus others

7. Funding?

- District support funds (*$1.50 per student for schools fully implementing the Student Database in 2002–2003*)

- School-based (*Phase III, PTA, trade time, school budget, etcetera*)

8. Yet to be developed:

- Individual student report (*Word document*)

- Excel baseline training content (*data entry; database management; instructional application*)

Elementary Electronic Student Database

Dubuque Community School District

_____ School

REGISTRATION FOR TRAINING

■ Data Entry Person _____

This staff member will enter the school's data into the database in Excel. This person should have familiarity with Excel and/or a level of technical competency to be readily trained in data entry in Excel. This person could be a paraprofessional, secretary, or teacher.

■ Database Manager(s) _____

_____

One or two teachers will work with other faculty, as well as with the principal and Site Council at the school, to analyze, interpret, and apply the Student Database for effective diagnostic teaching and diagnostic school improvement purposes. Database managers will be included in training in the technical aspects of Excel as well as in how to apply the database at both school and classroom levels. These persons may be general or special education teachers, TAG facilitators, reading specialists, IMS, guidance counselors, or strategists.

Please complete and return this registration to Nancy Bradley at the Forum by September 20.

Elementary Electronic Student Database

Calendar of Data Availability for Entry

Implementation Year: 2002–2003

Note: Math basic fact assessments are important student achievement data. However, *no math data will be entered* into the district's core template for the Elementary Electronic Student Database pending recommendations from the Elementary Math Study Committee for implementation beginning in the 2003–2004 school year.

Ongoing Updates: (may be entered now for current status, but will need to be updated for each child as services are initiated)

IEPs	Reading Services
PEPs	■ Title I
504 Plans	■ Reading/Writing Reinforcement
ELL	■ Reading Recovery
Problem Solving	■ Early Success
Health Plans	■ Soar to Success

Calendar of Availability for Data for Database Entry

August:	
September: Mid-September	Observation Survey Results...grade 1
October: Early October Early October	BRI Results...grades 2–6 Early Literacy Assessment Results...kindergarten

November:	
December: Mid-December–Mid-January	Iowa Tests of Basic Skills (ITBS)...grades 3–6
January:	
February: First of February First of February	Observation Survey Results...grade 1 BRI Results...grades 2–6
March: Late March	Kindergarten Screening Results
April: ??	Cognitive Abilities Test (CogAT) grades 3 and 5
May: Mid-May Mid-May Late May	Observation Survey Results...grade 1 BRI Results...grades 2–6 Early Literacy Assessment Results...kindergarten
June:	

Appendix D

Dubuque Community School District

District Intervention Plan...a Plan for District-Wide Continuous Focus on Student Achievement and School/District Improvement

---

I. Expectations for School and District Monitoring of Student Achievement

---

This document seeks to define and describe the Dubuque Community School District's expectations and protocol for monitoring student achievement, using data to guide instruction and increase student learning. The plan will be reviewed annually and revised as needed to reflect the state's interpretation of federal legislation intent and application.

In order to have a collaborative culture in pursuit of high student achievement for all students at all levels, standard practice throughout the Dubuque Community School District includes:

A. District Level

1. District personnel will provide ongoing Data Coach Training with special emphasis on working with federal, state, and district data requirements and expectations relating to student achievement.

2. District personnel will monitor district and individual school-level student achievement. Disaggregating will include gender, SES (socioeconomic status), race/ethnicity, special and nonspecial education, ELL (English Language Learners), and length of time in the district.

3. District personnel will support and monitor adopted curriculum for full implementation in all schools through analysis of student achievement data (both general and special education) and collaborative data analysis with principals and other school personnel. Monitoring will include

   - standards and benchmarks

   - assessments

   - materials

   - instructional strategies

4. District and school personnel have a yearly conversation about the school's student achievement, including data coming from the school's Electronic Student Profile.

5. District personnel will report district and school student achievement data to the Board of Education, the Iowa Department of Education, the community, and the schools.

B. School Level

1. The principal, with the Site Council and faculty, will continually monitor both aggregated and disaggregated student achievement data in reading, writing, mathematics, science, and social studies. Further disaggregation will occur for gender, SES, race/ethnicity, special and nonspecial education, ELL, and length of time in the district.

2. The principal will provide **special** school-wide monitoring in reading and mathematics.

3. The principal will support and monitor the district-adopted curriculum for full implementation for both general and special education students throughout the school through school and classroom data analysis and classroom observation. Monitoring will include

   - standards and benchmarks

   - assessments

   - materials

   - instructional strategies

4. The principal and teachers will monitor student achievement at the school, grade, classroom, and individual student levels. Data will include that found in the school's Electronic Student Database.

5. The principal will provide school-based structure for and assure the accomplishment of classroom-level expectations, e.g., discussions at team meetings, faculty meetings, and grade/department meetings.

6. The principal will provide assessment information to district personnel and the Site Council as well as teachers, parents, and the school community.

C. Classroom Level

1. Each teacher (general, special education, specialist) will gather and analyze existing individual student achievement data at earliest contact with each

student, e.g., CogAt, ITBS/ITED, kindergarten screening, curriculum-based assessments, student portfolios, agency and parent reports, attendance information, problem-solving reports, IEPs, and PEPs.

2. Each teacher will use diagnostic information to plan appropriate instruction to maximize student learning.

3. Each teacher will continuously monitor student performance, including data found in the school's Electronic Student Database, through appropriate assessments and adjust instruction accordingly.

4. Each teacher will provide assessment feedback to students, parents, and the principal.

5. All teachers and support personnel will collaborate and communicate with each other to support individual student learning based on identified needs.

II. Intervention Plan for Schools in Need of Improvement in Reading and Mathematics

(All Title I, Non-Title I, Elementary, Junior High, and Senior High Schools)

A. "Internal Alert" for Low Student Performance in Reading and Mathematics

1. Criteria for "Internal Alert"

   An internal alert will be made by the school and/or district when one or more of the following conditions are present:

   a. when the school's percentage of low performing students on any indicator exceeds the state average of low performing students at grades 4, 8, and/or 11

   b. when the percentage of low performing students at any grade level increases for that same grade level over the previous year, i.e., same grade level over time (achievement analysis)

   c. when a group of students fails to show a year's growth in a year's time (grade equivalency analysis)

   d. when other performance indicators suggest learning concerns

2. Required Response to "Internal Alert" Status

   a. Student Achievement Intervention Plan (*designed by the principal in collaboration with school and district personnel and requiring Superintendent approval*)

The principal and school staff will

    1) identify the individual low-performing students and enter each into the problem-solving process

    2) analyze the effectiveness of current instruction

    3) determine the intended improvement outcomes for identified students

    4) identify needed changes in instruction and additional interventions

    5) determine staff development for needed improvement to occur

    6) monitor with school and district personnel the implementation of interventions/modifications for intended improvements in student learning

The principal will assure that all school staff contributes to efforts to achieve the intended outcomes of the Student Achievement Intervention Plan.

   b. The principal, with the faculty and Site Council, will analyze disaggregated student achievement data in areas of the alert to determine if an increase in low performance can be tied to any specific disaggregated group(s). If this is determined to be the case, the school will design interventions for the group(s).

   c. The school's Comprehensive School Improvement Plan must include a focus in the area(s) of alert for low performance (*district approval of plan required*). The Student Achievement Intervention Plan (as outlined above) becomes a priority in the school's CSIP.

B. **Federal/State Identification for Schools in Need of Improvement for Low Student Performance in Reading and Mathematics**

   1. First Year Identification as a School in Need of Improvement

    a. Student Achievement Intervention Plan (*designed by the principal in collaboration with school and district personnel and requiring Superintendent approval*)

The principal and school staff will

1) identify the low-performing students

2) determine the intended improvement outcomes for identified students

3) analyze the effectiveness of current instruction

4) identify needed changes in instruction and additional interventions

5) determine staff development for improvement needed to occur

6) monitor with school and district personnel the implementation of interventions/modifications for intended improvements in student learning

The principal will assure that all school staff contributes to efforts to achieve the intended outcomes of the Student Intervention Plan.

b. Participation in State Program Improvement (*if eligible*)
The school and its entire staff will participate in full in the State Program Improvement Plan as defined by the Iowa Department of Education.

c. The school's Comprehensive School Improvement Plan must include a focus in the area(s) of alert for low performance (*district approval of plan required*). The Student Achievement Intervention Plan (as outlined above) becomes the priority in the school's CSIP.

2. Second Year Identification as a School in Need of Improvement

a. Student Achievement Intervention Plan (*designed by the principal in collaboration with school and district personnel and requiring Superintendent approval*)

The principal and school staff will

1) identify the low-performing students

2) determine the intended improvement outcomes for identified students

3) analyze the effectiveness of current instruction

4) identify needed changes in instruction and additional interventions

5) determine staff development for improvement needed to occur

6) monitor with school and district personnel the implementation of interventions/modifications for intended improvements in student learning

The principal will assure that all school staff contributes to efforts to achieve the intended outcomes of the Student Intervention Plan.

b. Participation in State Improvement *(if eligible)*

The school and its entire staff will participate, if eligible, in full in the State Program Improvement Plan as defined by the Iowa Department of Education.

c. Addition of Instructional Strategist (.5–1.0 FTE)

If the district's budget permits, an Instructional Strategist will be added to the school staff if none already exists. The purpose of that additional leadership support will be improvement of instruction leading to increased student achievement. The Instructional Strategist will report to an identified district person, will work collaboratively with both district and school personnel, and will assist the principal in working with school staff to improve student achievement.

d. The school's Comprehensive School Improvement Plan must include a focus in the area(s) of alert for low performance (*district approval of plan required*). The Student Achievement Intervention Plan (as outlined above) becomes the priority in the school's CSIP.

3. Identification as a School in Need of Improvement for Three or More Years

From the ESEA Reauthorization: *No Child Left Behind Act of 2001*...

a. Corrective Action

"...strengthens corrective action (required after two years in school improvement) to include actions more likely to bring about meaningful change at the school, such as replacing school staff responsible for the continued failure to make AYP, comprehensive implementation of a new curriculum (including professional development), and reorganizing the school internally. Corrective action schools also must continue to provide choice and supplemental services options to their students."

b. Restructuring

"...adds a new **restructuring** requirement for schools that fail to respond to corrective actions. If a school fails to make AYP after one year of corrective action, it must begin planning a restructuring, which involves fundamental change such as reopening the school as a public charter school, replacing all or most of the school's staff, or turning operation of the school over to a private management company with a demonstrated record of effectiveness, and implement its restructuring plan the following year. Schools identified for restructuring also must continue to provide choice and supplemental services options to their students."

Appendix E

Elementary Instructional Strategist

Dubuque Community School District

Focus: School-based staff development for instructional improvement to enhance student achievement

Through a collaborative effort among the Instructional Strategist, district and AEA staff, and school staff, school-wide instructional leadership and support will be provided by the Instructional Strategist in the following areas:

- Best practices in instruction and assessment of student learning

- Instructional interventions and strategies based on regular student data analysis and interpretation

- Action research

- Problem solving

- Student behavior management and instruction related to student achievement

- Study skills

In-school leadership functions of the Instructional Strategist include the following roles:

- Model effective teaching practices in classrooms

- Conduct regularly scheduled meetings with individual teachers as well as grade-level teams to address teaching best practices and student achievement

- Assess individual students

- Work with staff to collect, analyze, interpret, and apply student achievement data

- Plan and create interventions for use with students

- Evaluate student progress with teachers

- Provide short-term direct service to students to select, refine, and model interventions (1–3 days)

- Observe and provide feedback to teachers on teaching and learning

- Observe students with unique learning needs

- Support school staff and parents in collaborative efforts for improved student achievement

■ Gather resources for teachers, e.g., materials, instructional strategies

■ Provide professional development for school staff in aspects of diagnostic teaching and assessment of student learning

Professional Development Needs of the Instructional Strategist:

■ District curriculum

■ Application of problem-solving philosophy and process in the classroom

■ Student assessment, e.g., standardized, curriculum-based, teacher-made

■ Progress monitoring

■ Curriculum-based measurement

■ Data collection, analysis, interpretation, and application *(Data Coach training)*

■ Instructional interventions and strategies

■ Collaborative coaching skills (from ETS PATHWISE Induction Program)

■ Kansas Strategies

■ Study skills

■ Behavior competencies that relate to student achievement

Professional Development Plan for instructional Strategies:

■ Summer Institute

■ First Trimester: one-half day per week

■ Thereafter: one-half day twice monthly

Compensation:

Instructional Strategists will receive their regular DCSD salary and benefits plus:

■ .5 consultant stipend *(per Schedule I of the Master Agreement)*

■ Three additional contract days *(for before and after regular contract length)*

Appendix F

Dubuque Community School District
Systemic School Improvement Initiatives, 2001–2003
Nancy Bradley with Consultation from the Learning Group
January 2002

In order to ensure that school improvement focuses on student learning in the classroom AND becomes systemic within the district, efforts are being made at four levels: the district, the school, the classroom, and the individual student. This year's school improvement initiatives are designed to address each of these levels.

The District

Chapter 12 Committee

In refining the district-level efforts to create and sustain school improvement that will benefit the entire district while supporting the other levels, the Chapter 12 Committee has been the catalyst. In addition to providing a forum for discussing the effects district initiatives in school improvement have at the school level, this year's work has expanded and refined the process of data collection and dissemination. The committee has identified currently collected and maintained records and information, their sources, and availability. In a district this size, the effort is formidable, but the benefits are numerous in creating a clear and predictable means of communication of important and relevant information that is readily accessible for each level and for multiple purposes. Thus, when the database as envisioned is in place, the district will have access to the information about student learning at every level correlated with efforts to improve instruction to impact learning. Conversely, the school will have a clear understanding of the information that is collected at the district level and the appropriate use of that data to identify strengths and challenges for the school.

The Schools

Data Coaches

In order to provide clarity in developing the district database and appropriately interpreting it for use to improve instruction and learning, there have been regularly scheduled training/working sessions with Data Coaches. Representing each school as Data Coaches are the principal and two or more professional employees (usually teachers, but they might also be assistant principals and/or counselors). Their efforts have been focused on developing expertise in the collection, analysis, and interpretation of relevant information, understanding the process of school improvement, and developing the skills and opportunities for engaging all staff in the school in the improvement effort and in the development of expectations and skills of working with school and district data for accountability.

Site Council Visits with Critical Friends

An additional effective means of providing the understanding, skills, and insights necessary to implement school improvement at the school level has been the biannual Site Council Visits with Critical Friends. These sessions have provided additional assistance in the same vein as the Data Coach training, but involve a more inclusive and representative group. The benefits have been evident as the Comprehensive School Improvement Plans (CSIP) have become more refined and focused and have been more and more actively used as a road map for implementation at the school level. The SCIP is no longer a "plan" that is put on a shelf or in a filing cabinet as a requirement for compliance, but it has become an "on the wall" action plan for activities and initiatives—one that has the capacity for editing, improving, and interpreting as appropriate. Most importantly, the CSIP is now a blueprint for improving student learning based on school, classroom, and individual student achievement data.

Dubuque High Schools Project

The Dubuque High Schools Project is another district-wide initiative at the school level that is having an impact on school improvement implementation. As part of the combined efforts of all three high school teams, information about ninth grade students is being compiled in order to identify problems and needs that are challenging young people entering Dubuque's three public high schools. In addition to the work that is common to all three schools, each high school has also had the opportunity to work on analyzing the data specific to that school that is impacting student learning, and subsequently, developing a clearer understanding of the possible actions that could be taken to improve the situation. The next step will be to develop action plans for implementing the identified "solutions" to the problems and/or interventions that will impact the challenges and bring positive benefits to students involved.

The Classroom and Students

Classroom Action Research

In order to assist with the implementation of improvement initiatives at the school level, Classroom Action Research is being piloted at Bryant, Irving, and Marshall Elementary Schools on a school-wide basis. This involves teachers' systematic investigation of some aspect of their work in order to solve a problem or to improve their effectiveness in the classroom. Action Research involves identifying a problem and collecting and analyzing relevant data to assess the impact of new instructional strategies and techniques on intended student outcomes. For example, teachers have charted their students' test results on several different tests, then identified the areas where students needed instructional assistance to improve, initiated that assistance, then re-tested and charted again. This effort can be expected to engage students and parents in more direct analysis of progress in learning for that individual student. It is this diagnostic approach that will be school improvement at the student level. In the three schools where this process is being piloted, the project includes several educators working together, which is collaborative action research.

This systemic approach that the Dubuque Community School District is taking to school improvement is addressing the needs of all the students in the district and is unique in the state and perhaps in the nation. This district is proud of its commitment to providing continuous school improvement for the sake of its students and the community.

Notes

These materials are being sponsored by the Elementary and Secondary Education Division of Educational Testing Service (ETS), a not for profit organization. One of the division's goals is to serve teachers' professional development needs by providing products and services that identify, assess, and advance good teaching from initial preparation through advanced practice.

Our mission is to help advance quality and equity in education by providing fair and valid assessments, research and related services. Our products and services measure knowledge and skills, promote learning and performance, and support education and professional development for all people worldwide.

We welcome your comments and feedback.

E-mail address: professionaldevelopment@ets.org

Professional Development Group
Elementary and Secondary Education Division
Educational Testing Service, MS 18-D
Princeton, New Jersey 08541